the vegan gardener

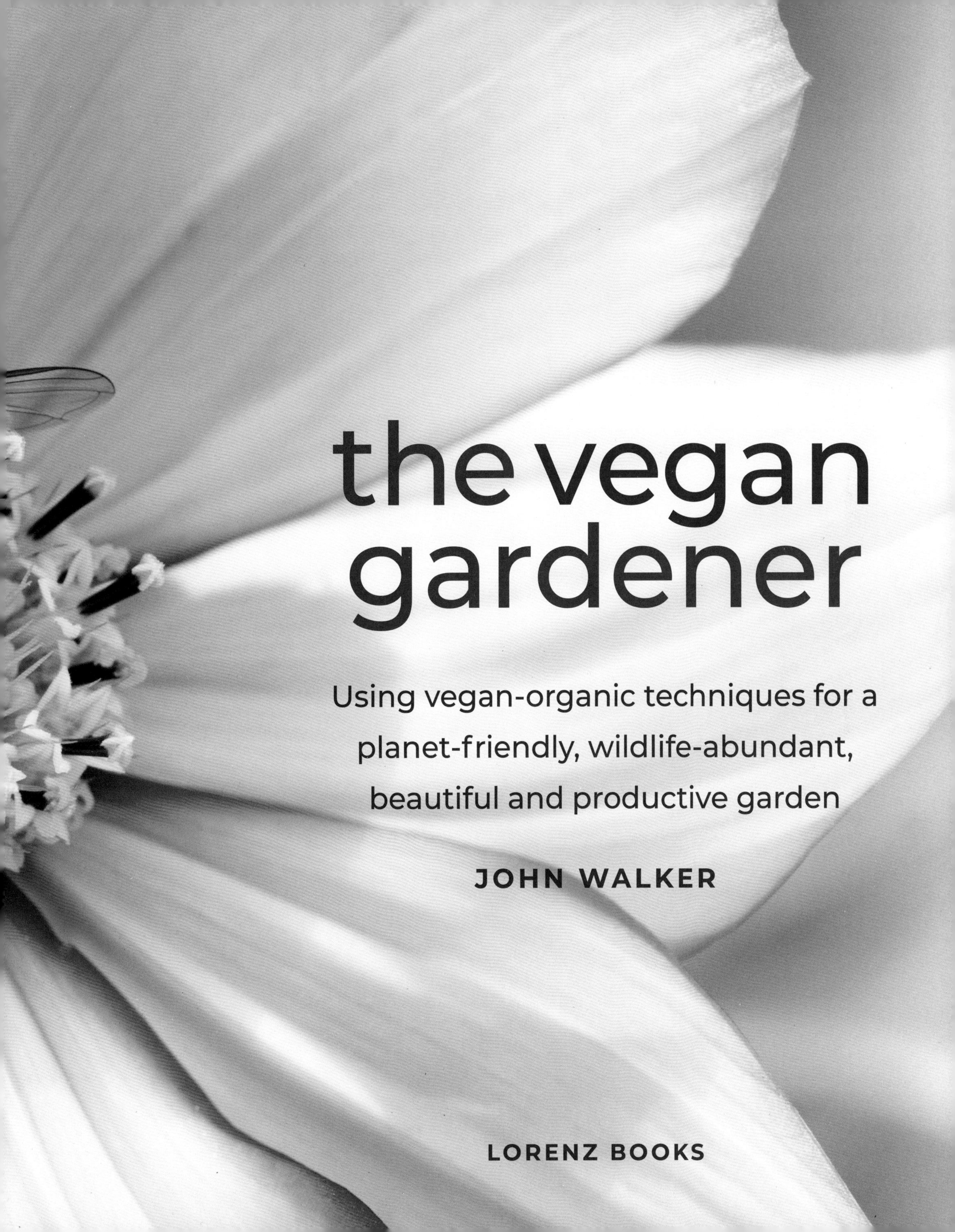

the vegan gardener

Using vegan-organic techniques for a planet-friendly, wildlife-abundant, beautiful and productive garden

JOHN WALKER

LORENZ BOOKS

Contents

Foreword: a veganic gardening journey

Opposite, clockwise from top: Wild birds such as blackcap (Sylvia atricapilla) are drawn to insect-rich veganic gardens. Make as much garden compost as you can. Fresh home-grown vegetables can be free of any animal inputs. Butterflies (this is a comma, Polygonia c-album, on a buddleja) thrive in pesticide-free gardens.

Below: Innovative veganic techniques encourage soil life, such as these plant-friendly fungi, to flourish.

When I first began coaxing my current garden from a bracken-riddled hillside, I dreamed of being able to secure hot and steaming heaps of farmyard manure to dig into my virgin soil to – as the gardening lingo goes – 'improve its fertility'. I dreamt on, but no heaps were to be found: I live and garden deep in sheep farming country (their manure does not get piled into delivered-by-trailer heaps). My soil was raw, hungry and needy.

I found that chopped fresh bracken and long grass mixed with spoiled straw made wonderful big and hot compost heaps (they steamed at night) which produced rich, dark garden compost in just a few months. My soil devoured it, but it was never enough, and I still hankered for manure. I imported a local-ish source of rich and dark green waste soil improver, made from composted garden i.e. plant waste. I also sowed a test strip of various living plant mulches (green manures or cover crops), to see which might thrive here; buckwheat and mustard were early winners on my infant soil, quietly helping to give it body using nothing but the power of sunshine.

I made more and more compost, slowly and quickly, inviting compost worms to join in. After two autumns busily raking, I started to reap the rewards: lashings of soil-boosting leaf mould.

Regular sowings of living mulches carried on doing their thing. Without realising it, I was no longer importing any fertility into the garden, and my manure-filled dreams ebbed away. All of this soil-bolstering goodness is made by plants themselves using sunlight and carbon dioxide sucked from the air; it then makes its way into the soil as rich compost and crumbly, mouldered leaves, or through the decaying shoots and roots of living mulches.

My flowers and vegetables grew like mad. I am still making and using compost and leaf mould, and sowing living mulches, but they have been joined by another plant-powered way of invigorating garden or allotment soil, using home-grown chopped-up and sappy 'green wood chips'. Watching microbial life bloom when green wood chips are added to soil is a revelation; you *must* give them a try and see it for yourself (the flushes of little toadstools are a treat).

By harnessing the power of plants to grow more plants, my garden – which at the outset was always intended to be organic – quietly became vegan by stealth. Realising I had crafted a vibrant, nature-filled and no-dig garden from scratch, and was able to sustain it without lifting a forkful of manure, or any of the other grisly byproducts (dried blood, bonemeal) of the animal-exploiting meat, dairy, poultry and fishery industries, filled me with an unexpected buzz. That same buzz has taken my growing, as well as my thinking about how what I do in my garden affects our natural world, way beyond just organic gardening.

My vegan-organic (or veganic) gardening journey delights and surprises, and teaches me something new each day, and I know of no better way to bring beauty and abundance into our beleaguered, changing world. I hope you will enjoy exploring the pages of this book, and be tempted to set out on a journey of your own.

John Walker

Introduction

Our natural world is undergoing profound and irreversible change, with implications for every living thing on earth. To meet humanity's greatest challenge – our global climate crisis – we must rethink and reshape every aspect of our everyday lives, including the way in which we cultivate our gardens. This book explains a mindful, beautiful, gentle yet powerful way of gardening that is in harmony with nature.

*Opposite: Bumblebees (*Bombus *spp.) forage on simple, pollen- and nectar-rich flowers, such as summer-flowering* Verbena bonariensis.

However enthusiastic we are, it can be hard to find rewarding ways of doing our bit to ease the mounting pressure on our natural world; simply going about our everyday lives incurs some environmental cost. We know we should recycle, use our cars less and public transport more, make our homes more energy-efficient and try to eat locally-grown food – while trying to grow some ourselves. Yet all these 'green' and eco-conscious activities – important though they are in light of our unfolding climate crisis, and as our life-supporting ecosystems falter around us – often leave us feeling frustrated and deeply unfulfilled.

However, when you step out into your own precious piece of paradise – your garden or allotment – that lack of fulfilment ebbs away. Here, working hand in hand with nature, you can choose to garden in a way that is both personal and intensely satisfying, but which also allows each of us, in our own way, to do that extra bit towards easing planetary burdens. Even when our actions seem small and insignificant, the positive vibe they give is considerable and meaningful; there are tens of millions of gardeners across our planet and our collective actions are a green – and gathering – force for good.

No other activity gives such lifelong joy, gets us so up close and personal with nature – daily and in every season – or inspires us to enrich and add beauty to our fragile living world, in the dirt-under-the-fingernails way that gardening does. This book is about what is arguably the deepest green, the most ethical, responsible and thoughtful, as well as the kindest, most rewarding and modern way of gardening there is.

The following pages explain what veganic gardening is, and how it builds on the spirit and philosophy of organic gardening – but goes way beyond it. We discover how our garden (or allotment) is actually a living, dynamic ecosystem in its own right, and how wildlife, in all its guises, is crucial to creating a healthy ecological balance. Climate-friendly gardening is explored, along with examples of how to take practical steps – by reducing our 'gardening footprint' – to help temper climate breakdown. The concept of a veganic, closed-loop garden, self-sufficient in everything it needs – from soil-building compost to plant supports – is shown in action.

'Veganic basics' provides all of the information you need to start growing vegan-organically. This section covers choosing vegan-friendly kit, tools and materials; sourcing veganic and peat-free compost, and mixing your own ultra-local blends; how to avoid plastic pollution by growing plastic-free, and choosing pesticide-free plants; and harvesting, storing and using water wisely. How to protect vulnerable plants from pests using harmless techniques, and learn to love, use and gently curtail weeds without using chemical weedkillers, are explained.

'Growing spaces' looks at the practicalities of using containers if you do not have access to a garden, how to take on and maintain a veganic allotment, utilising a greenhouse or polytunnel to capture free and renewable sunlight; and how to integrate your greenhouse into a garden's wider ecosystem by making it wildlife-friendly. Detailed plans showing how a veganic food garden can be made in an ordinary back garden, over a five-year period, are accompanied by practical growing techniques.

'Sun-powered soil' shows you how to determine exactly what type of soil you have, describes the pros and cons of each, and explains the vital role animal-free organic matter plays in nourishing your soil, while helping it to lock away atmospheric carbon. This section also covers the many benefits of respecting soil life by adopting a no-dig, less work approach, showing you how to lay a sheet mulch to clear weed-ridden ground, and giving practical advice on growing no-dig vegetable crops. Everything you need to know about making soil-building garden compost – using a cool and slow, or a hot and fast method – is explained, together with advice on setting up a 'wormposting' bin. If compost is in short supply, the innovative veganic technique of using locally-found green wood chips to improve and build soil, while boosting its microbial life, is clearly illustrated.

Practical steps are given for making your own free (and annually renewable) leaf mould, and advice on finding and using different types of soil-hugging mulch, along with tips on producing your own versatile mulches using a powered shredder. The vital role of living plant mulches in enriching and protecting soil, capturing nitrogen from the air, and benefiting wildlife is described in detail. Useful tips are given on using fresh or dried seaweed as a valuable source of animal-free garden fertility. The importance of feeding plants via the soil is explained, together with a step-by-step guide to making your own home-grown plant tonics.

'Welcoming nature in' urges you to treat your garden as a safe, nature-friendly no-kill zone, to rely on wild bugs as your most important natural allies in a balanced garden ecosystem, and encourage more of them by building insect hotels. How to choose the best types of plant to boost pollinator populations is explained, together with recommended flowers to grow for every season.

There are tips for growing dandelions to help bumblebees and other insects, and for encouraging and befriending pest-catching spiders, especially in a greenhouse. Building a wildlife pond using free and found materials is shown in a step-by-step sequence. Allowing parts of your garden to go wild and break the rules, the value of growing self-reliant plants which sow themselves, and letting your lawn grow long and become a wildlife haven are all explored alongside practical advice.

'Must-grow plants' contains a selection of the best and most attractive plants to grow in a veganic garden to sustain bugs, pollinators and other wildlife all year round – from fast-growing annual flowers to long-lived shrubs and trees. An extensive list of flowers proven to benefit pollinating insects (including moths and other night-flyers) is included, together with pest- and disease-resistant vegetable varieties. Finally, a useful checklist summarises key seasonal jobs in the veganic garden.

Gardening in the 21st century requires a willingness to jettison traditional practices and to explore new, yet proven and truly earth-friendly ways of nurturing beautiful, bountiful and nature-rich gardens. This book's ambition is to empower everyone to do that.

Above: *Peacock butterfly* (Aglais io) *foraging on the tall stems of* Verbena bonariensis, *one of many summer-flowering plants you can grow to encourage wild pollinating insects to visit your veganic garden or allotment.*

Opposite: *Fresh, pesticide-free and ultra-local veganic food can be grown in even a modest-sized garden, using renewable, plant-derived materials such as compost and leaf mould to build and nurture your no-dig soil.*

What is veganic gardening?

Veganic gardening is the most ecologically and ethically sound way of growing plants there is. It combines the values of a vegan life and diet – which exclude all forms of exploitation of and cruelty to animals for food, clothing or any other purpose – with the key tenets of organic and sustainable gardening: avoiding the use of all synthetic chemical pesticides and artificial fertilisers.

Below left: *Farmyard manure can pollute soils and watercourses, and importing it into your garden risks contaminating your soil with residues of antibiotics, hormones, veterinary medicines and plant-damaging weedkillers.*

Below middle: *Spreading animal slurry on land releases nitrous oxide, a powerful 'greenhouse gas' that is helping to drive our global climate emergency.*

VEGAN + ORGANIC = VEGANIC

Although organic gardening eschews the use of synthetic chemical pesticides and fertilisers, it still often relies on farmyard manures, on fertilisers derived from the bodies of slaughtered, or, in the case of fish, suffocated animals, to nourish soil and feed plants, as well as on other animal-derived products.
The veganic approach goes beyond organic gardening by avoiding:

• All fertilisers derived from animal byproducts of any kind. Dried blood, fish meal (ground fish offal), bonemeal and 'hoof and horn' (ground up animal bones, hooves and horns), pelleted poultry manure, feather meal, and ground shells (from the seafood industry), are often used in an organic garden. They are sold individually, or in blends such as 'blood, fish and bone'. The vast majority of these seemingly benign products are all ultimately derived from the exploitation and commonplace suffering of intensively-farmed animals; although a byproduct, it is impossible to know exactly how much suffering buying them supports.

• Vermicompost (worm castings) produced by the intensive farming of captive compost worms – although we can invite live worms to help us make soil-nourishing garden compost.

• Gardening products made from wool, such as certain composts and plant ties, and leather, found in many gloves.

• The use of any seeds or plants resulting from genetic modification (known as 'GM' crops).

Growing veganically allows us to dissociate our gardens and allotments from the meat, poultry, fishery and dairy industries – and from the inherent exploitation of other sentient beings those embody.

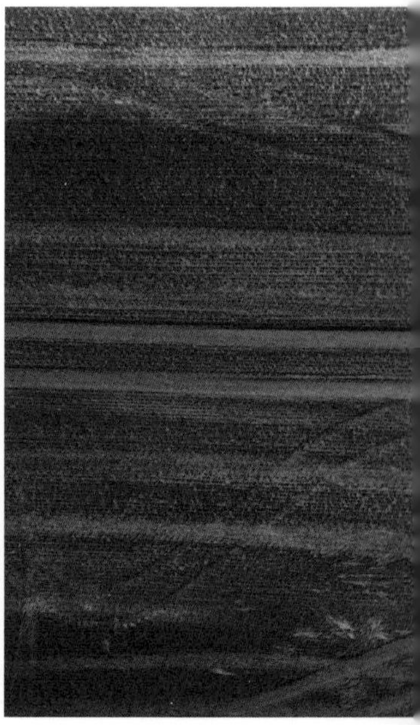

EASING OUR ECOLOGICAL CRISES

Cutting demand for animal-derived products helps lessen the wider damage done by industrialised animal farming to our natural world. Deforestation is increasing where tropical forests are cleared to grow food for animals; fish stocks are being depleted by overfishing; water pollution is caused by both by the use of synthetic fertilisers, especially nitrogen, used to grow crops to feed to animals, and by spillages of the slurry and effluent generated by increasingly intensive mega-farming. Animal wastes also generate large amounts of gases which help drive our climate crisis: methane (from bovine burps and flatulence), and ammonia (nitrous oxide) from manure and slurry.

Veganic gardening severs all links with a chain of events which both exploits animals and threatens the future resilience of our life-supporting ecosystems.

RESPECTING ALL LIFE

Killing other living things which interfere with our gardening – those we regard as 'pests' – is considered acceptable in organic gardening, as evidenced by the range of 'natural' pesticides on offer (which indiscriminately kill even beneficial creatures). In a veganic garden, we take another important step beyond organic growing, by adopting a hands-off, stand-aside approach. By treating our plots as strictly no-kill zones, where all life is revered, we actively encourage nature to find its own ecological equilibrium, so that any one species never becomes a pest problem in the first place. By adding some simple, key elements – such as a pond – we welcome nature into our gardens, and then tempt it to make its home there. Harmless exclusion, by using physical barriers – such as wire mesh cages to protect ripening fruit crops – is also used in veganic gardens. At times it may test our gardening resolve, but nature becomes our ally, rather than our adversary.

WHAT'S WRONG WITH MANURE?

Steaming heaps of farmyard or stable manure (or any bagged animal manure) are not necessary for a beautiful and productive garden or allotment. Using manure to improve the fertility of a garden relies on animals to eat plants, extract much of the goodness from them, and then pass on what is left in their faeces and

Below right: *By avoiding fertilisers made from animal byproducts you decouple your veganic garden or allotment from the suffering and exploitation inherent in the intensive farming of animals.*

Above left: *Gardening veganically means adopting a gentle, nature-friendly approach which encourages a rich mix of wild species that support a healthy and balanced garden ecosystem.*

Above right: *Veganic gardening avoids any need to use animals to generate fertility – such as manure – but instead adds it directly to the soil through the power of plants.*

urine. The residues of anything the animal has been treated with – such as growth hormones, antibiotics, other veterinary medicines, and even weedkillers used on their fodder – can find their way into our garden soil. Not using manure of any kind decouples your garden from the risk of potential contamination.

Instead, in a veganic garden we avoid the use of animals as third-party fertility providers, and choose to tap directly into the power of plants to build and nourish the soil. Garden compost, leaf mould, living plant mulches, and soil-boosting green wood chips all add their fertility straight into the soil; they do not have to pass through an animal first – one which may be leading a short, confined and miserable life.

PROVEN TO SUCCEED

Veganic growing has been practised by an increasing number of vegetable farmers (who often refer to it as 'stockfree'), smallholders and gardeners for many years, with proven success. Long-term on-farm trials and experimentation have shown that it is entirely possible to grow an abundance of edible and flower crops without importing any animal-derived fertility – including manure – on to the farm; almost all of the fertility needed by plants can be generated *by* plants, within a self-reliant farm or garden.

Opposite: *Anyone can use veganic techniques to make and maintain a beautiful and abundant plot.*

WHERE ARE YOU NOW?

This book is for everyone who wants to garden in a more mindful, ecologically aware and climate-friendly way. Veganic gardening will work for you whether you are a lifelong vegan, are quietly switching to a plant-based diet, or an omnivore. The plants you grow will look just the same as those you grew before you went veganic. But you will learn some different and innovative new techniques along the way, which can be applied, tweaked and refined wherever you are, to suit your garden's own unique circumstances. As veganic gardening gains momentum worldwide, it needs each and every one of us all to start experimenting with veganic techniques. You will soon come to hold the buzz of wildlife in your garden in awe, and derive joy from knowing you are gardening in a way that is kind to our earth.

Your living garden

Rather than seeing your garden or allotment as a collection of unconnected elements and of different independent gardening problems to solve, think of it instead as an interconnected, dynamic and diverse community of living organisms large and small – including you – all adapting to and interacting with their surroundings. Establishing and nurturing a rich and vibrant ecosystem, packed with all kinds of life, is the foundation of a beautiful and flourishing veganic garden.

WHAT IS AN ECOSYSTEM?

An ecosystem is a biological community of living things and the physical surroundings in which they live and interact with each other. Mature oak woodland, which supports a wide variety of life, is a good example of a natural ecosystem. In oak woodland, birds make their nests and feed on grubs and insects, which themselves are feeding on the oak leaves. Bird droppings fall to the woodland floor where they are broken down, along with fallen leaves, by worms and other soil life, becoming part of the soil that supports and feeds the tree roots. The fissured bark of the trunk is home to insects and other creatures which are eaten by birds or mammals. After dark, bats, which roost in cracks in the tree's trunk, feed on night-flying insects, while owls hunt small mammals over the woodland floor below.

LEARNING FROM NATURE

Veganic gardeners observe the way nature works and then weave together as many different kinds of life and physical habitats as possible, so that they work together for the benefit and health of the entire garden or allotment. With a guiding hand from us, nature will quickly put in place its own checks and balances. Increasing the overall variety of life in your garden – its biodiversity – helps it to become a self-sustaining and vibrant ecosystem in its own right.

WEAVING YOUR GARDEN WEB

Everyone can encourage birds into the garden by providing nesting habitats, winter food and shelter. Small birds such as blue tits will forage for aphids and caterpillars, which can eat our plants, feeding them to their chicks, while thrushes will eat snails (noisily smashing them open on stones). Beneficial insects such as hoverflies, whose larvae eat aphids, are attracted by growing simple, single flowers rich in pollen and nectar. Pollinating solitary bees are drawn to bug hotels, where they will build their nests. Perennial stinging nettles *(Urtica dioica)* attract aphids, which adult ladybirds will eat when they emerge from hibernation. Nettles are also eaten during the summer months by the caterpillars of several butterflies. Adding even a small pond will dramatically increase the life in your garden, and is a self-contained aquatic ecosystem in its own right. Slug-eating frogs and toads will use it to breed, as will newts and dragonflies. Birds, small mammals and bees will all drink there.

Your garden might already contain other mini ecosystems, such as a compost heap or bin, where garden and kitchen waste is turned, by compost worms, bugs and microbial life, into a rich material for nourishing soil. If you want to grow some of your own veganic food, as well as other plants, nurturing the soil's own dynamic ecosystem is vital. Adding garden compost to your soil feeds earthworms and the soil micro-organisms which then create humus – the decomposed organic matter that makes soil dark, and helps us lock away some carbon.

Opposite, clockwise from top left: Peacock butterfly (Aglais io) *feeding on devil's bit scabious,* Succisa pratensis. *Common toad* (Bufo bufo). *A redwing* (Turdus iliacus) *eating berries in winter. Honey bee* (Apis mellifera) *foraging* Verbena bonariensis. *Speckled wood butterfly* (Pararge aegeria) *taking nectar on* Inula hookeri. *Peacock butterfly caterpillars feasting on stinging nettle.*

Garden life

Creating a range of mini habitats with their accompanying wildlife is key to making a successful, bountiful and rewarding veganic garden. In this average-sized urban plot all the different elements overlap, blending together to create a thriving ecosystem where living things are constantly on the move, interacting and benefiting each other.

1 Pollinating insects flock to the flowers on the shed's living roof.

2 Shrubs such as firethorn (Pyracantha) provide pollen and nectar for insects in early summer, and its berries provide autumn and winter food for thrushes and other birds.

3 A dense, spiky holly bush is an ideal nest (and roosting) site for blackbirds.

4 Birds roost in this silver birch. A mature tree is an asset in the garden.

Clockwise from above: *Nest boxes attract insect-eating birds such as blue tits (Cyanistes caeruleus). Aphids on stinging nettle (Urtica dioica) in spring attract beneficial insects such as lacewings and ladybirds. Including waterlilies (Nymphaea spp.) provides shade and cover for pond-dwelling wildlife.*

5 Hedgehogs hibernate in piles of dry leaves left in undisturbed corners.

6 Insect hotels lure in beneficial and pollinating insects.

7 Slow worms, grass snakes, common lizards, frogs, toads, and ground-dwelling bugs such as slug-eating centipedes live in piles of rotting logs.

8 Sunflowers provide pollen and nectar for beneficial insects, such as bumblebees, followed by food for seed-eating birds such as goldfinches.

9 Sparrowhawks prey on smaller birds.

10 Compost heaps are mini ecosystems in themselves, and help feed the soil.

11 Nest boxes attract birds such as tits.

12 Multipurpose weeds such as stinging nettles attract pest-eating insects, feed butterfly caterpillars, and their young leafy shoots can be turned into liquid plant feed.

13 Ground and rove beetles hide in longer, uncut grass during the day, then forage at night, feeding on slugs, the eggs of cabbage root fly, and other ground-dwelling bugs.

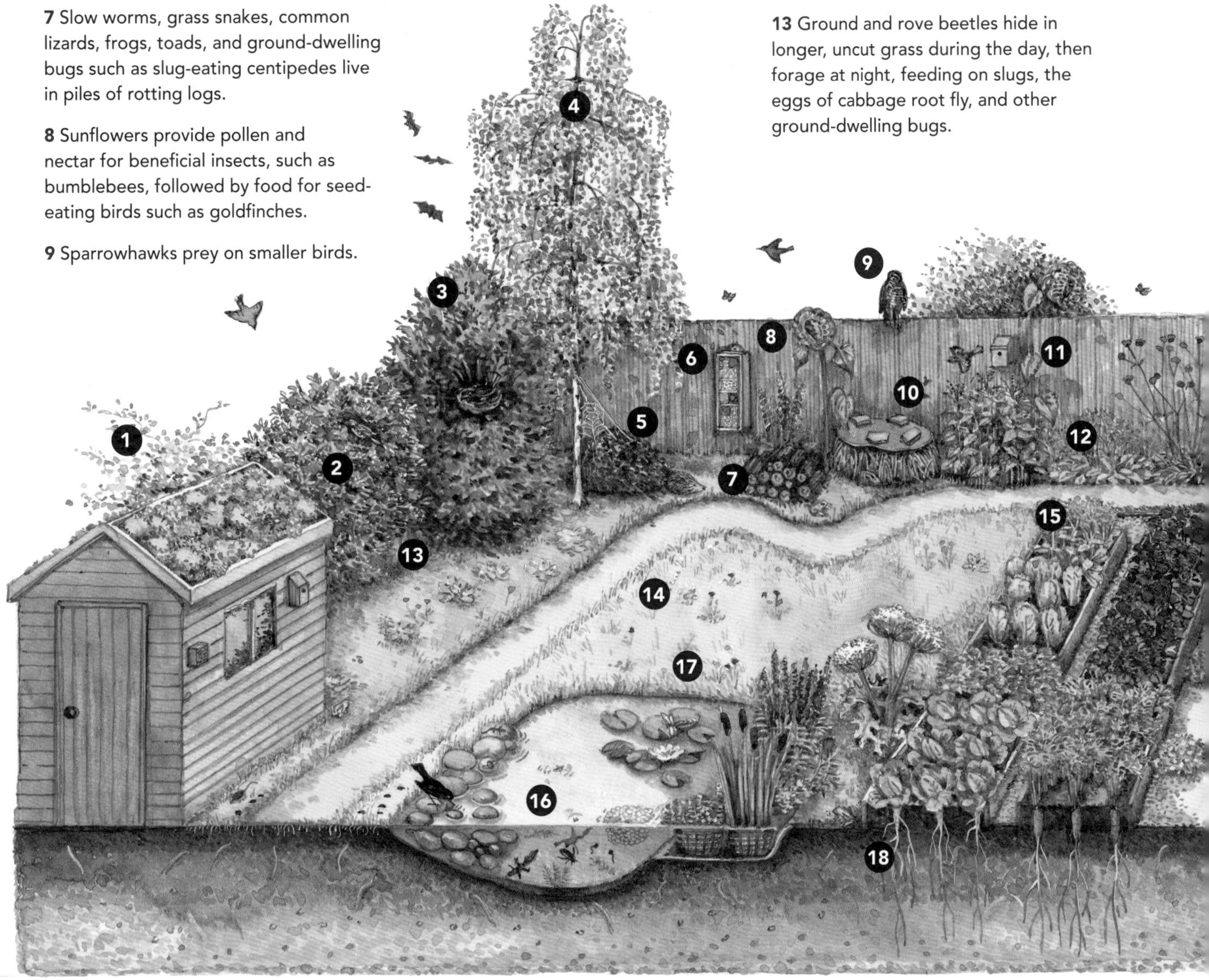

14 Letting a lawn go 'wild' and grow longer, allowing weeds such as dandelions to bloom, and introducing wildflowers and bulbs, creates habitat for plant- and ground-dwelling bugs.

15 Self-sown flowers growing among the food crops attract beneficial insects.

16 A pond is a mini ecosystem. Frogs, toads, newts, beetles and dragonflies will breed there, while birds, mammals and insects drink and bathe in the shallows.

17 Bats feed on moths and other night-flying insects drawn to the garden, especially by the pond.

18 Healthy no-dig soil supports the garden's entire ecosystem and teems with microbial life.

Climate-friendly gardening

Gardeners worldwide are dealing with the everyday effects of human-made climate chaos. Hotter summers, wetter but milder winters, droughts, and sudden, frequent flooding, together with palpable shifts in seasons are among the increasingly extreme weather events we now experience. Veganic gardening is a practical, positive and empowering way of making your own individual contribution to helping mitigate the growing impacts – near and far – of dangerous climate breakdown.

Above left: Consider carefully the essential tools and equipment you actually need for your veganic gardening; much garden-related paraphernalia is sold in response to fads and if it cannot be recycled, will probably end up as landfill.

OUR CLIMATE EMERGENCY

What happens to our shared global climate affects every living being on earth. Overwhelming scientific consensus agrees that a build-up of carbon dioxide and other greenhouse gases in our planet's atmosphere is due to human activities, primarily the burning of the fossil fuels coal, oil and natural gas. This unseen pollution acts like an insulating blanket wrapped around the planet, trapping in heat energy from the sun, resulting in global warming. It is this heating effect which is now driving climate breakdown and the disruption of weather patterns everywhere. Some effects are already apparent: perhaps the most familiar is the rapidly accelerating melting of polar ice and glaciers. Unless we drastically reduce carbon emissions within decades, average global temperatures will keep rising, leading to dangerous, irreversible changes which will hit the world's poorest and least developed populations the hardest.

Gardeners can do more than simply adapt to climate breakdown by growing different types of plants, and by changing how and when we do things. We can make informed, mindful choices which do not add to the problem, and which can help slow its pace. Veganic gardening combines simple and practical gardening solutions which are inherently climate-friendly.

REDUCING ENERGY USE

Using powered garden equipment requires energy and creates pollution, especially when petroleum is burned. The most climate-friendly garden equipment is powered by

renewable electricity from a 'green' supplier. Synthetic fertilisers and pesticides (insecticides, fungicides, weedkillers) use raw materials and energy in their production, packaging (predominantly plastic) and transport. Synthetic weedkillers generate more carbon emissions than any other garden pesticides.

Veganic growing aims to minimise energy use. Instead of relying, for example, on insecticides, we encourage nature itself to keep any harmful bugs in check, by fostering a vibrant, diverse and self-balancing garden ecosystem.

LOCKING UP CARBON

One way we can reduce the concentration of atmospheric carbon is to lock up some of it in our garden soil and in the plants we grow. Adding organic matter to your soil leads to a build-up of dark humus, which can store some carbon for long periods. All plants absorb carbon dioxide from the air, storing it in their tissues. Veganic techniques aim to transfer the carbon and other substances found in plant tissues (living and dead) directly to the soil, such as when green wood chips are incorporated to add fertility (page 142). Adopting a no-dig approach, where soil disturbance is minimal, is also a key veganic technique.

Trees and shrubs store large amounts of carbon for long periods; large, fast-growing trees are most effective at locking carbon away in the woody parts of their roots, trunks, branches and stems, as well as their leaves (which we turn into leaf mould, page 147). Look after your trees: if they die their stored carbon is then released as they decay or when they are burnt.

GROWING VEGANIC FOOD

The food you grow in your garden or allotment requires few energy inputs. Apart from constructing the garden, harvesting might be most energy-intensive job you do. Food from your veganic plot does not need synthetic, oil-derived fertilisers and pesticides to grow, will not require packaging, refrigeration and processing, or transporting thousands of miles – it might travel just footsteps from plot to plate. Home-grown food will reach your table at 'peak freshness' and with its nutritional content intact.

In contrast, modern food production uses energy and resources – including the by-products of animal farming, such as manure and slaughterhouse-derived fertilisers – that generate the greenhouse gases exacerbating our climate emergency.

Above middle: *More frequent and severe flooding is a direct consequence of increasingly intense and extreme weather events driven by accelerating climate breakdown.*

Above right: *Food grown veganically, without any animal by-products, breaks free from the long, energy-intensive chains involved in modern food production, and leaves only a tiny gardening footprint.*

Below, clockwise from left: *These tomatoes were grown in a greenhouse warmed only by renewable sunshine. Self-seeding plants such as foxglove require almost no inputs from us, have a minuscule gardening footprint, and are magnets for bumblebees. In this simple compost heap made of wooden pallets, plant material decays slowly over several years.*

MAKING GARDEN COMPOST

When once-living, organic waste materials are buried in landfill they rot in the oxygen-starved conditions, releasing methane, a heat-trapping greenhouse gas 20 times more powerful than carbon dioxide. Veganic gardeners see garden and kitchen and household waste differently – as an invaluable, soil-nourishing, readily available and ultra-local resource. Using your organic household and garden waste to make garden compost, whether using cool and slow, or hot and fast methods, or by 'wormposting', will transform it into a wonderful rich, cost-free, soil-building compost, which helps sink some carbon into your soil.

RETHINKING OUR LAWNS

Because they remain undisturbed, and because their fibrous roots add organic matter to the soil, lawns can store carbon. But maintaining them can be energy- and resource-intensive, cancelling out any benefits. Applying an annual round of synthetic weedkillers and fertilisers, using a petrol lawn mower, and watering with tap water are all energy-intensive and emit carbon dioxide. Using nitrogen fertilisers can release nitrous oxide, another powerful greenhouse gas.

Climate- and wildlife-friendly lawns are those where most grass is allowed to grow long, and wildflowers are given the chance to flourish

(page 204). A push mower, or an electric model powered by 'green' electricity, can be used to maintain any paths. A quiet, muscle-powered scythe can be used to mow long grass.

REDUCING GARDENING CONSUMERISM

Gardening is now a globalised, high-value industry which is dependent on encouraging gardeners to constantly consume more new products, often regardless of whether they actually need them (or whether they actually do the job). Constantly creating new trends combined with relentless advertising is one way in which gardening consumerism is perpetuated.

Veganic gardeners will occasionally need to buy some everyday gardening essentials, such as a set of basic tools, quality peat-free compost (soil mix), pots, organic flower and vegetable seeds, and plants. But there is much we simply do not need, or some we can grow and/or make for ourselves, such as soil tonics, home-made peat-free compost, and plant ties. Many gardening products use resources and energy in their manufacturing, which often takes place overseas, before they are shipped around the globe to retailers, which all adds to mounting carbon pollution.

Constantly asking ourselves if we really need some of these products and avoiding non-essential ephemera is a vital step toward gardening more thoughtfully.

Above: Self-reliant, low-input veganic gardening is inherently climate-friendly; be discerning in your buying habits, focusing only on equipment, products and materials that are essential.

YOUR GARDENING FOOTPRINT

A 'gardening footprint' is a useful way of visualising how much impact (positive or negative) a certain object, plant or gardening activity has. A small, light footprint means less resources and energy are used, with minimal negative and maximum positive environmental impact. A large footprint indicates the opposite: more resources/energy are used, meaning a greater negative impact. As an example, consider two foxglove plants (*Digitalis purpurea*).

One plant starts life as a self-sown seedling in your garden, germinating in early summer. It grows bigger, forming a leafy, overwintering rosette, then flowers the following spring. Aphids start feeding on the flower buds, but hoverfly larvae soon devour them. This plant needed no pot, label, potting compost, artificial heat, or any kind of pesticide treatment. All you had to do was let it be. Its footprint is tiny.

The other is bought from a garden retailer, a car journey away, in spring, before it flowers. It is in a plastic pot, grown in climate-damaging peat-based compost, with a large plastic label. It was reared in a heated greenhouse, alongside thousands of identical plants. To protect it from pests and diseases, it was treated prophylactically with insecticides and fungicides (you do not know this when you buy it, despite the label promoting it as 'good for pollinators'). After planting, a plastic pot and label are left, to reuse or recycle. This plant required raw materials and energy before arriving in your garden. Its footprint is substantial.

Closed-loop gardening

Nurturing your soil and sustaining a balanced, healthy garden, by relying entirely on ultra-local and renewable resources found within your own environment, is an exciting challenge. Instead of depending on animal manures or slaughterhouse byproducts to build soil fertility, veganic gardening taps into the potential of the plants themselves – which are powered by sunlight – to improve and bolster your garden soil, allowing you to grow an abundance of food and flowers.

WHAT IS A CLOSED-LOOP GARDEN?

The underpinning ethos of closed-loop gardening is that your plot should become as self-sufficient as possible in everything it requires in order for you to be able to grow strong, healthy plants – for food or ornament – year after year. The concept of the closed-loop system is that it creates a virtuous gardening circle, where you neither import fertility from outside your garden or allotment (e.g. green waste compost), nor export it as 'waste' (tough weeds or woody prunings). This is achieved by growing various types of plant which can be used to enhance your garden in different ways, and by composting every scrap of material that will either rot down into garden compost, or can be turned into mulch.

In a mature closed-loop garden, every plant you grow is utilised in some way:

- Trimmings, and dead flowers, leaves, stems and roots, are turned into garden compost, which is used to improve your soil. Woody prunings can be shredded and used as mulch (pages 150 and 154).
- Living mulches (cover crops) protect bare soil while capturing sunlight and absorbing carbon dioxide from the air.
- Coppiced hazel (*Corylus*) sticks can be used as plant supports, then shredded into mulch for beds or paths, while fresh green wood chips can be used to boost soil life (page 142).
- Leaves which fall on your patch can be collected up, slowly turned into leaf mould, then used as a microbe-rich mulch on no-dig soil.
- Comfrey (*Symphytum*) is grown as a leafy 'green' for composting, and can be turned into a nutrient-rich liquid plant tonic (page 166).

With thought and planning, you will be able to keep all valuable plant-derived materials within your garden's own loop. There is a modest gain when it comes to making compost (pages 126–141), because we add imported materials – such as the skins and peelings of bought fruits and vegetables along with paper and card (both made from wood pulp) – to the composting mix.

ALLOW FOR KINKS

Achieving a self-sustaining, closed-loop garden takes time. At the outset, be easier on yourself by allowing some 'kinks' in your garden's loop to help speed up the process. If a neighbour offers you their autumn leaves, dead stems or woody prunings (which would otherwise be put out for collection), or any other organic material of plant origin, gratefully accept them. If lawn mowings are offered, check first they have not been treated with chemical weedkiller, as any residues will damage plants.

Kinking your loop by importing some locally-made soil improver at the outset will give your garden a head start, but check it is made from garden waste, not from general food waste (which may contain animal remains).

Above, clockwise from top left: *Twiggy hazel shoots are ideal supports for peas. Home-grown hazel is a rich, ultra-local resource. Use hazel poles for climbing beans or as a feature in their own right. Reused roofing tiles used as bed edging. Turn dead leaves into leaf mould.*

Opposite: *In autumn hazel twigs and the sweet peas they supported can be shredded into mulch.*

A closed-loop garden in action

This typical urban back yard, surrounded by a wooden boundary fence, is shown in midsummer. Veganic techniques have been used to create a self-sustaining, no-dig garden buzzing with wildlife, where the focus is on growing food. Everything needed to sustain soil fertility is found within the plot's own closed loop, and every scrap of organic 'waste' is recycled into compost, which then nourishes the soil.

Allowing an occasional kink in the loop means the gardeners can import wood chips to top up the paths (which slowly rot down). Another regular import might be vegan-friendly peat-free multipurpose compost, to be used, alongside home-made potting mixes, for raising plants in a lean-to greenhouse at the back of the house.

Below: Even a small and fish-free pond will draw wildlife to your veganic garden, including iridescent damselflies, which might breed there, too.

1 No-dig beds, edged with reused terracotta roof tiles, grow fresh fruit and vegetables. Each bed is 1.2m (4ft) wide and is accessible from all sides. The soil in the beds is never trodden on, is rich in organic matter, dark and alive with an abundance of earthworms. The majority of beds are used to grow vegetables year-round, including no-dig potatoes. Self-sown single flowers are growing at random among the crops, attracting various beneficial bugs.

2 The all-weather paths between the beds are 45cm (18in) wide.

3 Devoted to a permanent planting of black/redcurrants and raspberries, this bed is edged with strawberries. In summer, old cotton net curtains are draped over the bushes to protect the ripening fruits from birds.

4 Buckwheat (*Fagopyrum esculentum*) is being grown as a living mulch, to both 'rest' the bed's soil and increase its organic matter. Pollinators flock to its summer flowers.

5 Paving slabs, lifted to make room for the mixed borders near the house, are reused to make paths.

6 Coarse woody chips, donated by a local tree surgeon, form durable paths between the no-dig beds.

7 An imported barrowload of fresh wood chips from a neighbour are used to top up the paths.

8 Perennial flowers and shrubs are packed into the beds near the paved area, and chosen to attract a range of garden bugs, especially pollinators.

9 A small wildlife-friendly pond is used by frogs, toads and newts for spawning, and will be visited day and night by birds, mammals and insects.

10 Leaf mould is made in a three-bay 'cage' constructed from wooden stakes and 2.5cm (1in) gauge galvanised mesh. The three-year-old mould in the right-hand bay is ready to use.

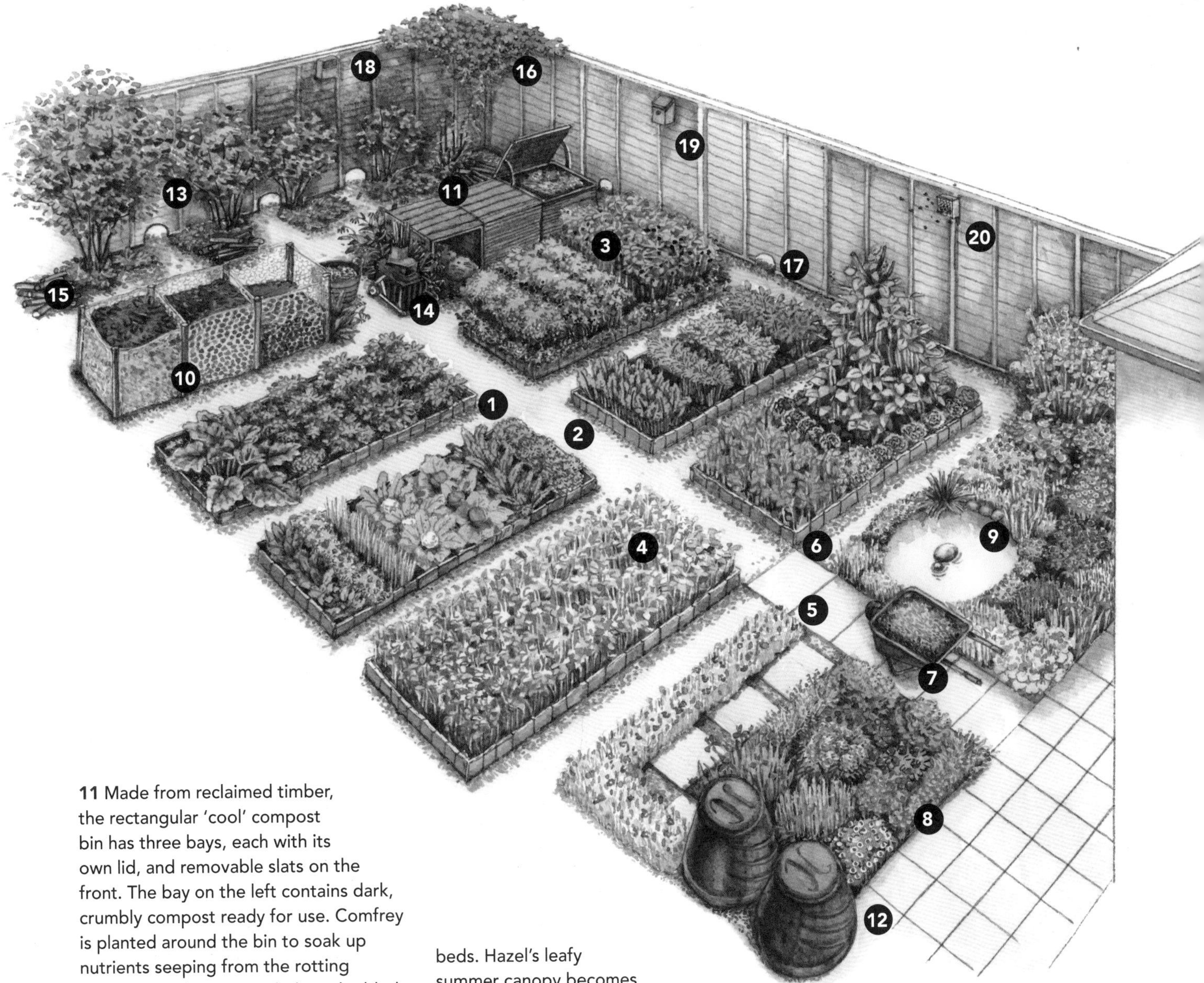

11 Made from reclaimed timber, the rectangular 'cool' compost bin has three bays, each with its own lid, and removable slats on the front. The bay on the left contains dark, crumbly compost ready for use. Comfrey is planted around the bin to soak up nutrients seeping from the rotting compost, and is cut regularly and added to the compost mix going into the bag currently being filled.

12 Recycled plastic bins are used for wormposting all kitchen and household waste (page 138).

13 A mini hazel coppice is used to grow poles for climbing crops, twiggy sticks for pea supports, and shoots for shredding into soil-building green wood chips (page 142). One plant is coppiced (pruned to the ground) each spring, providing a constantly renewing supply of material. The longest shoots, harvested in spring, are used to support runner beans in the beds. Hazel's leafy summer canopy becomes a wildlife refuge, providing valuable cover for birds.

14 A small electric shredder is used to chop up tough, woody stems for use as mulch and/or for paths, and to provide green wood chips.

15 Log piles (made from donated wood) and a layer of dead, rotting leaves create habitat for wildlife. Clumps of primrose (*Primula vulgaris*) bloom in spring, before the hazel canopy opens.

16 A thicket of ivy (*Hedera helix*) climbing over the fence is used by birds for nesting and roosting. Its autumn flowers provide pre-hibernation fuel for butterflies and other insects.

17 Holes 13x13cm (5x5in) cut around the base of the fence panels allow foraging hedgehogs to move freely between gardens.

18 Nest box with open front, used by birds such as robins.

19 Closed wooden nest box for insect-eating blue tits.

20 Home-made timber nest box to attract wild solitary bees and wasps.

Veganic garden basics

This chapter contains all the information you need to get started in veganic gardening. It offers down-to-earth tips on choosing everyday kit – from clothing made without animal-derived materials to plant ties made from compostable plant fibres. Advice is given on vegan-friendly and peat-free sowing and potting compost, together with simple recipes for mixing your own. The problems of plastic pollution, plastic-free growing solutions, and the importance of buying pesticide-free plants are all explored. There are practical, clearly illustrated ideas for harvesting, storing and using rainwater wisely, protecting vulnerable plants in harmless ways, outsmarting slugs and snails, and learning to cherish, utilise and gently curtail garden weeds.

Left: *Garden scarecrows can be an effective yet harmless way of deterring birds, but make sure they wear only 100% cotton clothing to avoid microplastic pollution.*

Choosing vegan-friendly kit

What you actually wear to do your gardening in, and the tools and equipment you use, can also be guided by the vegan and organic ethos. Choosing clothing and products wisely, and focusing on pre-loved items, especially those made from natural, mostly plant-based materials, will break links with animal exploitation, reduce your gardening footprint, and help to combat the global problem of plastic pollution.

Above left: Choosing pre-loved clothing shrinks your gardening footprint and is usually more comfortable to work in.

Above right: Gloves made of 100% cotton are a sensible choice for veganic gardening. They can be buried in your compost heap once they wear out.

PRE-LOVED AND SECONDHAND

We all tend to reserve our older and worn-out clothing for gardening, because it does not matter if it becomes permanently soiled, or torn and ripped from our everyday activities. Often there is the fun in the challenge of seeing how long we can keep on wearing something until it, quite literally, falls to pieces.

If you need a specific bit of gardening kit – say a warm pullover – it makes sense to find a secondhand one. Pre-loved clothing abounds in charity shops, which are a rich source of inexpensive, and often unusual and eye-catching kit for gardeners. Choosing something pre-loved also helps us reduce our own gardening footprint: the energy and raw materials needed to create that item of clothing are already embedded in it, so buying it does not stimulate any fresh demand.

It is important to check what garments are made from: wool (all types), leather (animal skin) and silk (from insect cocoons) are derived directly from the farming and exploitation of animals. Vegan-friendly, plant-derived and animal-free choices include clothing made from cotton (preferably organic), linen (flax fibre), hemp and bamboo. Raffia and other palm fibres are used to make gardening sunhats, and bamboo is used to make socks (usually combined with synthetic fibres to add 'stretchiness'). Check that clothing is actually made of 'pure' or '100%' of the stated fibre, because much modern clothing is a blend of natural and man-made materials. Labels on pre-loved clothing are often faded, so if you are in doubt about what something is made of, choose something else.

AVOIDING SYNTHETICS

Try to avoid clothing made wholly or partly of synthetic fibres, such as polyester, nylon and acrylic, which are made from fossil fuels. Garments such as polyester fleece jackets are lightweight, durable and long-lasting, but they are constantly shedding tiny microplastics (page 46) when worn, and when we wash them. Research has shown that tens of thousands of unseen fragments can be shed during a single machine wash, which enters our river systems and eventually our seas. Even 'green' fleeces, made from recycled plastic bottles, pollute our natural world.

Thick cotton pullovers or jackets can replace synthetic fleeces. Cotton fibres are biodegradable, rot away in the soil, and do not pollute our waterways when the clothing is washed. If you decide to buy new cotton, or any other plant-based clothing, try to choose those which are certified as organic (cotton crops are treated with more pesticides than any other).

Waterproof clothing, even a vegan-friendly option, invariably contains a mixture of synthetic and natural materials. For most gardening needs, a simple waterproof cape or poncho – which allows you to move freely beneath it – is a sensible choice. Stored dry and away from sunlight, it should last for many years.

GLOVES AND FOOTWEAR

The majority of gloves and gauntlets sold to gardeners contains leather, made from processed animal skin (usually from cattle) which is tough and hardwearing. Gloves made of faux 'vegan' leather are available, made of various synthetic materials which are non-recyclable and will need to thrown away when they wear out. Bamboo fibre gloves exist, but they are usually combined with a coating of synthetic rubber, which will break down as the gloves wear out, contributing to microplastic pollution.

One hundred percent cotton/hemp gloves contain no animal byproducts, can be washed (they do not shed harmful fibres), and are compostable when they wear out (note that synthetic stitchings are sometimes left behind once the cotton has rotted). Cotton gloves coated with natural rubber are tougher and waterproof, and can also be added to compost, although they take some time to break down. The rubber will remain after the cotton has rotted away (do not compost cotton gloves coated in or dotted with synthetic rubber). Those made from organic cotton and fairly traded rubber are the most ethical choice.

If you need fully waterproof gloves or gauntlets, a good quality, long-lasting pair made from synthetic rubber (or similar) is a pragmatic, animal-free option.

Vegan-friendly footwear suitable for gardening, such as work boots, or Wellington boots or gumboots made with natural rubber, do exist, although they are often expensive.

Above: *Gardening clothing made entirely from pure plant fibres, such as organically-grown cotton, avoids the risk of microplastic pollution caused by synthetic fibres.*

USE WHAT YOU HAVE

When you switch to veganic gardening, it is sensible to make the best use of the kit you already have, exploring vegan-friendly options when you need to. There is little to be gained by throwing out a pair of trusted leather-containing gloves or work boots (right) – unless you feel strongly that it is the right choice for you. You may as well use what you have until it wears out (the raw materials and energy needed to make the item are already embedded in it).

Clothing is more of a conundrum: continuing to wear (and machine wash) even a favourite and well-worn polyester fleece jacket means microplastic pollution will still be shed into the air, water and soil. The only solution is to dispose of the fleece (it cannot be recycled) and switch to clothing made from biodegradable plant fibres, such as cotton.

Tools and materials

Tending to your garden requires some basic, quality tools, as well as other materials. If you look after, maintain and have tools repaired when needed, they should last your gardening lifetime – or even longer. Where you can, choose robust tools made as locally as possible, from long-lived wood and metal, rather than plastic. Plant ties, supports and labels derived from plants can easily replace polluting plastic options.

OLD OR NEW?

You will often find pre-loved garden tools for sale in junk and secondhand shops or thrift stores. They are an ecologically-sound choice because buying them helps reduce the demand for new (often cheap and plastic) tools, and therefore avoids the resources and energy required to manufacture them. Tools with plastic components will eventually break down in sunlight and might become a source of widespread pollution (page 46).

Cherished tools passed from one generation to another are a good example of reuse in action; the older tools are sometimes superior to their modern equivalents, having better balance or longer handles which are easier to use.

CHOOSING TOOLS

It can be difficult to find out where many new tools are made. Generally, the cheaper tools are likely to have been mass-produced and will be short-lived. Whenever you choose tools, get a feel for what they will be like in use. Is it heavy or light? Will a long or short handle be easier? What is the balance like? Is it easily adjustable? Does it offer good grip?

USING COPPER TOOLS

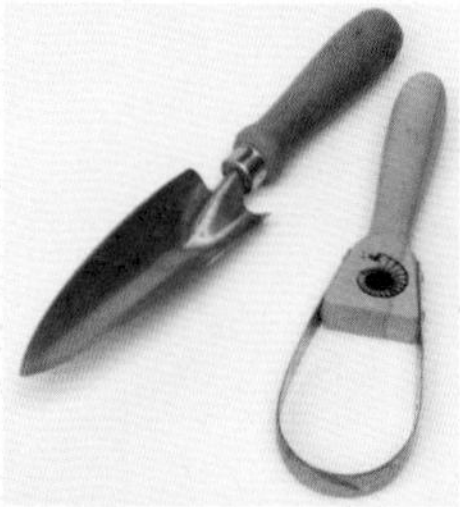

Gardeners who use tools made of copper, such as this trowel and weeder, often find that their plants are less prone to slug and snail damage. One theory is that copper tools do not, unlike those made from iron, disturb the soil's natural magnetic fields. Using copper for cultivating soil and for planting and weeding is thought to impart deterrent qualities (this effect has been shown to be limited when copper rings and tapes are used as deterrents). You can also get copper spades, forks and hoes.

Tools for the veganic garden

The veganic gardener's ethos of adopting a no-dig approach (page 114) in which the soil's own unique ecosystem is disturbed as little as possible, influences the set of garden tools you will need (and how you use them).

SPADE

Not used for digging, but for moving compost, green wood chips, leaf mould and mulches around, and spreading them over the soil, loading up a wheelbarrow, and for chopping up weeds and sappy garden waste before it is composted. Stainless steel blades (and tines on forks) stay rust-free and are easy to clean.

GARDEN FORK

Used for loosening the soil surface and mixing in garden compost, green wood chips and leaf mould, for building a 'cool' compost heap, and mixing the ingredients in a 'hot' one. Use a fork to loosen the soil around large weeds with deep tap roots, and around root vegetables such as parsnips. A fork is useful for moving around piles of garden debris.

TROWEL

Used to make planting holes for small or 'plug' plants and bulbs, and for sowing larger seeds.

HAND FORK/WEEDER

Useful for loosening and lifting smaller weeds.

SECATEURS

For pruning shoots of woody plants such as shrubs, removing dead flowerheads and for cutting back faded perennials. Bypass types that cut like scissors are better than the anvil types that work by pressing a sharp blade against a solid surface. Always keep the blades clean and use a biodegradable oil for lubrication.

Clockwise from top left: Stainless steel fork. Pre-loved wood/metal hand tools. Sturdy steel trowel. Strong steel loppers. Cotton string. Slate plant labels. Wooden boxes, terracotta pots, wooden plant labels, cotton string and other items of plastic-free garden equipment.

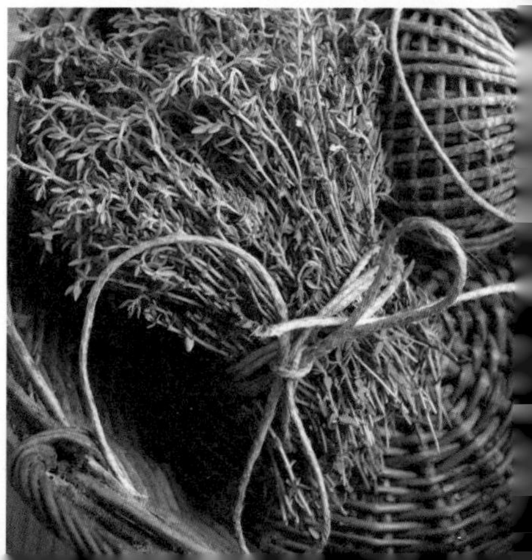

Clockwise from top left: Wood/steel planting dibber. Metal tags and raffia ties. Wooden label. *Cordyline australis* leaves make strong home-grown ties. Jute twine. Selection of pre-loved wood/metal tools.

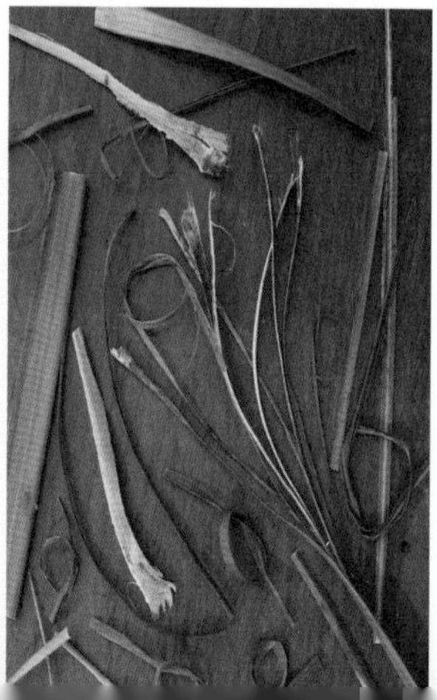

LOPPERS

More powerful than secateurs and used with both hands to cut through the thicker branches of trees and shrubs.

SHEARS

Their scissor-action is useful for trimming soft young growth on hedges and for clipping back long grass, causing minimal harm to any wildlife. Also useful for chopping up any soft weeds ready for composting.

GARDEN KNIFE

Useful for taking plant cuttings, for cutting twine, removing dead flowerheads, and for harvesting food crops.

LEAF RAKE

Essential for quickly gathering up large quantities of fallen leaves to turn into leaf mould, and for general tidying up. Invest in one with a wooden shaft and a fan-shaped head of sprung metal tines.

PLASTIC-FREE PLANT LABELS

Labels remind us of what we have sown or planted, and where. Most are made from plastic, which breaks up after a few years in the sun. Unless you recycle or dispose of perished plastic labels when they snap (use them until they do), they add to microplastic pollution in the soil (it is unwise to make your own labels from household plastics because they break down in the sun within a few months). Labels made from plant-derived and other materials are available, but usually cost more than plastic. Recycled plastic labels are also available.

Labels made from wood and bamboo are widely available (write on them using a non-toxic marker pen) and can be composted when they wear out. Twigs 1.3–2.5cm (½–1in) in diameter and split lengthways make effective home-grown labels. Aluminium, copper and galvanised steel labels have a bigger gardening footprint, but do not pollute in use, and are a good choice for long-lived plants such as trees and shrubs. Write on them using a non-toxic marker pen.

PLANT TIES AND SUPPORTS

Synthetic materials such as polypropylene, and reused agricultural baler twine, are widely used for both supporting climbing plants and for tying stems to supports. In time these degrade in sunlight and fray, shedding copious clouds of microplastic pollution.

Nylon hosiery is often used for DIY plant ties, but these soon fragment in sunlight, so avoid using them.

Renewable plant fibres offer effective, pollution-free and compostable options for supporting plants. Most fibre-producing crops grow in warm climates, needing few fertiliser or synthetic pesticide inputs, and some are grown organically:

- Jute/hessian twine, made from the fibres of *Corchorus* spp. is soft, easy to use, and is also available in netting form for peas and climbing beans.
- Sisal is made from *Agave sisalina* fibres, and turned into a tough, hardwearing and 'hairy' fibrous twine.
- Hemp rope/twine is made from soft and pliable *Cannabis sativa* fibres. Available from do-it-yourself and craft stores.
- Flax twine made from *Linum usitatissimum* is strong, smooth and ideal for tying in woody plants trained on walls.
- Raffia is made from flat strips of palm leaves, which are soft and pliable.
- Cotton twine/string is flexible, soft and easy to use.

Home-made ties can also be made from old 100% cotton clothing; strips 10–12.5cm (4–5in) in length suit most tying-in jobs.

Below: *Home-grown bamboo stakes and ties made from the fibrous leaves of New Zealand flax are used to support dahlias. Both can be shredded and/or composted after use.*

GROW YOUR OWN PLANT TIES

You can easily source your own plastic-free, ultra-local and infinitely renewable plant ties by growing plants with tough, fibrous leaves. New Zealand flax (*Phormium* spp.) and cabbage palm (*Cordyline australis*) are tough and long-lived, with narrow, elongated leaves which can easily be torn into strips to make small and large, thick or thin ties, in whatever lengths you need. Tying them around plants stems is easy, they look attractive, and can be composted when they wear out.

1 Cut New Zealand flax leaves to the length needed, then split them.

2 Put the tie around the stem and cross them to form a separating loop.

3 Secure the tie to the support by tying the ends with a knot.

Vegan-friendly composts

To sow seeds, and to pot-up and grow young plants in pots, trays and containers, we need compost (soil mix) made from genuinely renewable raw materials. There are different kinds available, but only a few of these are entirely free of animal byproducts and therefore suitable for veganic gardening. All composts have some environmental impact in their production, but it is the peat-containing mixes which cause maximum harm.

COMPOST EXPLAINED

The seed, potting and multipurpose composts which we buy ready-mixed (usually in plastic bags), are different from the garden compost produced in a compost bin or heap, or by 'wormposting' (page 138). Purchased peat-free composts are free of weed seeds and pests and diseases, although the most successful composts are still 'alive' with beneficial microbial life. Always aim to buy fresh compost, rejecting any faded, torn or waterlogged bags.

Garden compost, and/or 'wormpost', can be used as part of a home-made mix. It will contain weed seeds, and possibly pests or diseases (unless it has been made using a 'hot' technique – page 134), and is best used for potting up/on larger plants with already well-developed root systems. If you are new to gardening, bought composts are a more reliable option for sowing and then growing on young seedlings, and for potting up young mail order plants. As your experience grows, you can begin to experiment with home-made mixes (pages 42–45), which have only a modest gardening footprint.

WHAT IS 'VEGAN-FRIENDLY' COMPOST?

Unless a compost is labelled as 'vegan', 'vegan-friendly' or 'suitable for vegans', it will almost certainly contain one or more fertilisers made from slaughterhouse byproducts, such as dried blood, bonemeal or 'hoof and horn' (ground-up animal bones, hooves and horns). Poultry manure and ground shells from the seafood industry are also used as fertiliser. Composted cattle manure is sometimes used in compost mixes (or sold as a product in its own right). Mixes containing composted sheep's wool are not suitable for veganic gardening. Check the information on bags before you buy, or ask the retailer for more information.

Opposite: Sown and then potted in a modern vegan-friendly and peat-free compost, these healthy and strong-rooted Dahlia *'Bishop's Children' are ready to plant out.*

Vegan-friendly, peat-free compost is available for all kinds of plants, including acid-loving plants which need an ericaceous (lime-free) mix. If finding suitable compost proves difficult, an online search for 'vegan compost' will help you to find local stockists, or provide mail order options. Choosing a compost that is certified organic gives extra reassurance that it has been manufactured without the use of artificial fertilisers, pesticides or other chemicals.

RENEWABILITY MATTERS

The most ecologically sustainable composts are those made from genuinely renewable raw materials, which can be grown and harvested repeatedly, while causing minimal environmental impact. These materials are often byproducts of other industries; fine bark and wood fibre (from conifers such as spruce pine trees), and coir, the granular pith from the outer husks of coconuts, are key components in modern peat-free composts used widely in commercial horticulture (and by veganic gardeners).

Green waste compost, made locally from composted plant material (prunings, lawn

Above: Tree bark is graded into small fragments before being blended with other ingredients to make peat-free gardening composts.

WHAT DOES 'ORGANIC' AND 'VEGAN ORGANIC' MEAN?

In its purest sense 'organic' refers to anything that is derived from once-living matter; leaf mould is 'organic' in that it forms from decayed leaves. In this sense, all composts are organic by nature, but some are also *certified* as organic. This means they have been manufactured to a set of 'organic standards' defined by an organisation, showing the compost has met strict criteria in the sourcing of its ingredients, and in its production. This generally means the compost is made without the use of artificial fertilisers, pesticides or other chemicals, or genetically-modified organisms, although some animal-derived ingredients will still be used. Organically-certified composts which are also vegan-friendly take this a step further, by excluding the use of *any* animal-derived materials. Composts which meet the criteria set by certifying bodies (which inspect the manufacture of the compost) can display those logos on their bags.

Above, left to right: *Garden compost is simple to make and full of plant nutrients. Hollyhock (Alcea) seedlings thriving in a vegan and peat-free multipurpose compost.*

Opposite: *Cordon tomatoes and other crops thrive in the author's greenhouse.*

mowings, weeds), collected from gardens, is sometimes included in composts, and also sold as a soil improver (check that it is derived from plant material, and contains no food waste of animal origin). Another plant-derived and vegan-friendly material is digestate, a renewable byproduct of green energy generation, which is showing promise as a nutrient-rich addition to potting composts and as a soil improver.

SIGNS OF LIFE

There is no need to worry if you open a bag of bought compost and find pale moulds coating either the compost, or the inside of the bag. These moulds grow in certain conditions and will not harm plants (or you). Fresh bags of compost can sometimes feel warm when you by them. As with mould, this a positive sign that the compost is healthy and 'alive' with microbial activity.

At home, leaf mould, wood chips, garden-made compost, and wormpost are all 'renewable' because we can make them repeatedly from plant and other household materials, and we can be certain they do not contain any animal inputs, such as food scraps. Because deciduous trees unfailingly shed their leaves each year, mature leaf mould is one of the best, ultra-local, plentiful and free raw ingredients, both for making home-made vegan sowing and potting compost (pages 42–45), and for feeding and mulching no-dig soil.

VEGAN-FRIENDLY COMPOST INGREDIENTS

Coir

Although coir is imported from tropical climates, it is dried and compressed into blocks first. Efficient sea freight transport gives coir a relatively modest gardening footprint. It is available in pure form, which can be used in home-made compost mixes, or as a ready-to-use compost, complete with fertilisers.

Composted bark

Small woody chips of bark taken from conifers such as spruce (*Picea* spp.) is used in quality peat-free potting mixes, often with wood fibre and coir, and helps to keep the compost well-aerated and free draining. Bark can also be used in home-made potting mixes.

Leaf mould

Ultra-local and easy to make in quantity, well-rotted, 2–3 year-old leaf mould is an ideal base for making your own veganic composts. It primes home-made mixes with microbial life and is easy to store outdoors, covered with a sheet, or in bags. Sieve it first before using.

Garden compost

Made slowly in a cool heap, or more quickly in a hot heap, crumbly mature garden compost is rich in plant nutrients. It can be sieved to remove lumps and used as part of a home-made potting mix. It teems with beneficial microbial life, stimulating healthy growth.

Wormpost

Fine, dark and crumbly, wormpost is made up of the organic materials added to a compost bin and eaten by composting worms. The resulting wormcasts are rich in plant foods/growth stimulants and beneficial microbes, and produce reliable home-made potting mixes.

Wood chips

Green wood chips (page 142) which have been stored in a heap, where microbes and fungi have partly broken them down, will add bulk to home-made composts, and also help to keep such mixes open and well-drained.

Digestate

Anaerobic digesters are fed a mixture of chopped forage maize and other grasses to produce biogas (methane), which is used as an energy source. Digestate is the crumbly, sweet-smelling material left over once digestion ends. It can help boost the performance of bought peat-free composts and can be used in home-made mixes.

Peat-free compost

Bought peat-free composts are generally made from a mixture of bark, wood/plant fibre, coir and fertiliser, or just coir. Some will contain horticultural sand, loam and green waste compost. Always check they are vegan-friendly. Compost not labelled as peat-free could contain up to 100% peat.

Peat-free gardening

Going 'peat-free' in your garden means not using compost, soil improver, or any other products containing either sphagnum moss peat, or sedge peat. Healthy and undamaged peat bogs are among earth's most important carbon stores. Draining and effectively 'killing' bogs, then mining their peat to make compost, releases their carbon, helping drive climate breakdown. Modern peat-free composts, made from genuinely renewable materials, help your veganic garden thrive.

Above, left to right: *Peat mining is carried out on an industrial scale. Carbon-storing sphagnum mosses. Dahlia seedlings thriving in peat-free compost.*

WHAT IS PEAT?

Peat (peat moss) is a pale brown, spongy material formed from the partial decomposition of decaying mosses growing in bogs found in moist climates. It forms, at a rate of 1mm (0.04in) a year, in the waterlogged, anaerobic layer below the green carpet of living moss carpeting the surface of a healthy, functioning bog. Together, the world's peatlands lock away more than twice the amount of carbon stored in all of the world's forests.

'Sphagnum moss peat' is the main type of peat used to make sowing and potting composts, and is mined, on an industrial scale, from lowland raised bogs (upland blanket bogs are not generally used for compost-making). Brown-black sedge peat consists of the decaying remains of sedges, reeds and other plants, and is used much less. Sphagnum peat is a fossil fuel which, if left undisturbed, eventually forms coal.

When peat is processed by milling, it turns into a fine, crumbly material which both holds water and keeps compost mixes open and aerated. Peat is a cheap raw material to extract and has been used successfully for growing plants for many decades. Nonetheless, the mining of peat has negative, harmful impact on our natural world.

PEAT-FREE CARNIVOROUS PLANTS

Pitcher plants (*Sarracenia* spp.) and sundews (*Drosera* spp.) grow naturally in nutrient-poor acidic sphagnum bogs. They get their food by catching and digesting insects, either in or on their leaves. Despite growing in bogs containing peat, these and many other carnivorous plants can be grown easily and successfully in gardens, using bespoke peat-free potting mixes (usually a blend of fine composted bark and perlite).

THE PROBLEM WITH PEAT

The mining of sphagnum peat from lowland raised bogs causes damage at both a local and a global level:

• Before peat can be mined, the site must be drained to allow access for machinery. Stripping off the thin living moss layer, and digging drainage channels, kills the bog. Air entering the drained peat (which can be 6m/20ft or more deep) causes it to oxidise, releasing carbon dioxide which may have been safely stored away for millennia. More is released when the peat is mined, stacked and eventually milled, exposing it to the air. This adds to atmospheric carbon, helping to further exacerbate our global climate emergency.

• Killing a bog prior to peat mining completely destroys a natural, established ecosystem that was habitat for sometimes rare species of mammals, birds, insects, plants, and many other kinds of wildlife. Mining leaves behind a barren, lifeless landscape. Restoring stripped bogs so they can 'live' again, soak up carbon and become a functioning, wildlife-rich ecosystem, is a long-term and often expensive process.

• Peat mining can damage adjacent wildlife habitats because of the dramatic drops in water tables when lowland bogs are drained. Localised floods can also be exacerbated by the removal of sphagnum bogs which while healthy and intact act like a giant waterlogged sponge. If the bog no longer exists, the water it once stored, and then gradually released over time, has to go somewhere else, contributing to increasingly intense flooding events.

PEAT IS NON-RENEWABLE

An average harvest from a drained bog removes around 20cm (8in) a year. In a lowland sphagnum bog, peat forms at a rate of 1mm (0.04in) per year. The loss cannot be made up because the bog is dead; no live moss is present and no fresh peat can form – there are no commercial peat operations where peat is forming on one part of a bog at the same rate as it is being removed elsewhere. Peat is a finite and non-renewable material. Our peatlands are now far more valuable – ecologically and societally – as undisturbed carbon sinks and wildlife habitats, than as potting compost.

GOING PEAT-FREE

Modern peat-free composts, made from renewable materials, can grow plants equally as well as, or in some instances even better than, those containing peat. An increasing number of professional growers now run their businesses using peat-free mixes (and the resulting plants are often widely available for gardeners to buy). The quality of peat-free composts can vary, and you will generally get what you pay for. The inexpensive mixes might seem tempting as a money-saving bargain, but they are more likely to give you poor, disappointing results. It is far wiser to invest in a top-quality compost clearly labelled as 'vegan friendly'. As you gain more experience, you can experiment with making your own peat-free blends (pages 42–45).

An increasing number of plants sold by garden retailers are now grown in peat-free compost. Young peat-free plug plants, especially vegetables and salads, are available by mail order. Some are also certified as organic.

Sourcing plants that are both peat-free and vegan-friendly can prove challenging. The best solution is to raise as many plants as you can yourself, from seeds and cuttings, using sowing and potting composts (including your own mixes) guaranteed to be free from both mined peat and also any animal byproducts.

USING 'GREEN' PEAT

Acceptable 'green' peat compost uses fine particles of upland peat (eroded from blanket bogs) and leaf/plant matter, which are washed by streams and rivers into lakes and dams, where they collect. The silt-like material is removed, via specialist water filtration systems, then blended with fertiliser to make an eco-friendly peat-based compost. Unlike composts containing sphagnum moss peat, no peat is deliberately mined to make them. Some 'green' peat mixes are vegan-friendly and also certified organic.

Below: *No garden plants need peat to succeed. These tulips are thriving in a 50:50 mixture of mature leaf mould and sieved garden compost, both of which are easy to produce at home.*

Home-made sowing and potting compost

Gathering the raw materials and mixing your own sowing and potting compost is one of the most eco-friendly and satisfying aspects of veganic gardening. Your own compost will be unique; its makeup will be determined by the ingredients you have to hand, and you can be certain it is free of animal byproducts. Home-made mixes can be used for seed sowing, propagation, potting up, and for filling containers.

Below: *Making your own veganic sowing and potting composts helps keep your gardening ultra-local and reduces your gardening footprint.*

LEARNING COMES FIRST

Although it is tempting to jump straight in and start making your own compost mixes, it is far better to learn the basics of how sowing and potting composts work when starting out, by using a quality purchased peat-free mix. Bought composts are formulated to give good results, regardless of our level of gardening experience. Using a purchased mix first allows you to become familiar with the way composts perform in general, whether you are sowing seeds or potting up young plants. Importantly, you will learn how to spot when a plant needs more water, both visually – when leaves and stems wilt in the sun – and by feeling the weight of the pot (lighter pots indicate dry compost that needs watering and vice versa).

Because they are made from varying ingredients, home-made composts are less predictable in how they will perform, so it takes longer to get used to growing successfully in them. Starting off with a bought compost means you can acquire the skills needed to make the most of your home-made mixes later on.

Far left: Sieve raw garden compost to remove any woody or unrotted lumps or stones before mixing it with other vegan-friendly ingredients.

Left: Tiny toadstools growing around the sides of biodegradable pots (these are made from compostable paper pulp) will not harm your plants, but are a sign that the compost is filled with beneficial microbial life.

If you cannot wait to try out your own compost blends, then test them alongside a bought peat-free compost; sowing and growing most of your plants in purchased compost will avoid the risk of losses if your first attempt at a home-made mix fails. You will also see how bought compost differs from home-made when it comes to day-to-day care, such as watering.

TEEMING WITH LIFE

One characteristic of home-made composts is that they are full of unseen (and usually harmless) microbial life, which encourages strong plants that are less prone to pests and diseases. Quality peat-free mixes are also biologically 'alive', and encourage strong and healthy growth.

If you are using garden compost or wormpost as part of your home-made mixes, compost worms and other large, easily spotted creatures can be gently removed when you are mixing the ingredients together. Some of the small, pale eggs of compost worms will be left in the mix, but these are nothing to worry about; worms living in pots rarely harm plants.

BEATING WEED SEEDS

Every home-made sowing or potting compost will contain some seeds of weeds and other self-seeding plants. This can be a problem when you are sowing seeds, because the weeds are likely to germinate (below), and start to grow amongst the seedlings of the plant you are trying to raise. Small seedlings of plants you have sown can easily be swamped by vigorous weeds germinating around them.

A simple solution is to use a quality bought peat-free compost in the top quarter of the pot or tray (use more for larger seeds). Bought mixes will be free of weed seeds. Part fill the container with home-made mix, tap to settle, add a layer of purchased compost, sow the seeds, then cover them (if necessary) with the recommended depth of the same mix. The seedlings which subsequently appear will be those you have sown; they should all be identical and will usually appear all at the same time. When you pot them up, you can be certain they are the plants you want and nothing else. The same technique can be used when planting up larger containers.

Among the microbial life in both bought peat-free composts (especially those containing bark and wood fibre) and home-made mixes, are soil-dwelling fungi. These do not harm the plants you are growing, but encourage healthy growth through symbiosis; they both digest and break down woody materials in the compost, releasing useful plant foods, while their mycelium (fine, pale filaments often seen spreading through the compost when you tap a plant from its pot) help the plant's roots to absorb it.

You might only be aware of how active these fungi are when small toadstools sprout from the compost in the tops of pots, sometimes right next to the stems of strong, healthy plants. They often start to appear in spring, and then in flushes throughout summer, but they cause zero harm to plants and do not need to be removed.

TAPPING INTO LEAF MOULD

Dark and crumbly 2–3-year-old leaf mould is the ideal base for home-made compost, so make as much of it as you can (page 147). It is usually free of weed seeds, but contains plenty of beneficial microbes. Leaf mould is naturally low in plant foods and can be sieved and used on its own for sowing seeds, which need few nutrients for germination. But to produce a general-purpose compost suitable for potting seedlings or young plants on, and to sustain plants grown in larger containers, it needs to be mixed with other more nutrient-rich materials, such as wormpost. Leaf mould stores well indefinitely, so a surplus can be carried over from year to year.

BASIC COMPOST RECIPE

The raw ingredients available, the kinds of plants you want to grow, trial and error, and experience will all help you refine your home-made compost. If, for example, you tend to grow a lot of hungry greenhouse crops in pots, then a mix rich in plant foods will give the best results. Keep notes and/or a visual record, so you can check back on what blends give the best results.

This recipe for a home-made peat-free mix can be used for sowing seeds, for potting up young plug plants, and for planting up

Left: *Tomatoes thriving in a home-made vegan-friendly potting mix.*

Below, top to bottom: *Composted bark. Part-decomposed wood chips. Mature leaf mould. Digestate.*

containers. If you cannot find all the ingredients, substitutes are suggested:

- 1 part mature leaf mould (or coir, but without fertiliser added).
- 1 part sieved mature garden compost/wormpost, or some of each (or nutrient-rich digestate, page 39).
- 1 part decomposed green wood chips, page 142 (or composted fine bark).

Wood chips/composted fine bark are not essential, but they do improve the mix. A basic 50:50 mix of leaf mould and garden compost/wormpost will usually give good results.

Garden compost, wormpost and digestate are rich in plant foods, and will sustain most plants for several weeks. Seaweed meal (page 160), which is vegan-friendly, can be added sparingly to the mix, to give it an extra boost of a wide range of plant nutrients.

Mixing is easy. Spread the materials out thinly on a cotton sheet, then pick up each corner in turn, rolling and blending the ingredients together. When you cannot identify any of the individual ingredients, the compost is thoroughly mixed. For large quantities, mixing can be done using a shovel.

Opposite: *Plants raised in healthy, biologically 'alive' compost will grow strongly when planted outdoors.*

Avoiding plastic pollution

Plastic pollution is a serious and accelerating global problem affecting all parts of the earth. While plastic litter is ubiquitous, smaller, often unseen microplastics are also present in our air, soil and water, and have been found in all of nature – from remote mountain ranges to the depths of the oceans. Reducing and eliminating plastic use in our gardens helps to reduce the harmful effects on other life, large and small.

Opposite: A sturdy metal watering can could last you a gardening lifetime, and is a wiser environmental choice than a cheap, short-lived and potentially polluting plastic one.

THE PLASTICS PROBLEM

Our gardening activities use large amounts of various types of plastic, almost all of which are made, via energy-dependent manufacturing, from crude oil. The most iconic symbol of gardening's long reliance on plastic is a heap of empty, often faded and cracking plant pots. Much of the plastic used by the gardening and horticulture industries, including that used for pots, is 'single use', meaning it has only one useful purpose before it is either thrown away or, hopefully, recycled into another product. Gardeners can reuse pots over and over again (multi-use) until they eventually wear out.

Horticulture's self-made plastic problem is its extensive use of cheap black plant pots, which cannot be recognised by the optical technology used in recycling, which means that kerbside collection schemes reject them. Although some black plastic is recycled, much is still sent to landfill (where it can take centuries to degrade) or incinerated. Changing the colour of pots can increase recycling rates, but it does not stem the endless flow of plastic into our gardens.

Although pots are a large part of the problem, plastic also enters our gardens and allotments as seed and watering trays, plastic (or part-plastic) tools, cell trays, wheelbarrows and other equipment, hosepipes and watering systems, plant labels, liquid feed and other containers, watering cans and buckets, plastic-coated wire and plant ties and twine, mail-order packaging, plastic film-coated seed and plant packets, propagators, compost bags, bubble wrap greenhouse insulation, shade netting, crop covers and fleece, weed-blocking membranes, planters, potato and patio sacks, outdoor furniture, tool stores, non-glass mini greenhouses, cloches, polytunnel covers, rubberised gloves, trugs, and artificial grass.

Ultraviolet (UV) radiation in sunlight degrades and weakens anything outdoors made from plastic. In time, plastics fade, become brittle and crack, often shattering completely when handled. Gardening plastics are usually treated with UV-stabilisers – which extends their life outdoors – but they do eventually break down. Repurposing plastic food and drink containers for sowing seeds and potting-up plants seems a good way of reusing household plastics, but because they often have no UV protection, and degrade after only a few weeks in sunlight, they are best avoided.

A sun-weakened plant pot or tray, or a faded watering can, could shatter into multiple obvious shards. We can gather most of these up, but there are always smaller, less obvious fragments which fall to the soil, or wash into drains. When a plastic item is lost, by being blown into a corner of the garden, or further afield reaching a stream, river or the sea (pot fragments are regularly found on beaches), where it breaks

Below left: Unseen microplastic pollution in soil can affect the organisms that live there. Some species of earthworm lose weight when they eat tiny fragments of plastic.

Below right: Plastic-free growing – these comfrey plants were grown in biodegradable plant fibre pots using vegan-friendly, peat-free compost. The cardboard box and newspaper they were mailed in can be added to a compost heap or bin.

Top: *Plastic pollution is now ubiquitous in marine ecosystems and affects wildlife such as birds, that can mistake it for food.*

Above: *Plastic plant pots which have escaped from our gardens are a common sight on beaches. Take any pots you find home to reuse, reuse, reuse…*

GOING DARK

The most important action you can take to prolong the useful life of plastic is to keep it in total darkness, away from sunlight. This prevents UV radiation from degrading plastic and shortening its life. Garden sheds, garages or other storage spaces are ideal pot stores (they do not need to be frost-free). Never leave unused plastic pots, trays or plant labels outdoors in the sun, or in your greenhouse; as soon as you have finished using them, store in the dark.

up, we do not get the chance to pick them up. Larger pieces are routinely eaten by wildlife; marine life, including mammals such as whales, as well as fish, will ingest plastic, mistaking it for food, and seabirds will eat plastic detritus and feed it to their young (with often fatal results). Over time, the bigger fragments are broken down into ever-smaller fragments known as 'microplastics'.

WHAT ARE MICROPLASTICS?

Microplastics are bits of plastic less than 5mm (0.2in) across. They are now present everywhere in soil, water, air and, perhaps most conspicuously and colourfully, on beaches, mixed with grains of sand. Tiny microplastics (nanoplastics) can be carried over long distances, in water and by air currents; plastic found in our oceans can return to the land via aerosols generated by crashing waves on the shoreline. Microplastics are also found in mains tap water.

Scientific understanding around the potential harm done by microplastics is in its infancy. We do know they can absorb and concentrate toxic chemicals, and that they are entering and moving up through food chains: if an animal eats another containing microplastics, the concentration of plastic trapped in its tissues will increase, and so on.

WILDLIFE AND PLASTIC POLLUTION

Research shows that soil polluted with microplastics has an adverse effect on some earthworm species, causing them to lose weight, due to either plastic particles irritating the worms' guts, or chemicals in the plastic interfering with their digestion. No one yet knows what the knock-on effects might be if, for example, a bird eats an earthworm which has ingested microplastic present in the soil. Emerging research has found that leaf-cutter bees, *Megachile* spp., are using sections of plastic tape, rather than plant leaves, to seal their nests, which is likely to cause stagnant air inside the nest and a higher risk of fungal-disease problems for the bees' larvae.

TACKLING PLASTIC IN YOUR GARDEN

Eliminating all plastic from your garden can feel daunting, if not impossible. Alternatives are limited, sometimes expensive, and may be difficult to source locally (an online search for 'plastic-free plant pots' will give mail order options). If your garden feels as if it is awash with plastic, applying some simple, realistic practices will help you reach a sensible balance as you work towards becoming plastic-free.

1 Reuse, reuse, reuse

For now, the most pragmatic approach is to keep making good use of the plastic you already have, especially plant pots and trays, by reusing them over and over. Provided they are stored correctly (see Going Dark, opposite), and are not brittle and/or cracking, they will last for many years, often decades, and cause no harm when plants are grown in them. Globally, hundreds of millions of pots already exist, so we ought to utilise them. If you run out, ask neighbours and friends if you can take their pots off their hands.

2 Recycle worn-out plastic

Never use plastic items which are cracked or breaking up. Put suitable plastics out for kerbside collection (ask your local recycling facility for advice on any you are unsure about). Some non-recyclable hard gardening plastic will inevitably go to landfill or incineration. Just do the best you can.

3 Reject new plastic

Impose a strict 'no more plastic' rule on what enters your garden and where they exist, seek alternatives (page 32). This might mean finding a get-around solution. There are no plastic-free versions of hosepipes (yet), so a solution would be to use a metal watering can instead, which is recyclable at the end of its (long) life. Plastic fruit-cage netting can be replaced with its long-lived wire mesh equivalent. Where possible, swap short-lived plastic hand tools for those made of metal and wood.

4 Choose plastic-free alternatives

There are alternatives to plastic, especially for sowing and growing, often made from natural and non-polluting plant-derived materials, that are readily compostable – pots that rot naturally, made of paper: see the suggestions given overleaf. Choose containers such as wood, metal and ceramic instead of plastic.

5 Use recyled plastic as a last resort

Some plastics can be recycled into other useful gardening equipment: a growing number of pots and trays, and heavyweight plastic 'lumber' used for constructing garden beds, is made from 100% recycled, durable plastic. Although purchasing these products stimulates demand for waste rather than new plastic, it still brings plastic, with all of its potential to pollute, into your garden or allotment.

Above left: Plastic sheeting left out in the sun will eventually perish and break down into soil-polluting fragments.

Above right: Look after plastic plant pots and prolong their life by storing them in the dark.

Below: Leaf-cutter bees (Megachile spp.) have been observed using sections of plastic tape instead of leaves (shown here) to seal their nests.

Growing plastic-free

Reusing and responsibly recycling gardening plastics is an important step in reducing pollution, but if you want to minimise or get rid of plastic from your garden altogether, there are various plastic-free sowing and growing options. Ready-made and vegan-friendly products are available to buy, or you can easily make your own for little or no cost, using everyday household materials such as newspaper.

Above left: Roots growing through the base of a pot made from coir fibres, a vegan-friendly byproduct of the coconut industry. Coir pots slowly decompose in the soil.

Above right: Young Cosmos bipinnatus *plants ready for planting, grown in pots made of newspaper, which is starting to rot where the roots are pushing through.*

POTS THAT ROT

Plant pots and trays made from natural, plant-based materials, which rot away either in the soil, or in your compost heap or bin, are pollution-free and add organic matter. These biodegradable pots can be made from paper (see opposite), paper/wood fibre, card, recycled wood pulp, the fibres of coir, bamboo and hemp, natural rubber, rice husks, and straw. The softer options, such as paper and coir fibre pots, can be planted straight into the soil when roots push through the sides of the pot. Harder pots are used just like plastic ones, except that at the end of their life they can be broken up and composted. Always check that biodegradable pots are peat-free, and are not made from animal manure.

Fungi found in microbially-active peat-free composts sometimes feed on pots made from wood/paper pulp, and toilet-roll tubes, resulting in a flush of tiny toadstools. These rarely cause harm, but can steal nutrients from the plants as they break down the pulp. If your seedlings or young plants turn pale when toadstools appear, you can give them a dilute liquid tonic (pages 163 and 166).

Making your own paper pots

1 A wooden pot-maker and newspaper is all you need to make low-impact pots. Use a tin can or bottle to make larger pots.

2 Tear the newspaper into strips according to the size of pot you want, then, on a flat surface, roll them around the pot-maker.

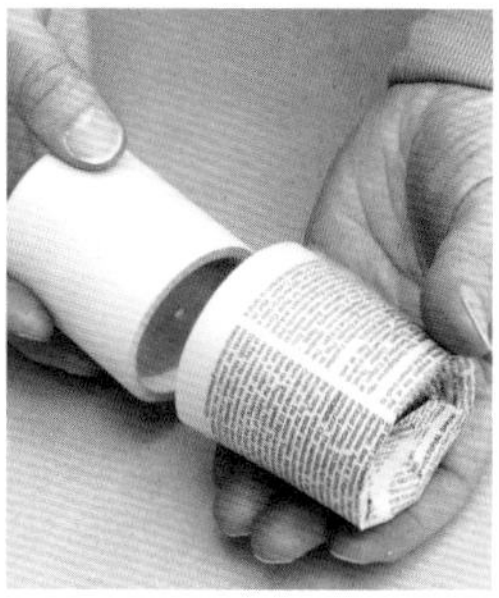

3 Fold the overlapping paper over, firming it to form the pot's base, then slide the newly-made pot from around the pot-maker.

4 Overfill the paper pot with peat-free compost, tap it gently to settle, then lightly brush off excess with the flat of your hand.

5 Sow large seeds by laying them on the compost and pushing them in. For smaller seeds, make holes with a dibber.

6 When roots grow out through the starting-to-rot paper pot, simply plant outdoors or pot-on into a larger container.

Some biodegradable pots are considerably more expensive to buy than others. Those made from a mix of bamboo fibre, rice husks and straw, as well as those made from long-lived natural rubber, are also heavy, adding to their gardening footprint if they are imported from overseas. Home-made paper pots are light, with only a tiny footprint.

METAL AND CERAMIC CONTAINERS

Food-grade aluminium foil trays and dishes, including those used for takeaway food, are good, inexpensive substitutes for plastic seed trays. Drainage holes are easy to puncture in their base, they are not degraded by exposure to sunlight, can be used indefinitely, and aluminium is infinitely recyclable. Ceramic baking dishes (or similar) also make effective seed trays, provided holes are drilled in their base first. Metal and ceramic containers do require energy and resources to make, but they can be reused for many years, and cause no pollution when in use.

CLIMATE-FRIENDLY

LESS PLASTIC, LESS HARM

Both reusing plastic pots and switching to plastic-free options can help ease our climate emergency. Reducing demand for new plastic pots means demand for oil and its refining falls, less pots are made, and the climate-harming emissions from their manufacture and transport decline. Fewer discarded plastic pots entering our ecosystems means less pollution. Plastic-free pots still require energy to make, but do not require oil. Plant-derived materials will instead have absorbed carbon dioxide from the atmosphere, storing it in their roots, stems and leaves.

WOODEN TRAYS

Lined with newspaper, wooden trays can be used for sowing seeds, or growing leafy salad or other patio or balcony crops. Keep them dry when not in use, to prevent rotting and prolong their life. Large trays with carrying handles are useful for moving pot-grown plants around.

CHOOSE PRE-LOVED TERRACOTTA

Terracotta or clay pots are an obvious plastic-free alternative, but they are heavy, and smaller diameter pots dry out rapidly in high temperatures. Terracotta pots are also resource-hungry, requiring raw clay to form them, and then high temperatures – achieved by burning fossil fuels – to fire them.

The most eco-friendly terracotta option is to choose pre-loved containers, especially larger ones (found in junk and salvage stores). The energy used in their manufacture is already 'embedded' in them, so buying them does not trigger fresh demand.

MAKING COMPOST BLOCKS

An entirely plastic- and pot-free option is to make compost blocks using peat-free compost and a metal blocking tool. The tool is pushed into wet, mud-consistency compost, compacting it, and the blocks are extruded into a seed tray. Each block has an indentation in the top, where either a seed/seeds can be sown, or a seedling can be planted. The blocks sit side by side and no pots are required. When roots fill the block of compost, the plants are carefully separated and planted or potted.

You will need to experiment with the compost you are using. Adding crumbly, mature leaf mould will increase stickiness in the compost, helping blocks to form (mix 25% leaf mould with 75% bought compost). Natural cellulose wallpaper paste (free of fungicides and other additives) helps bind compost into blocks; thoroughly mix a teaspoonful of dried paste with a bucket of compost, before you add extra water.

Below left: *Using pre-loved terracotta pots will help to wean you off plastic pots, but you will need to pay more careful attention to regular watering.*

Below right: *Wooden boxes lined with sheets of newspaper are useful for making successional sowings of quick-growing salad crops.*

PLASTIC-FREE PLANT SUPPLIERS

Some plant nurseries offer a plastic-free option: they will remove (and reuse) the pots the plants are growing in, either when you buy them, or before they are sent out. Buying bare-root plants also helps avoid plastic. These plants are grown outdoors, are lifted during the dormant season, and are supplied without any soil around their roots. They are lighter in weight, reducing their gardening footprint, and should be planted as soon as you receive them.

Mail order suppliers (check they use vegan-friendly peat-free compost) espousing a plastic-free ethos will also use compostable packing materials, such as shredded paper and paper-based wrapping tape.

Right: Buying plastic-free will help stem the flow of plastic into your veganic garden or allotment. These hardy geraniums are wrapped in compostable waxed paper.

Pots that rot

All of these pots will rot down when planted in the soil, or added to a compost heap or bin.

Toilet roll tubes Free and ideal for raising vegetables such as brassicas and sweetcorn.

Coir fibre Coir fibres bound with natural latex make sturdy pots.

Recycled paper pulp Use in trays, and separate by gently pulling them apart.

Bamboo fibre Break up and add to your compost heap when worn out.

Paper and coir (left) Roots easily grow through the pot's base and sides.

Hemp (right) Renewable and biodegradable hemp fibre.

Natural rubber cells (right) Tough, yet flexible and reusable, natural rubber is a long-lived and sustainable option.

Choose pesticide-free plants

Most of the plants and bulbs we purchase from gardening retailers, including by mail order, are treated with pesticides – insecticides and fungicides – during their production. Pesticides kill things, often indiscriminately, and can harm the bugs and other wildlife that veganic gardening embraces as part of a healthy and balanced garden ecosystem. Not using pesticides, choosing organically-grown seeds, bulbs and plants, or growing your own, avoids harm to other living things.

Opposite: This globe thistle (Echinops) was grown organically and contains no traces of chemical pesticides which could harm honey bees or other insects.

Below left: Plant nurseries which use no synthetic chemical pesticides are often also using peat-free compost.

Below right: These Narcissus cyclamineus are well established. Any pesticide residues which the bulbs may have contained originally will now have gone.

CHEMICAL COCKTAILS

Most pesticides are synthetic chemicals, often derived from crude oil via energy-intensive and polluting manufacturing, which kill bugs (and fungi) that can damage plants. A few organic pesticides are made from plant extracts, but they still kill living organisms. All pesticides contain an ingredient which kills its intended target, mixed with other substances that help it penetrate and stick to plants. Some pesticides work by killing on contact, while other more insidious chemicals work systemically, by entering and polluting the plant's sap, rendering all parts of the plant poisonous.

Commercial growers use pesticides on their plants, often as a cocktail of different chemicals. Pesticide safety is generally assessed on a chemical-by-chemical basis; little assessment is made of how different substances interact with each other, or how they might affect other non-target organisms. There is no compulsion for growers to list what synthetic pesticides their plants may have received and you cannot tell by looking at a plant whether it has been treated.

Gardeners can buy pesticides freely and use them in any combination, when, where, and however they choose (they need no training in their use). Pesticides pollute our air, water and soil; the residues of some can persist in nature for many years. Globally, there are hundreds of different pesticides in use.

POISONING THE GARDEN FOOD CHAIN

Using a pesticide has potentially harmful knock-on effects for garden wildlife that is not its primary target. For example, if an aphid sucks the sap of a plant treated with a systemic

Clockwise from top: Tulip 'Rococo'. *Minute traces of neonicotinoid insecticide can harm bees and butterflies such as this common blue (*Polyommatus icarus*). Organic flower bulbs. Teasel (*Dipsacus fullonum*) seedlings sown in peat-free compost.*

pesticide, it absorbs that chemical (which pollutes the plant's sap) and is killed. If a bird such as a blue tit then feeds on poisoned aphids, it takes small but accumulating doses of pesticide into its own body. Birds cannot tell whether their prey is tainted with pesticides and might feed polluted food to their young.

Mass-produced spring-flowering bulbs, such as tulips, are routinely treated with systemic insecticides, and fungicides, whose persistent residues can be stored in the dormant bulbs. When the bulbs grow and flower, traces of pesticide will be present not just in the sap of the plant, but also in the flower's petals, pollen and nectar. When insects such as bumblebees forage on the contaminated flowers (they cannot tell if pesticides are present), they will ingest some toxic nectar themselves, and carry that polluted nectar and pollen back to their nests to feed their offspring.

Neonicotinoids are a much-studied group of pesticides used widely in horticulture, which act as neurotoxins – they attack insects' brains, causing paralysis and death. Research has shown that minute traces of these chemicals can impair bumblebees' ability to forage (they become 'lost') and impede the size and development of their colonies, resulting in fewer worker and queen bees, and increasing the risk of disease.

CHOOSING ORGANICALLY-GROWN PLANTS

All gardeners need to buy plants at some point (and it can be fun). The only certain way of obtaining plants guaranteed to have been grown without the use of synthetic pesticides is to choose those certified as organic. This means the grower has raised the plants without the use of any human-made chemical pesticides. Instead, organic growers combine good plant husbandry with naturally-occurring predators and pathogens to keep pests in check.

Various organic bodies offer certification schemes. Growers who meet a strict set of standards can use logos on plant labels and packaging to signal that their plants are pesticide-free. Organic growers might be using animal inputs; check they are using vegan-friendly and peat-free compost, and be prepared to compromise (vegan-organic certification schemes are still in their infancy and do not extend as yet to everyday garden plants). Organically-grown plants can be difficult to find in general retailers, but are easier to locate by searching online.

GROWING YOUR OWN PLANTS

The only way to be certain that your plants are free of both animal inputs and pesticides is to grow them veganically yourself – from seeds, cuttings, offsets, or by division. Raising your own plants gives you complete control over how they are grown; you can be absolutely sure they are raised in a suitable compost (possibly home-made), in an appropriate pot, using only minimal inputs. Home-grown plants require no packaging and might travel only footsteps from where they are sown to where they are grown, giving them a negligible gardening footprint.

Choosing organically-certified seeds, or those from an ethical supplier – or saving and sowing your own seeds, or growing self-sown seedlings – guarantees a pesticide-free start. Mature garden plants are unlikely to contain harmful levels of systemic pesticides and can be safely increased from cuttings. Long-established perennials can be increased by splitting them up (see below).

The best source of new, cost-free and locally-sourced plants for stocking your own garden is the garden of someone you know who does not use any pesticides at all.

Organically-grown bulbs are becoming more widely available, but can cost more than their mass-produced equivalents. If you cannot obtain organic bulbs, as an imperfect compromise you can plant non-organic bulbs but remove their unopened flowerbuds for the first one or two growing seasons. This lessens the risk of insects foraging on potentially contaminated pollen or nectar. By the third growing season, any traces of pesticide residue will have diminished to levels unlikely to cause harm. However, while this is a useful approach for long-lived bulbs such as daffodils (Narcissus) and crocus, it does not work for tulips because their best display is in the spring following planting.

Dividing perennial plants

1 In spring, use a fork to lift a clump as it is just starting to grow. This is an established astrantia.

2 Use a spade (or a knife) to slice through the tough rootstock and divide it into fist-sized clumps.

3 Keep as much soil as you can around the clumps and check that each one has some shoots and roots.

4 Plant the clump and firm the soil in around the roots, leaving a slight depression around the plant.

5 Fill the depression so that water soaks down around the roots. The leaves will wilt at first.

Be water-wise

Water brings the garden to life: seeds and plants need it to grow and flourish, it creates a habitat for wildlife, and it can delight the senses by creating sound and movement. Together with sunlight, rainwater is the most abundant, free and renewable natural resource anyone can harvest. Using it instead of energy-intensive tap water helps us to reduce the impact of our gardening activities on the natural world.

A PRECIOUS RESOURCE

Fresh water is a finite and precious natural resource. Human activity in many parts of the world is consuming it faster than it is being replenished by nature. All living things – including plants – require water to exist. Less than 1% of all the water on earth is available for use; the remainder is either sea water, or water that is held in a frozen state, mostly at the North and South Poles.

As human populations expand and urbanisation accelerates, the demand for safe, drinking quality (potable) water is growing, intensifying pressure on nature. To supply our homes, fresh water is extracted from our environment then sanitised in large purification plants, before being piped to our taps, which all requires energy and resources. Storing large amounts of fresh water in dams can drown and destroy entire ecosystems and displace human communities, while extracting water from rivers and lakes can have an adverse impact on aquatic systems – such as when rivers run dry. Drawing water from underground aquifers can lower water tables, degrading otherwise fertile land. Fresh water is also used for agriculture and horticulture, and for many industrial processes.

Increasingly extreme weather events driven by

Right: *Free and abundant rainwater is worth capturing in any way you can. Rain falling on this shed is collected in a recycled tank that simply overflows into another when full.*

Far right: *Water can be delightful as well as functional. The rainwater in this recycled copper tank is circulated by a solar-powered pump.*

climate breakdown determine how water affects our gardens in two main ways. Firstly, flooding, when rivers burst their banks after prolonged rainfall, or flash floods following rainstorms, can inundate flood-prone gardens and allotments, leaving them underwater for hours, days or even weeks. Over a prolonged period this can have an adverse effect on the soil ecosystem, and flooding can also contaminate gardens with sewage and other debris washed from overwhelmed drains.

Secondly, scarcity of water is a problem that affects gardens more widely, because with too little water over a prolonged spell of often high temperatures, most plants simply fail to grow. Droughts and heatwaves, erratic, muddled seasons and sudden swings in temperature are becoming more commonplace as our climate moves to a newer and more volatile phase. Shifting weather patterns are making gardening more unpredictable, whether we are growing plants for either ornamental value or for food. We can learn and adapt, to a degree, to change, but what is an inconvenience for a gardener growing for pleasure, might be a matter of life and death for someone gardening for their survival. Climate breakdown will inevitably hit the world's poorest and most vulnerable 'gardening' communities the hardest.

Domestic water use is increasing, with a growing amount being used in gardens. Veganic gardening's ethos is to create a beautiful, bountiful and as far as possible self-sustaining garden which has only a minimal impact on our natural world, and also to provide a diverse range of garden habitats for wildlife, which is also being impacted by climatic change. Reducing or stopping your reliance on mains tap water rather than rainwater is one of the easiest ways to keep your garden's overall 'footprint' small, and help your garden be climate-friendly.

HOW WE USE WATER

Water is essential for plants to carry out photosynthesis and respiration (the biological processes by which they grow, flower and fruit)

Above: Wildlife ponds add a dynamic, aquatic ecosystem to a veganic garden or allotment. They can also help alleviate flooding in urban areas as they 'top up' during spells of extreme rainfall.

Right: *A leak-proof wooden barrel stores a generous amount of rainwater diverted straight from this workshop roof. The water can be used either by dunking a watering can in the top of the barrel, or via the tap at the base.*

and to absorb mineral nutrients from the soil through their roots. As gardeners we use water in many different ways, for example:

- Watering seedlings and pot-grown plants.
- Wetting soil grooves (drills) before sowing seeds outdoors.
- Moistening hard and dry, baked soil to make planting easier.
- Settling in newly-planted pot-grown plants or bare-root transplants after planting outdoors.
- Regular watering of lawns, established plants and crops (outdoors and under cover).
- Making and diluting purchased or home-made liquid plant feeds and tonics, and applying these to the roots of plants, and as foliar feeds.
- Creating and topping-up wildlife ponds, bog gardens, water features and bird baths.
- Keeping garden compost heaps or bins moist, and wetting the mix of ingredients during 'hot' composting.
- Watering hanging baskets and container-grown plants (indoors and out).
- Washing soil from hands, boots, tools and harvested root crops.
- Damping down paths in greenhouses to cool them and raise humidity.
- Cleaning greenhouses, polytunnels and paths.
- Blasting away pests with strong jets of water.
- Scrubbing pots and containers.
- Providing a low pressure supply to automatic and semi-automatic watering systems.
- Creating sound and movement (water features such as fountains).

Abundant and cost-free rainwater serves almost all of these uses, but convenience means it is often easier to turn on a tap – which also has a financial cost if your water is metered. Automatic watering systems often require high-pressure mains water to work effectively, but are among the most efficient watering methods. Other non-garden (but often substantial) uses include filling paddling or swimming pools, and washing vehicles.

Sources of water in a garden

A typical garden uses water from various sources. Some comes directly from the sky, as rain, hail and snow, some is straight from the tap, while some is recycled tap or 'grey' water. Much of the water moving through a garden ultimately enters the local drainage and/or sewage network. In a self-reliant veganic garden, the goal is to harvest, intercept, divert and store as much usable water as possible.

Above, left to right: *Use harvested rainwater to wash down a greenhouse or polytunnel; wet the surface with water first, to loosen dirt, and rinse while it is still wet.*

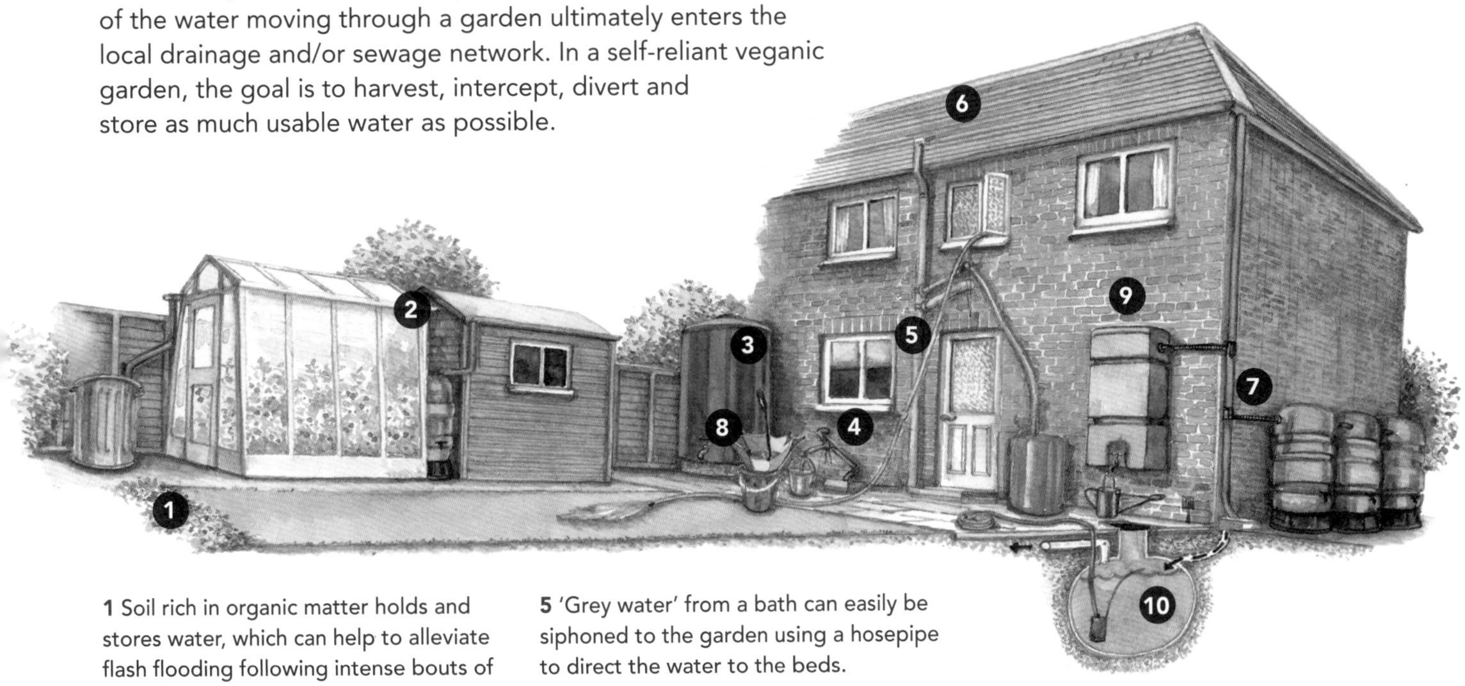

1 Soil rich in organic matter holds and stores water, which can help to alleviate flash flooding following intense bouts of rainfall in urban areas.

2 Greenhouse and shed roofs intercept rainwater to fill tanks or water butts.

3 Downpipes can be plumbed directly into large tanks made of recycled plastic.

4 Fit outlet pipes from kitchen sinks and bathrooms with a diverter so you can easily redirect suitable 'grey water' (see page 64) into a bucket or watering can to use in the garden.

5 'Grey water' from a bath can easily be siphoned to the garden using a hosepipe to direct the water to the beds.

6 House and garage roofs are the single biggest potential source of harvested rainwater.

7 Rainwater diverters fitted to downpipes are easily plumbed into several linked water butts. When one butt is full, it overflows into the next.

8 An old umbrella with holes in it can capture modest but useful amounts of water during rainstorms.

9 Space-saving wall-mounted water butts store rainwater, which can be used for filling watering cans (allow room for cans beneath the butt).

10 In drier climates an underground rainwater storage system can be a substantial but worthwhile investment; the water is pumped out as needed.

Harvesting and storing water

Harvesting and storing as much rainwater as you can is straightforward, costs very little, and is the most climate-friendly and low-impact way of meeting your garden's water needs. Almost any kind of container can be used for storage; water tanks or butts are adaptable and convenient and are often made from recycled plastic, or metal. Some household or 'grey water' can also be used for watering.

Above: *The roofs of our homes are the biggest areas we can harvest rainwater from.*

WATER IN THE SOIL

Soil is one of the most overlooked stores of water in a garden. Once it is improved with garden compost or other sources of organic matter, such as green wood chips, it can absorb and retain large amounts of water which plants can then use. Although it can soak up large quantities of rainwater during heavy rainfall, soil will eventually dry out, especially during prolonged dry spells or drought. Plants will then need a further supply of water to keep them growing and healthy.

CAPTURING WATER

Most harvestable water falls on the roofs of buildings, sheds and greenhouses. This normally runs into the gutters, then the downpipes and on into the drainage network. You can intercept rainwater by tapping into the flow of water in the downpipe. A rainwater diverter is easily fitted to a downpipe, as is shown in the sequence overleaf. On smaller structures such as sheds, a downpipe can simply feed water into a tank, through a lid, or be plumbed directly into a large water tank. To filter out any debris, fix an old cotton sock or cloth over the tank inlet pipe with a jubilee or hose clip. Ensure that any overflow water is directed into a drain, or preferably to a pond or bog garden.

Polytunnels can be fitted with adhesive 'guttering' to harvest rainwater (there may be no other water source nearby).

WATER STORAGE

Rainwater can be stored in any watertight container. Custom-made tanks or water butts usually come pre-fitted with a lid and an outlet tap, and sometimes a base to raise

Clockwise from above: *Rain from a greenhouse is stored close to where it is needed. Water storage using a watertight wooden barrel is both functional and an attractive garden feature. Connected water butts. On/off tap on a plastic butt.*

Above, left to right: Old metal water tanks can look good used in the garden. The roof of even a small shed is worth turning into a rainwater-harvester. Dunking is a quick way to fill a watering can. Only use 'grey' water if you also use vegan-friendly, biodegradable washing-up products.

them off the ground so that a watering can fits under the tap. Wooden barrels also make attractive storage solutions, provided they are watertight. Wall-mounted water tanks save on space. Always choose repurposed containers (search for them online) or those made from recycled materials; check they are free of any contaminants and scrub them out first. Garishly-coloured containers can be disguised using hessian (burlap) sheets wrapped around them (which also gives them some protection from the plastic-degrading ultraviolet (UV) rays in sunshine). Well-fitting lids prevent evaporation and also deter algal growth and breeding insects. Wide and removable lids allow you to easily dunk watering cans or buckets to fill them up.

Although it is desirable to reduce the amount of plastic entering your garden (page 46), most water storage containers will be made

USING 'GREY WATER'

'Grey water' is any used domestic water other than sewage, including kitchen and bath or shower water. It is readily available and useful for general garden watering. It should not contain excessive detergent, fat, or highly perfumed toiletries. Always use vegan-friendly biodegradable products in your household water. Never use chemical-laden dishwasher or washing machine water.

Use grey water immediately, as it quickly smells unpleasant if stored. Never bring it into contact with any edible part of a plant (including root crops); use it around fruit trees, and with care around other crops. Avoid using it under cover or for container-grown plants, and rotate its use around different areas of the garden.

Kitchen and bathroom waste pipes can be fitted with special grey water diverters for filling watering cans or buckets. The water from an upstairs bathtub can be siphoned through a hosepipe straight to the garden, or into a temporary holding tank.

from plastic, so you will need to be pragmatic. Plastic containers experience little wear and tear (reducing the risk of plastic pollution) and should last for many years. Several allotments might be able to share one large storage tank, which will help to spread the initial cost.

The amount of water you store will depend on the size of the garden and how much water it needs: no-dig veganic food gardens will tend to use more than deeply mulched borders of ornamental plants. Greenhouses and polytunnels also increase garden water use because the plants in them are entirely dependent on you for their water needs. Aim to store as much rainwater as possible, as close as possible to where it will be most needed. You can always add extra capacity by linking together additional water tanks.

For safety, all water storage containers, especially larger ones, should sit on a firm, solid and level base (not soil) that is able to carry their weight when full. For larger tanks, this might mean building a brick or block base. Drain the containers before winter to stop them cracking, as water expands as it freezes. They can be scrubbed out while empty.

Installing a rainwater diverter

1 Remove a section of downpipe and fit the diverter. The downpipe will still carry water to the drain when the water butt is full.

2 A leaf trap inside the diverter prevents any leaves and other debris washed down from the roof gutters from entering the butt.

3 Use flexible pipe to connect the diverter to a butt. It should be below the top of the butt so that any unharvestable water drains away.

4 Check the leaf trap by lifting the top section of the diverter. The trap will need emptying at least once a week during autumn leaf fall.

Watering techniques

There are various ways of getting harvested and stored rainwater or tap water to the roots of your plants. They range from the simplest – using a watering can – to installing a fully automatic irrigation system which will do most of the work for you. Low-tech watering methods, involving minimal use of energy and resources, and often using recycled materials, are the natural choices for a veganic garden.

Below: *Filling a shallow, saucer-shaped depression around new plants ensures that water (and any rain that falls later) soaks down deep into the soil around their roots.*

WHY WATERING MATTERS

When plants run short of water, the most visible symptom is wilting: the leaves, stems and flowers flop and sag. This occurs when there is too little water available in the soil or compost to sustain healthy plant growth.

When plants run short of water, they become stressed and can suffer from various problems. Food crops become less productive, resulting in smaller plants, lower yields and the premature dropping of flowers and fruits. Plants are more prone to pests and diseases, and to nutrient deficiencies. Annual plants will 'bolt' (flower prematurely) while only small, and trees and shrubs may shed their leaves early.

USING WATER WISELY

The golden rule of watering is to reduce the need for it as much as possible. This keeps stored water in reserve for periods of real need, and it saves time. Choosing climate-appropriate plants, adopting a no-dig approach, improving soil with garden compost and green wood chips, using mulches to avoid bare earth, removing weeds (which compete for water), shading seedlings from hot sun and sheltering plants from drying wind, all reduce the need for watering. When it does become necessary, apply these simple rules:

- Only water if needed.
- Water in the early morning or evening.
- Prioritise seedlings and new plants (use fresh tap water for seedlings to avoid fungal 'damping off' disease).
- Apply water to the soil or compost, not the leaves, which helps avoid fungal diseases.
- Water soil before you cover it with a mulch.
- Use automatic or semi-automatic systems with a timer to control time and duration of watering.
- Avoid using sprinklers or fine-spray watering lances: they use lots of tap water and much of it is lost through evaporation.
- Do not water no-mow lawns or other wild, grassy areas during dry spells; they will turn brown, but soon recover.

SIMPLE WATERING TECHNIQUES

Water stored in a tank or butt can be transferred to where it is needed in different ways. The simplest way is to fill a watering can or bucket and carry the water to the plants. Various semi-automatic devices are available for watering containers. These turn empty plastic drink bottles into mini reservoirs; water seeps through a spike pushed into the compost, or through an adjustable dripper, over several hours.

A body of stored water can produce enough pressure to make water flow along a hosepipe, provided the water level remains above the final outlet (water will not flow uphill). The larger the body of water, the greater the pressure; raising tanks on a base at least 30cm (12in) off the ground can help. This lets you use a hosepipe to water directly from a tank, or to fill up a tank or butt elsewhere in the garden. The low water pressure makes the rate of flow easily controllable by placing your thumb over the hose end (or use an attachment).

ADVANCED SYSTEMS

Some semi-automatic systems operate using filtered, tank-only pressure water. Dripper pipes, tapes or tubes are laid on the soil (usually in a food garden), and dispense water through holes or nozzles over their entire length. They are easily moved around. A network of porous

DIFFERENT WATERING TECHNIQUES

Watering can Use a can to pour water around plants or for watering containers; you can use a 'rose' fitted on the spout for a fine spray of water.

'Leaky pipe' Water seeps through pores in the recycled rubber pipe, which is buried 5–10cm (2–4in) deep in the soil or under a layer of mulch.

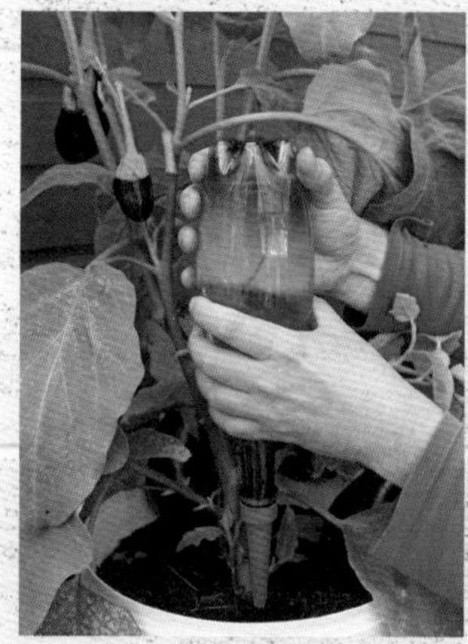

Watering spike This screws on to a repurposed plastic bottle and is pushed into the compost, where it slowly releases water over several hours.

Drip waterer An adjustable dripper regulates the flow of water to the compost from a reservoir of water stored in a repurposed plastic bottle.

Porous pot A buried terracotta water dispenser, fed by a low-pressure water supply (such as a large tank of water) releases moisture into the soil or compost.

Bottle top waterer A screw-on attachment repurposes an empty plastic drinks bottle into a handy waterer for use on young plants and delicate seedlings.

terracotta pots, linked by flexible tubing, will also operate from a tank. Water fills the buried pots, then percolates into the soil or compost.

High-tech drip irrigation systems carry water to individual plants or containers through plastic pipes to special drip nozzles, and they need fitting with a non-return valve. Using a timer allows watering for a set period. These systems need mains tap water pressure to work, so are inherently less climate-friendly than those using stored rainwater. They also introduce more plastic and other materials into your garden. Timers will need batteries to power them.

Recycled rubber 'leaky' pipe releases water under pressure, through its pores. It is covered with soil or mulch, so evaporation losses are minimal, making it an efficient way of watering permanently planted beds and borders.

Protecting your plants

Veganic gardens are no-kill zones but we sometimes need to find ways of protecting plants, especially our food crops, from pests. Simple techniques can be used to deter many pests. The most effective solution is to use physical barriers. You might need to protect your whole garden from larger pests, such as rabbits, with a fence, or prevent butterflies from laying their eggs on your cabbages by using netting.

Above, left to right: Fruit-seeking birds are determined, so double-check there are no gaps between the wire mesh and the soil. A simple barrier of home-grown willow sticks stops pigeons from walking on to the beds from the paths. Food cans around the base of brassica crops, such as these kohlrabi, helps protect them from cabbage root fly and cutworms.

KEEPING OUT LARGER PESTS

Rabbits can cause serious damage to plants by eating them. Installing a 90cm (36in) tall boundary fence of wire mesh, with holes 2.5cm (1in) or less in diameter, is the best way of rabbit-proofing a plot. There should be no gaps and the mesh must be buried 15cm (6in) deep.

Birds will eat both vegetables and fruits. They sometimes peck at crops such as onion sets after planting (usually out of curiosity) but will leave most crops alone once they start growing. To protect vulnerable seedlings and young plants from birds, use sections of wire mesh bent into tunnels or domes and laid over them. Fruit crops are especially prone to being taken by hungry birds and squirrels. Both can strip fruit bushes and trees in hours.

If you grow soft fruit, such as blackcurrants, it is pragmatic to assume that both birds and squirrels will be a problem, and build a permanent walk-in fruit cage, comprised of a metal (or wooden) frame covered with galvanised wire mesh (squirrels can bite through plastic mesh, and sun-degraded mesh can become a source of plastic pollution). If you grow only a small amount of fruit – perhaps strawberries in a raised bed – you can cover them with a smaller, temporary cage, when they are most vulnerable.

OUTSMARTING SMALL MAMMALS

Voles and mice are fast-moving garden cohabitants, which eat and damage our plants. They tend to avoid open spaces, preferring to move around under the cover of plants. Growing food crops such as brassicas in beds with wide paths around them can help to deter them, but is not foolproof; a single vole can nip off an entire bed of young transplants. Voles are active year-round.

A more reliable solution is to surround vulnerable crops with a 45cm (18in) high barrier of 13mm (½in) gauge galvanised welded mesh panels, which voles and mice will not climb over.

This kind of pop-up protection is more easily set up around beds with a defined edge (such as a raised bed). It makes sense to protect a single bed, and use it to grow crops you know are at risk. Voles are persistent and will burrow under the soil; if you see lines of loosened and lifted soil, firm it back down to deter them.

USING NETTING, MESH AND FLEECE

The adults of winged insect pests search out suitable plants on which to lay their eggs, which then hatch into larvae that feed on plants or crops. Protecting plants with a physical barrier, through which the adult pest cannot fly, crawl or push, prevents any egg-laying from taking place.

How you use a barrier depends on which part of a plant is most vulnerable. Cabbage white butterflies will land on and lay their eggs on the leaf undersides of cabbages, cauliflowers or other brassica crops, and the entire plant – or group of plants – must be covered.

If butterflies are the main problem, plastic netting is an effective solution and should be suspended above the crop, using sticks, canes and/or twine, making sure that no leaves are left exposed where butterflies can land.

To keep out other smaller pests, such as carrot and cabbage root fly, which attack the roots of carrots and brassicas, aim to use a barrier with smaller holes (less than 2mm/0.08in in diameter) through which the adult flies cannot pass. This sort of insect mesh is usually made from long-lived polyethylene, and is porous to light, air and water. It comes in varying lengths and widths.

Mesh can be used to make a permanent carrot-fly barrier by putting a fence 60cm (24in) tall around individual soil beds. The adult flies do not fly any higher than this, so the crop is protected. With other crops, the mesh can simply be temporarily draped over them and its edges buried.

Garden fleece is made from polypropylene, a light and finely spun-made porous material with tiny holes. It is laid over crops to protect them from small pests such as flea beetles, and the edges must be anchored in the soil.

Although highly effective, synthetic netting and pest barriers add to your gardening footprint because they require raw materials and energy to make. Fleece can shed tiny fragments, adding to microplastic pollution. If you do use synthetic materials, look after them; store them away from sunlight when they are not in use, and fix any holes. Do not be tempted to wash them; they will shed large amounts of microplastic down the drain.

Everyday plant-based materials with a smaller footprint make highly effective barriers. Faded and 100% cotton net or voile curtains can be sewn together to make excellent pest barriers, which are long-lived, washable, do not pollute, and can be composted when they wear out.

SOIL BARRIERS

Physical barriers will protect plants from soil-dwelling pests. Adult cabbage root flies lay their eggs around the base of brassicas, such as cabbages. The grubs then eat the roots, weakening and, in severe attacks, killing the plant, which wilts and turns yellow. A collar 15cm (6in) wide, made of cardboard, fitted around the stem, prevents egg-laying.

Empty metal food cans, with both ends removed (leaving no sharp edges) work in a similar way and will also protect plants from soil-dwelling cutworms (moth caterpillars), which feed on roots and bite through stems at soil level.

USING DETERRENTS TO SCARE PESTS

Where using netting is not feasible, larger pests, such as pigeons, can be deterred by pushing thin twiggy sticks 60–90cm (24–36in) long into the soil among any at-risk plants. This gives them a harmless fright as they try to land. A barrier of thin sticks, pushed into the soil around the edge of a bed of vulnerable plants, stops birds from walking on to the bed from the path. A combination of twiggy sticks and 'bed barriers' can be extremely effective. Scarecrows give only short-lived protection, especially in areas where pigeons and other wildlife have become used to human activity.

Below: Wire mesh is long-lived, recyclable and flexible enough to be moulded into a protective 'bell' which fits over plants in individual pots.

Bottom: A bed used solely for growing carrots can be protected by surrounding and covering it with fine mesh to keep out egg-laying adult carrot flies.

Slugs and snails

Of all garden pests, slugs and snails are potentially the most damaging. They attack many different plants, both above and below ground, quickly causing extensive damage. As well as adopting less slug- and snail-prone gardening techniques, the most nature-friendly ways of dealing with them are by encouraging a vibrant garden ecosystem, containing an abundance of natural predators, collecting and relocating them, and by using naturally-occurring nemotodes, or eelworms.

Opposite, clockwise from top: Song thrushes (Turdus philomelos) will noisily smash open large numbers of snails in spring while feeding their chicks. Garden snails (Cornu aspersum) are easy to spot, collect and relocate. Shattered snail shells on a stone or 'anvil' used by thrushes.

Below: Leopard slugs eat rotting plant material, but they will also prey on other species of plant-damaging slugs.

WHEN DO THEY DO DAMAGE?

Slugs and snails are active mostly at night when it is cool and moist, especially during wet weather. They move by secreting a layer of sticky mucus over which they slide – the familiar glistening slime trails. Once they find a food source, they will keep returning to it by following their own trails. Both slugs and snails feed using strong, rasping mouthparts. During daytime, when temperatures are higher and the air is drier, slugs retreat into the soil and under stones. Snails have shells which makes them easier to spot, and tend to hide in cracks and crevices. Most damage tends to occur during spring, summer and autumn, but slugs and snails often feed non-stop during increasingly mild winters and can stay active year-round in greenhouses and polytunnels.

Extreme weather events, such as a prolonged dry spell – when slugs and snails become less active – followed by sudden and heavy rainfall, can trigger spikes in the damage caused by slugs and snails. Be on your guard; as soon as conditions turn wet and more humid, they will be out looking for plants to eat.

ACHIEVING A BALANCE

No garden can be made entirely slug- and snail-free. These pests are constantly on the move, can travel surprising distances, and breed rapidly. In a veganic garden we try to achieve a healthy and balanced ecosystem, and slugs and snails are part of that living community. They provide valuable food for wildlife such as birds, frogs and hedgehogs. Some larger slugs, which will live in cool compost bins, such as the leopard slug (*Limax maximus*), eat mostly decaying plant material. They pose little threat to healthy plants and help to break down organic matter, playing a part in the garden compost cycle.

Dealing with slugs and snails is always a balancing act, and using a mixture of different approaches will give the best results. Generally, the younger a plant is, the more alert you need to be in protecting it; seedlings and fresh transplants, especially of vegetables, are particularly vulnerable.

Growing as many plants as possible in pots of vegan-friendly peat-free compost and then planting them out is an effective way to make your garden less vulnerable to slug and snail damage. Larger plants are able to shrug off and recover from damage more easily, so there is less chance of the whole plant being destroyed.

GARLIC INFUSION

Using garlic can be effective when watered over at-risk plants such as hostas. To make your own (pungent) infusion, crush two whole garlic bulbs and then boil them in 2 litres (3.5 pints) of water for 10 minutes. Allow to cool, and then strain the liquid. To use, add one tablespoon to 5 litres (8.8 pints) of plain water and spray/water it over dry foliage in the evening. This leaves a coating that repels slugs and snails but is harmless to other wildlife.

*Above: Snails will hide among plants during the heat of the day – these are clinging to stinging nettle (*Urtica urens*) stems.*

SLUG AND SNAIL HUNTS

Using chemical slug pellets of any kind is against veganic gardening's ethos of respecting all life. The simplest and kindest way to reduce the number of slugs and snails in your garden is to catch and relocate them. They can be collected at night by torchlight, by hand (wear gloves as they are extremely sticky) or using barbecue tongs, and placed in a bucket. Snails have been shown to have strong homing instincts, so they must be relocated to a piece of wild ground or woodland at least 20m (67ft) from your garden. This approach requires more vigilance on an allotment, where slugs and snails are grazing across a large area, and readily move in from neighbouring plots.

Because they retreat to cool dark spots, a simple way of trapping slugs is to lay flat pieces of stone and wood around your garden, preferably with some slug-attracting bran underneath. Check below them each morning and relocate any slugs you find.

BOOSTING NATURAL PREDATORS

The song thrush (*Turdus philomelos*) will eat copious quantities of snails, especially in spring when they are busy feeding their chicks. Piles of broken snail shells can be found in your garden around stone 'anvils' where thrushes noisily smash them up. Putting some stones in open spots around your garden will encourage thrushes to feed there.

Adding a small wildlife pond (page 194) will attract slug-eating frogs, toads and newts, which may also breed there, boosting predator numbers. Hedgehogs living in a rewilded and undisturbed part of the garden will feed on slugs at night. Ground and rove beetles, and centipedes living in 'bug banks', long grass and log piles, will hunt down slugs after dark. Slow worms resident in compost heaps also prey on slugs.

BARRIERS AND DETERRENTS

Various physical barriers are frequently recommended as a means of keeping slugs and snails away from vulnerable plants. Many of

Clockwise from left: Slow worm (*Anguis fragilis*) in search of slugs. Slugs lured by bran are easily relocated. Slugs will not cross a 'moat' of water. Slug damage on carrots. Hand-pick any snails when you find them.

these – including the familiar copper tapes and rings – have been shown through research to be largely ineffective. Physical barriers only work for a short period; once rain falls and wets them, slugs and snails can slide straight over them (they are not deterred by sharp edges).

Water is a highly effective barrier because slugs and snails cannot swim and they will not cross it. Standing individual pots above a shallow reservoir of water (with their bases raised above it), or putting the legs of plant staging in containers of water, will stop slugs and snails from reaching them. Upturned pots stood in water, supporting wooden planks on which plants are placed, are a simple and effective way to protect large numbers of plants.

THE NEMATODE DILEMMA

If other interventions fail to reduce slug and snail populations – or if your garden or allotment ecosystem is still in its infancy – naturally-occurring nematodes (microscopic roundworms or eelworms) can be applied to the soil around slug-prone crops, such as potatoes, as a drench. They are most effective against small and pale slugs, not the larger, less damaging species, and do not control snails.

Nematodes are safe and easy to use, do not harm other garden wildlife (although it is best to apply them away from ponds to avoid any harm to water snails), and are effective on all but heavy soils. The nematodes, which occur naturally in soil, invade the slugs' bodies and secrete bacteria, killing the slugs from within, usually when slugs are hidden. Dead slugs then release more eelworms into the surrounding soil.

Nematodes' main drawback is that to meet demand from growers and gardeners, they must be mass-produced under specialised artificial conditions. They are held captive and are, effectively, being farmed, albeit it in a different way, just like other animals. This creates a moral dilemma for the veganic gardener: do you continue to try and curb slugs by deterring, catching and relocating them, or call upon a 'natural' but imperfect compromise, to rescue crops you may have invested time and money in raising?

Love your weeds

We usually think of weeds as causing problems in the garden or allotment. Some do, but others can be surprisingly useful and valuable assets. As well as providing clues to the kind of soil we have, weeds can help attract beneficial bugs and feed wildlife, be used for mulching and for making home-made liquid plant tonics, and as raw materials for producing garden compost. Weeds can be beautiful, too.

Right: *Left to their own devices weeds – wild plants – can soon transform neglected areas into floriferous havens for insects and other wildlife. Here, brambles, butterfly bush (Buddleja) and red valerian (Centranthus ruber) are thriving.*

WHAT ARE WEEDS?

Any plant growing where it is not wanted, and which competes for light, water and nutrients with the plants we do want to grow, is called a weed. Often, weeds are described as 'plants growing in the wrong place'. A patch of creeping thistle (*Cirsium repens*) colonising waste ground might be considered as growing in the 'right' place, but when its creeping roots invade a garden or allotment, it then becomes a weed. Weeds are grouped according to the length of their lifecycle, which varies according to the timescale (weeks, months or years) over which they germinate, grow, flower, produce seed and die.

• Annual weeds germinate, grow, flower, produce seeds and die within one year. Some, such as chickweed (*Stellaria media*) can repeat

GENTLE WAYS OF DEALING WITH WEEDS

Stop the spread
Remove weeds before flowering. This dandelion has airborne seeds.

Cut off seedlings
Use a razor-sharp hoe to sever the stems of young weeds just below the soil surface.

Pull them up
Remove shallow-rooted weeds by hand. Do this before they become well established.

Loosen and lift them
Use a fork to free up the soil around deep roots, then carefully ease them out.

Remove all fragments
Even a small piece of great bindweed (*Calystegia silvatica*) root can grow again.

Grow dense crops
Leafy pumpkins cast shade, which stops weed seeds from germinating.

Use ground cover
Low and spreading plants make an attractive, weed-suppressing blanket over the soil.

Sow a green manure
Fast-growing buckwheat smothers out any weed seedlings and improves the soil.

Rake them out
Moss is a common lawn weed which can be removed using a spring tine rake.

the whole cycle several times in a year and are called ephemerals. Annual weeds are predominantly found on bare, freshly disturbed ground. They appear less frequently in veganic gardens following a no-dig approach, because the soil is disturbed less often and rarely left bare and exposed.

• Biennial weeds germinate and produce a leafy clump or rosette in their first year, then lie dormant over winter. The following year the plant flowers, produces seeds and dies. Biennials are often found where the soil is undisturbed. A good example is ragwort (*Senecio jacobaea*).

• Perennial weeds, such as Japanese knotweed (*Reynoutria japonica*), grow for many years, often indefinitely. Some have tough, woody stems, while others such as dandelion (*Taraxacum*

Clockwise from top left: *Stinging nettles often grow around compost bins. Honey-scented creeping thistle flowers attract butterflies. Red soldier beetles (Rhagonycha fulva) foraging on hogweed for nectar, pollen and other insects. Bramble fruits in a neglected garden. Fast-spreading ephemeral chickweed. Dandelions draw in various insects, including flies.*

officinale, page 186) survive as deep-growing fleshy roots. Many perennial weeds can still flower and produce seeds, but also spread in other ways. They are often found in neglected gardens and overgrown allotments.

WHAT CAN WEEDS TELL US?

Looking carefully at the weeds in your garden will give you an idea of what type of soil you have, its fertility and its pH (how acid or alkaline it is). Chickweed (*Stellaria media*) suggests a rich, fertile soil, while creeping buttercup (*Ranunculus repens*) thrives in moist, poorly drained soil. Sheep's sorrel (*Rumex acetosella*) is a common lawn weed found on acid (low pH) soil. Thickets of perennial weeds, such as bramble (*Rubus fruticosus* agg) show that a garden has not been cultivated for some time.

MAGNETS FOR WILDLIFE

Most weeds are wild plants and have evolved alongside insects and other garden wildlife in mutually beneficial ways. Hogweed (*Heracleum sphondylium*) produces flat flowerheads to attract insects, which help with pollination and seed production. Some of these insects, such as hoverflies, are welcome in our veganic gardens because their larvae feed on aphids, which are sap-sucking pests.

Perennial stinging nettle (*Urtica dioica*) is a multipurpose weed which can be grown in clumps around the garden. In spring its leafy shoots attract aphids, which are a valuable food source for beneficial insects such as ladybirds emerging from winter hibernation. Later, in summer, red admiral and small tortoiseshell butterflies lay eggs on the nettle leaves, which the caterpillars eat. Clumps of stinging nettles also provide dense shelter for ground-dwelling garden predators such as frogs and toads.

WEEDS AS SOIL 'HEALERS'

Bare and exposed soil is uncommon in nature: it is usually found when a tree is uprooted, a landslip occurs, or when the ground has been charred following a grassland or heathland fire. In all of these situations, bare soil does not remain bare for long; within days seedlings begin to appear and cover the ground with a miniature green forest (shown above). A few months later the scar in the soil is barely noticeable. A year later you might not know it had been there at all.

We can contrast these natural examples of bare soil with those we create: ploughed fields and freshly dug-over gardens and allotments are obvious examples. Left to nature, even these often vast expanses of bare soil will soon turn green with a flush of small seedlings. The most neglected and jungle-like garden or allotment was once bare earth. In fields, gardens and allotments, on roadside verges and sports fields, along streets and on paths and pavements, we constantly battle to stop weeds growing. But all we are doing is keeping their healing powers at bay.

Weeds act like a living 'plaster' whenever soil is disturbed, either by nature or by us. When soil is exposed to sunlight, it is not just earthworms that quickly burrow back into the darkness; millions of microscopic soil organisms are also exposed to the sun's harmful rays. When carbon stored in the soil (as humus) is exposed to the air – during digging or ploughing – it oxidises, releasing climate-chaos carbon dioxide back into the atmosphere. The quickest and easiest way to trigger the process of healing bare, disturbed soil, especially in a new garden, is to let weeds grow. Then, while they are still young, they can either be hoed off and/or smothered under mulch as the ground is transitioned to no-dig status.

MULCHES, PLANT TONICS AND COMPOSTING

Freshly pulled up leafy weeds can be spread on the soil between crops as a temporary mulch, to stop more weeds germinating. Stinging nettles can be cut and steeped in water to produce a nutrient-rich brew which is diluted and used as a plant and soil tonic, while most fresh and leafy weeds, except tough perennials, are ideal for adding to a cool or hot composting mix (pages 130–137).

Tackling tough weeds

Almost all weeds can be successfully composted to produce ultra-local fertility for the garden, and most can be added straight to a cool or hot bin or heap, where they are an important source of 'greens'. However, perennial weeds, with tough, fleshy and creeping roots (rhizomes), and runners, should be dealt with first to make sure they are completely dead before being composted. Weedkillers are not used in veganic gardens.

Above left: Chopping up tough weeds makes them much easier to mix into compost heaps.

Above right: Plastic bins are ideal for drowning large amounts of tougher weeds. Here thick orange dock roots and Japanese knotweed stems are held down by a heavy stone. Putting the lid on cuts off all light.

Opposite, clockwise from top: Smash dock roots before composting them. Japanese knotweed roots being killed on a hot tin roof. Leafy weeds drying out and dying in the sun.

DRY THEM OUT

Whenever you pull or dig up weeds, try to leave them out in the blazing sun for several days, perhaps spread out over a paved area, so they weaken, shrivel and die. Annual weeds are easily killed this way and can then go straight into the compost heap or bin, although it is a good idea to wet them first to speed up rotting.

The leafy tops of perennial weeds such as dock (*Rumex* spp.) will dry out and die in hot sunshine, but this will not be enough to kill their thick roots. If you add these roots to a cool compost heap or bin the weeds will begin to regrow, surviving even in darkness – they could still be alive several months later.

Letting weeds dry out first is useful because their bulk and weight reduces considerably, which makes gathering them up and moving them around easier.

CHOP THEM UP

Crushing tough weed roots and breaking them into smaller pieces makes killing and then composting them much easier. Small amounts of thick, tough roots can be smashed using a hammer, or larger numbers can be passed through a shredder (make sure they have no soil or stones attached). Thick clumps of roots can be chopped up using a spade. Drowning is a slow but highly effective way to kill them prior to composting them.

Perennial weeds with masses of thinner roots, such as couch grass (*Elymus repens*) can be spread out and passed over with a mower. Leave the chopped up fragments in the sun until they feel crisp and dry, then compost them. If any regrow, put them back in the sun.

Problem perennial weeds can also be buried in the core of a large hot and fast compost

heap (page 134) where they are killed by being 'cooked' at high temperatures. This is one of the most effective ways of turning a large volume of tough weeds into useful garden compost. Chop them up and dry them out as much as possible first, several weeks before you build the hot heap. Any surviving fragments can be drowned.

FOOLPROOF SOLUTIONS

Some persistent weeds will cling to life whatever you do, but fortunately there are two ways to tackle them that guarantee success. You might want to treat all tough weeds this way. It is still a good idea to weaken weeds in hot sunshine, but crushing and chopping them up first is not essential.

- Submerging problem weeds in a container of water will cut off their air supply and drown them. This is an easy and relatively quick method (see opposite, top) which kills most weeds in four to eight weeks. Others, such as docks, will take longer – sometimes up to 12 months before their thick, orange roots finally turn dark and start to rot. The dead remains can be added to your cool compost heap or bin, or to a wormposting bin, to rot down further. Small amounts of tough weeds can be easily drowned in a bucket, but a lidded metal tank or recycled plastic bin is useful for dealing with large volumes.
- Sealing weeds inside a repurposed plastic compost bag starves them of light and they will eventually die, although this can take longer than drowning – usually 12–18 months. The bag used must not let in any light. Use a new bag and always recycle it responsibly afterwards. If left long enough, the dead weeds will turn into dark, crumbly compost which can be added straight away to your no-dig garden soil (see opposite).

CLIMATE-FRIENDLY

WEEDKILLERS POLLUTE

Tackling tough weeds without resorting to the use of synthetic weedkillers (herbicides) helps to keep your gardening footprint small, reduces pollution and is inherently climate-friendly.

All garden chemicals trigger demand for raw materials (commonly oil), require energy for their manufacture, and are sold in predominantly plastic packaging. Many 'convenience' weedkillers also come with extra components, such as hand-held pumps/lances powered by batteries, all of which require eventual disposal (by recycling, landfill or incineration). Avoiding weedkillers completely decouples our gardens from this energy-intensive chain of events and the emissions linked to it which are helping drive climate breakdown. Drowning and 'bagging' weeds in your own garden are benign activities resulting in a rich, pollution-free resource – garden compost.

Chemical weedkillers themselves also pollute our air, soil and water. Residues of the widely-used weedkiller glyphosate are now ubiquitous in many natural ecosystems. It is regularly detected in human urine and breast milk, having passed into our bodies via food (primarily bread) or drinking water. Weedkillers can percolate deep into the ground where they contaminate groundwater supplies and aquifers (requiring more energy use at water purification plants in efforts to remove them).

Spraying weedkiller pollutes our air, which can be breathed in by both us and by garden wildlife, including insects and other bugs. Glyphosate has been shown to affect the microbial communities found in the guts of honey bees, making them more prone to disease.

Drowning troublesome weeds

1 Pack tough perennial weeds down tightly in a bucket or barrel, then cover them with rainwater.

2 Put a heavy brick or stone on them so they are weighed down and remain submerged in water. Push any shoots back down.

3 The weeds are fully dead when they turn yellow and brown and are rotting. Pour the pungent liquid around plants as a soil tonic, and compost the darkened remains.

Killing tough weeds by 'bagging'

1 Chop up and wet the weeds and then pack them into an inside-out compost bag (with no large holes that will let in light).

2 Once the bag is full, but not too compacted, tie it off. Prick over the surface of the bag with a garden fork to allow in some air.

3 Put the bag in a shaded, out-of-the-way spot where the contents will slowly break down. Several bags can be stacked together.

4 Check progress every few months. Pale shoots like this mean the weeds are not completely dead and need more time in the bag.

Growing spaces

Whatever space you have for gardening, this chapter is packed with ideas and suggestions to help you make the most of it. Advice is given on growing plants in containers, even if you do not have a garden. There are tips on how to start growing on a veganic allotment, including ways of attracting nature with a 'perennimeter'. The joy of harvesting free and renewable sunshine in a greenhouse or polytunnel is explored, and how to integrate a greenhouse into your garden's wider ecosystem is clearly illustrated. Detailed, ideas-filled plans show how a prolific veganic food garden can be created over time in any growing space, alongside plenty of hands-on advice for sowing and planting.

Left: *Blending the ornamental with the edible – flowers with food – builds and then sustains a diverse and balanced gardening ecosystem.*

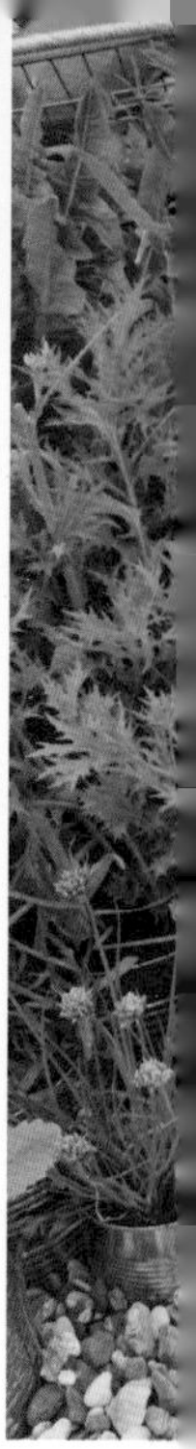

No garden, no problem

You do not need a garden or allotment to grow plants veganically. Almost all plants will grow successfully in a container filled with potting compost, provided it is not too small and allows water to drain freely from its base. The key difference between plants growing in soil outdoors and those in containers is that the latter rely on you entirely for their water and sustenance.

Above left: *Wooden boxes (with drainage holes in the base) make attractive planters for collections of herbs and can be stood on sunny steps.*

Above right: *Trailing nasturtium (Tropaeolum) growing in a repurposed chimney pot.*

TYPES OF CONTAINER

Any vessel capable of holding vegan-friendly, peat-free potting compost can be used to grow flowers, vegetables, herbs, salads, bush and cane fruits, and houseplants. Shrubs, such as camellias and blueberries, which need lime-free ericaceous compost, can also be grown successfully in containers. Fast-growing salad leaves might be in a small tray for a few weeks, dahlias a large pot for the summer months, while dwarf fruit trees occupy a sizeable tub for several years. Container growing is ideal if you only have a windowsill, a balcony, steps up to a flat (do not block fire exits), or a small patio or courtyard with only hard surfacing.

There are numerous types of container: pots, tubs, bowls, window boxes, hanging baskets, barrels, large square or rectangular (and often elevated) planters, plastic trugs, metal (galvanised) buckets, old sinks, and large repurposed tin food cans (with no sharp edges) will all hold compost. Salvage shops are a good source of quirky containers which can be adapted for garden use.

Permanent containers can be made of plastic (new or recycled), terracotta (glazed or unglazed), wood, metal or even concrete. Ephemeral containers made from biodegradable materials, such as wood pulp, will eventually rot down and can be added to your cool compost heap or bin. Growbags are plastic bags filled with compost in which plants are grown for several months.

Pre-loved terracotta pots have a smaller gardening footprint than new ones. If you already use plastic containers, it makes sense to use these wisely until they start to crack, then recycle them. The best way to avoid

contributing to microplastic pollution is not to acquire new plastic. If it is your only option, choose containers made from recycled plastic (and recycle them responsibly).

CONTAINER SIZE

As a general rule, the smaller the container you use to grow plants, the more dependent it is going to be on you for water. Leafy plants with well-developed root systems dry out rapidly on hot and sunny days, especially if they are in a sheltered suntrap – such as against a sun-soaked wall. Plants which run short of water will wilt, and can be damaged if they are not watered. It pays to err on the side of using a larger container than you think you might need. Small containers, and any which hold only small volumes of compost such as tin cans and guttering, cannot sustain plants for more than a few hours on hot summer days.

To grow flowering or food plants on a sunny patio, use pots which are a minimum of 30cm (12in) in diameter. Containers should be at least 30cm (12in) or more deep unless you are planting a box or trough for a windowsill (see the sequence overleaf). Shallower pots and bowls are ideal for water-storing succulents, such as houseleeks (*Sempervivum* spp.), which have only shallow roots and survive long spells without watering.

You need to consider how mobile your containers will be and how often you might need to move them; large plants growing in sizeable containers take effort (and more than one person) to move safely.

In a wind-prone garden, and if you are growing climbing plants up supports, using heavy containers with wide, flat bottoms and adding some heavy materials to their base – broken terracotta, slates or bricks, or stones – will add more stability and prevent them from blowing over.

Above left: *Tin food cans with any sharp edges removed, and with holes for drainage drilled in their base, can be used to grow smaller, clump-forming herbs and salad crops.*

Above right: *Sun-loving herbs such as rosemary thrive in pre-loved terracotta pots filled with free-draining peat-free compost. Pot feet raise the container off the ground so it does not sit in standing water during the winter months.*

POT-TOP MULCHES

Using a vegan-friendly mulch over the compost in containers slows down evaporation and drying-out of the compost. Wood chips or shredded prunings, digestate, lawn mowings, fine bark, seaweed, leaf mould, or even stones, can all be spread over several layers of wet newspaper or cardboard (and help to disguise it). The mulch on the container surface should form an even layer, at least 2.5cm (1in) deep.

Below left: *Edible crops such as sun-loving peppers will fruit heavily in most containers, provided they are watered regularly and fed weekly with a nutrient-rich plant tonic.*

Below right: *Growing strawberries in tall terracotta pots helps to keep the fruits off the ground and away from slugs, snails and small mammals.*

ENSURE GOOD DRAINAGE

Any container must have adequate drainage so that excess water drains away. If plant roots are submerged in standing water they will rot, and the plant will die. Containers do not always have pre-made drainage holes and you may need to add them; drill holes at least 13mm (½in) in diameter and 5cm (2in) apart in the base of the container (when drilling plastic, always dispose of the fragments). To increase drainage in terracotta pots, which may only have a few large holes, put in pieces of broken clay pots, flat stones or slate before adding the compost. Containers can be raised off of the ground using pot feet, stones or short lengths of wood.

SITING CONTAINERS

Position container-grown plants where you want them. Herbs and salads will be easy to harvest near a kitchen door. Ornamental plants in pots can be used to frame a doorway, or be used in an informal jumble for a riot of summer colour on a patio. In a shaded, sunless passageway between two houses, shade-loving plants such as ferns are a natural choice.

WATERING AND FEEDING

Containers do not capture enough rainfall during the summer to survive, and will rely on you for water and for extra plant nutrients. In autumn and winter, when growth slows down

and plants become dormant, regular watering is less critical. Adding seaweed crumb to the compost helps retain moisture (page 162).

Container plants can be watered and fed individually using a watering can, on an as-needed basis. The optimum time to water is either early in the morning, or late at night. Most composts run out of nutrients after 4–6 weeks, so it is worth making plant tonics (page 166) to keep container plants nourished.

If you have a large number of containers, using automatic or semi-automatic watering systems is easier and saves time (page 66). Standing pots in saucers or aluminium food trays allows roots to draw water up through the base.

Planting up a thyme herb trough

1 With its attractive patina, this 12.5cm (5in) deep metal box will sit on a hot, sunny windowsill. First it needs drainage holes adding to its base.

2 To ensure good drainage and to add weight, slate is laid over the base of the box (flat stones or broken terracotta can be used instead).

3 Fill the pot with a mix of three parts peat-free compost mixed to one part coarse grit. This keeps the mixture open and well-drained.

4 A few lichen-encrusted rocks are added, and golden thymes are planted between them. The plants will soon begin spreading out over the rocks and the box's rim.

5 To conserve moisture, any exposed compost is mulched with slate chippings, which sets off the thymes. Gravel or small stones could also be used.

6 The completed herb box is watered thoroughly and allowed to drain before being moved into position. Keep it near the kitchen for easy harvesting.

Plant-powered allotments

The natural progression from adopting a plant-based vegan diet is the desire to start growing some of your own vegetables, fruit and herbs, without using synthetic chemicals, or any animal-derived products. An allotment offers plenty of space to grow what you most enjoy eating – with full control over how it is grown. Flowers, ponds and other wildlife-friendly elements are also an integral part of an abundant allotment.

Below: Planting a patch of perennial comfrey (Symphytum officinale) *on an allotment provides the raw materials (leaves) to make your own liquid plant tonics.*

WHAT IS AN ALLOTMENT?

Allotments or community gardens are plots of rented land which vary in size and are used primarily for growing your own food. An average-sized, rectangular plot covers around 250 square metres (300 square yards). They are found in both urban and rural areas, and are usually clustered together in groups, numbering anywhere from a few dozen plots, to several hundred. Some long-established sites have been in constant use for many years, and their soil is usually rich and fertile.

A diverse range of gardeners are attracted to allotments, engendering a shared community spirit. Through food-growing, allotments also foster a keen sense of self-reliance. In urban areas, and for anyone who is gardenless, they can provide vital hands-on contact with our natural world.

Some allotments are supplied with piped tap water, electricity and vehicle access. Larger sites will often have a club allowing allotment holders to join forces and buy discounted bulk materials such as potting compost (soil mix).

KEEP TO THE RULES

Most allotment sites are administered by local authorities, but some are privately owned. Each plot of land is rented out, usually on an annual basis. Each allotment site will have its own set of rules governing what you can and cannot do on your plot. One of the most common stipulations is that the plot must be kept 'cultivated' – which basically means it must be used to grow at least some crops and not left to go wild.

Specific rules will also govern whether permanent structures – such as storage sheds (an important consideration if you are travelling any distance) and greenhouses or polytunnels – are allowed, or if wildlife-friendly ponds are permitted. Always study the allotment site rules before renting your plot, to avoid disappointment later.

Overgrown allotments are often sprayed with polluting glyphosate weedkiller as a well-intentioned favour to the person taking them on, so check first if you can and decline the offer.

An average full-sized allotment can be daunting if you are new to gardening. Sharing a large plot lessens the burden and helps sustain enthusiasm, especially when starting out. Some sites offer half-sized or even smaller plots, so always ask at the outset.

Sharing brings obvious social benefits, but it can also trigger curiosity around what you are doing on your plot, and why. 'How are you going to grow without using any muck?' is an obvious conversation primer.

GARDEN IN STAGES

The best way to avoid being overwhelmed by a large allotment is to tackle it in stages. At the outset, plan the position of a shed, greenhouse (and any accompanying water butts), compost bins or bays, leaf mould cages, wildlife ponds, pathways, bed edgings, and other permanent structures. Decide where long-lived plants such as bush and cane fruits will go, and what support systems they might need.

A wild and overgrown plot can be tamed by using a heavyweight mulch to clear it of weeds – see 'Sheet mulching', page 118. While the plot is deep-mulched, you can start growing food on just part of it, beginning with easy crops such as no-dig potatoes (page 125). Once the ground is cleared of weeds, more of it can be transitioned

Above, left to right: Adding a small, fish-free pond to an allotment attracts slug-eating wildlife such as frogs and toads. Sheds are invaluable for storing tools and equipment, and for shelter in poor weather.

to no-dig (page 114) and kept well mulched.

Allotment soil is usually already quite rich and fertile following many years of being improved by the annual digging-in of garden compost, animal manure and other organic matter. Such soils tend to be dark, have a fine, crumbly structure, and can easily be switched to no-dig straight away.

ADVANTAGE VEGANIC

Unlike allotments reliant on imported animal byproducts, energy-intensive synthetic fertilisers, and back-breaking digging, veganic plots are easier to nurture and are nourished by plants, and are powered by free and renewable sunshine.

- Avoiding animal-derived materials removes the risk of contaminating the soil with residues of damaging hormone weedkillers used on fodder crops (such as aminopyralid), or antibiotics and other drugs used in livestock farming, which are frequently present in manure.
- Switching to no-dig reduces physical work (literally, no more digging) and preserves the soil ecosystem. Carbon remains safely locked away in dark humus.
- Growing a comfrey patch to use for compost- and plant tonic-making, captures sunlight energy, turning it into a free and ultra-local source of plant nutrients. Locally-sourced green wood chips (page 142) can be used to boost soil microbial life.
- Unused parts of the plot can be sown with living mulches (page 156), which use sunlight to add organic matter to the soil.

PLANT A LIVING 'PERENNIMETER'

Derived from a combination of the two words perennial and perimeter, a 'perennimeter' is a wide, continuous bed buzzing with wildlife on the outer edge of an allotment or community garden. It is planted with annual, perennial and woody plants, including some crops, but also incorporates wildlife habitats: log piles (below), bug hotels, small fish-free ponds, and mulch. Self-seeding annual flowers and vegetables such as red mustard are spread randomly throughout a typical perennimeter. Herbs such as fennel and biennial teasel (*Dipsacus fullonum*) will attract adult hoverflies. Giant sunflowers with large flowerheads can provide summer pollen and nectar for butterflies, bees and other insects, and also autumn food for seed-eating birds.

Harvesting sunshine

Greenhouses and polytunnels capture the sun's free and renewable energy, creating a covered and sheltered indoor microclimate where you can sow and propagate plants, and grow those needing higher temperatures than are usually found outdoors. They also help stretch the growing seasons, letting you start plants off earlier and harvest them later. Using only 'modern' sunshine to warm a greenhouse causes none of the climate-changing pollution liberated by the burning of fossil fuels.

Right: *This lean-to greenhouse against a sunny wall warms up quickly at the start of the day. It then stays warmer at night because the heat energy absorbed by the bricks during daytime is radiated back out.*

Opposite: *A pre-loved, refurbished greenhouse heated only by renewable (and free) sunshine has only a small gardening footprint, and will allow you to grow a variety of flowers and food crops all year round.*

HOME-MADE MICROCLIMATE

In a greenhouse or polytunnel, you and your plants are protected year-round from wind, rain, frost, hail and snow, although temperatures can fall below freezing during winter. Covering a patch of earth alters it by giving it its own microclimate. The plants you grow there will be entirely dependent on you, because you are responsible for regulating the temperature and making sure they get enough water; no rain falls inside a greenhouse.

In spring, various vegetable crops can be sown under cover, in pots and trays, when the soil outdoors is too cold and wet. Later, when the soil warms, they are planted outdoors and get a head start on outdoor-sown plants. In autumn, the enclosed microclimate protects crops from early frosts, helping to extend their productivity for several weeks.

A polytunnel is especially useful for growing veganic crops year-round, even through the winter, when harvesting is possible regardless of the weather outdoors.

PRE-LOVED = SMALLER FOOTPRINT

Acquiring a pre-loved, pre-used greenhouse, as locally as possible, means it will come with only a modest gardening footprint. The

Clockwise from left: Cast-iron Victorian cloches are akin to small, mobile greenhouses and can be moved around the garden to protect individual crops, such as this frost-tender courgette. Glass bell jar cloches are used on individual plants. Greenhouses have a separate, miniature microclimate.

energy required for its original manufacture and transport is already 'embedded' in the structure itself. By reusing it, you are extending the useful life of that greenhouse (or polytunnel) indefinitely. Buying a new greenhouse would require fresh raw materials, and energy for its manufacture (meaning a bigger footprint).

Unused greenhouses are a common sight in gardens and on allotments; asking if the owners would be happy to part with it may yield a 'new' greenhouse for little or no cost – other than the time to dismantle it. Online sites often list pre-loved greenhouses as 'free on collection'. It is always wise to take plenty of photographs of a pre-loved structure prior to disassembling it, and to methodically label the glazing and the frame with an indelible pen and/or labels. This makes rebuilding it much easier (also, always check if the original manual is still available).

SITING YOUR GREENHOUSE

An open spot in full sun, away from the shade cast by trees or buildings, is ideal. Orientate the structure east–west so it harvests the maximum amount of sunlight. Plants can be grown directly in soil beds, or in containers. Soil-grown plants can root deep into the soil and are less prone to drying out than container-grown plants. In a polytunnel the ground is usually divided up into a series of soil beds with pathways between them.

Lay out soil beds where the vertical space above them is at a maximum, and use them to grow tall-growing crops such as cordon tomatoes. A central soil bed, with permanent paths either side (rather than a central path), often makes far better use of any vertical space available. Greenhouses can also be sited on paved areas, with everything being grown in raised beds or containers.

GREENHOUSE BASICS

When the sun's rays warm up the soil, paths and other surfaces inside a greenhouse, they warm the air, raising the temperature. We regulate this by opening the vents and doors during the daytime, letting warmer air out and cooler air in.

Right: Oriental salad greens thrive in cooler autumn days and will crop for several months given the protection of an unheated greenhouse or polytunnel.

Heat-absorbing surfaces release their warmth, radiator-like, at night, so closing doors and vents traps this heat, keeping the night temperature above that outdoors.

A greenhouse comprises a metal or wooden frame glazed with glass, or polycarbonate or acrylic, both tough plastics. The framework is usually made from rustproof aluminium, or naturally resilient western red cedar, and sits on a solid base. Greenhouses can be mini wall-mounted types, or larger square, rectangular, octagonal models, or even geodesic domes. Lean-to greenhouses are fitted to the side of a building. Covering a sunny wall this way is a highly effective way of using solar energy stored during the day, which is then released as heat by the wall at night.

A polytunnel is a series of galvanised metal hoops anchored in the ground over which a plastic cover is stretched tight. Usually there are doors at each end, and some designs have vents. Vertical tunnel sides maximise the growing space. Polytunnels are however less efficient at storing warmth at night. Covers deteriorate in sunlight and need replacing every five to seven years, and are best replaced and recycled before they shatter into small, polluting fragments. Polytunnels are generally less expensive than greenhouses.

A thermometer is useful to monitor temperature fluctuations. In high summer, a greenhouse can be shaded by laying leafy branches over the roof on hot, sunny days (remove them when it's dull). Sheets of hessian/jute or white cotton also work well. Avoid using plastic netting, which will eventually degrade into polluting microplastic. Opening vents and doors manually is the low-tech approach; automatic systems will open vents at pre-set temperatures. Wetting the paths inside the greenhouse on hot days will also boost humidity and has a cooling effect.

HEATING MATTERS

The most eco-friendly greenhouse is powered and warmed entirely by sunshine; working closely with the changing seasons is vital. In spring and summer, grow plants which need warmer temperatures and lots of sunlight, then, in autumn and winter, focus on those which tolerate less light and lower temperatures. It also means choosing not to grow plants which need constant high temperatures (and humidity) year-round, as these will require additional energy to heat the greenhouse.

Using a gas or paraffin heater, or using electricity generated from burning fossil fuels, releases carbon and so contributes to our climate emergency. The most climate-friendly way to keep a greenhouse (or preferably a section of it) frost-free is to use a simple fan heater powered by 'green' electricity from a renewable source. Set it to operate only if the temperature falls low enough. Polytunnels are not usually heated.

The living greenhouse

By its very nature, a greenhouse encloses a portion of your garden, creating a discrete, self-contained microclimate on that little piece of earth. But there is no reason why it needs to be treated as a separate entity, disconnected from the buzzing everyday life of your garden's wider ecosystem. Integrating a greenhouse helps you grow food and flowers, while providing habitat for a range of wildlife, large and small.

Above left: *Single-flower pot marigolds (*Calendula officinalis*) attract hoverflies.*

Above right, top to bottom: *Common frogs (*Rana temporaria*) will visit a pond to breed and spawn in spring.* Tagetes tenuifolia *protects tomatoes from whitefly by releasing limonene, a pungent oil.*

KEEP LIFE FLOWING

Veganic gardens bustle with life from spring through to autumn. Much of the beneficial wildlife surrounding plants grown in the open can be also coaxed into the sheltered microclimate of a greenhouse, benefiting the plants growing there. Flying insects are especially beneficial: they pollinate the flowers of crops, encouraging the formation of fruits, and help keep pests in check. Some do both.

Airborne adult hoverflies will flit between the flowers of greenhouse pot-grown strawberries, tomatoes and other crops in search of nectar and pollen (dislodging it as they go), which fertilises embryonic fruits. They can also 'sniff out' aphid pheromones, allowing them to find even small colonies hidden on the undersides of leaves. Female hoverflies then lay their pale, pill-like eggs among the aphids, which hatch into fast-moving larvae that eat them. Tiny parasitoid

wasps, which lay their eggs inside aphids where their larvae eat them alive, will go about their business unseen.

Your goal should be to encourage a steady, diverse stream of beneficial life to pass into and through your greenhouse, where it will flow around your plants.

INDOOR PONDS ADD LIFE

Including a small wildlife pond inside even an average-sized greenhouse embeds a self-contained aquatic ecosystem within the greenhouse's microclimate. A small fish-free pond can be fitted in one corner of a greenhouse, or a larger version can be built so that part of it is indoors and part of it out (see illustration overleaf). Polytunnels generally offer more space and scope to add a larger pond that teems with life.

Any inert, watertight container around 30cm (12in) deep buried in the soil is suitable for pond-making, and does not have to be round; square or rectangular containers work equally well and may be easier to fit in a limited space (pond dwellers are not fussy what shape a pond is). Any straight/ugly edges can be disguised by edging the pond with stones and/or logs, which also create nooks and crannies for wildlife to shelter in.

Frogs, toads and newts will be drawn to the pond, and may spawn there in spring. If they do, tread carefully on humid late summer nights, when tadpoles mature into froglets/toadlets/newtlets and leave the pond to start living on dry land. During winter, amphibians will hibernate in any edging around the pond, and you might also find them under stones, wood, plant pots or in other damp, secluded spots.

Above left: *Large red damselflies (*Pyrrhosoma nymphula*) are drawn to even small ponds, especially those which are half in, half out a greenhouse (see next page).*

Above top: *Leafy shoots from shrubs, long grass, or bracken fronds, shown here, can be used to instantly shade and cool down a greenhouse during hot spells.*

Above bottom: *Garden spiders (*Araneus diadematus*) will spin their webs between the foliage of any greenhouse crops, trapping any small flying insect pests.*

Bringing your greenhouse to life

A greenhouse set within your garden's wider ecosystem is much more than just a glazed structure. This pre-loved greenhouse, incorporating repurposed and recycled materials, has been thoughtfully laid out so that gardener and nature work together side by side, one benefiting the other, in a host of interconnected ways.

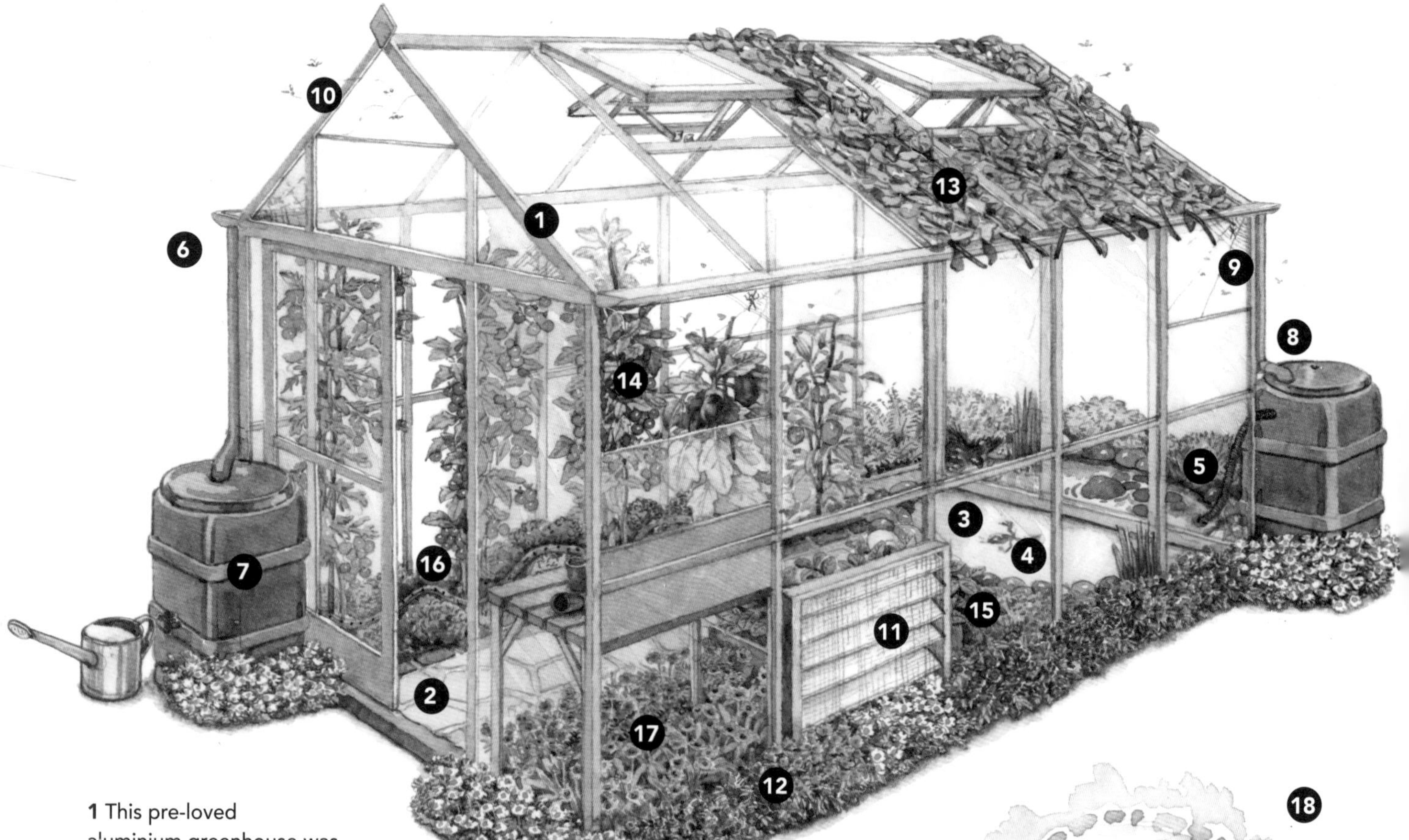

1 This pre-loved aluminium greenhouse was offered as 'free on collection' via a local community online noticeboard. A few glass panes needed replacing, requiring basic DIY skills. The greenhouse is 2.5m (8ft) long by 1.8m (6ft) wide, with a door at one end, top vents, and a low-level louvre.

2 The central path is made from natural stone and bricks rescued from a skip.

3 Half of this fish-free wildlife pond sits inside the greenhouse, the other half is outside. Amphibians such as frogs, toads and newts come and go via the aquatic corridor, and also spawn there. Dragonfly and damselfly larvae hunt below the surface, hidden by dwarf waterlily leaves.

4 Frogs and toads leave the pond and roam around the greenhouse and surrounding garden at night, when it is cool and moist, feeding on any slugs.

5 Birds and insects alight on stones set in the shallow pond margins, to bathe, drink and to collect mud for their nests.

6 Rainwater is harvested from the roof and fed into lidded butts made of recycled plastic.

7 The butt near the door is fitted with a tap for filling a watering can.

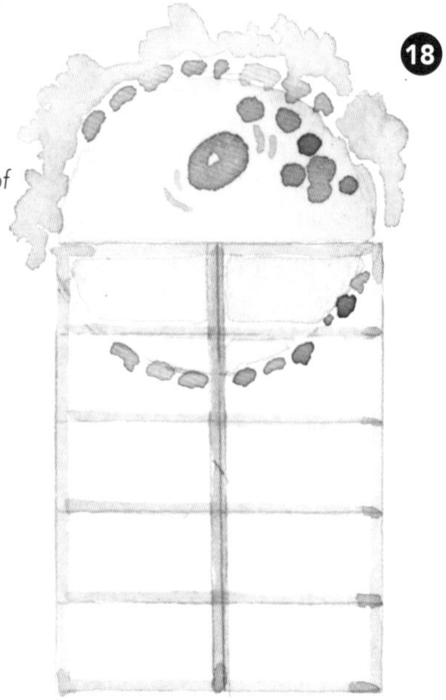

Right: Bird's-eye view of glasshouse and pond.

8 An overflow from this butt diverts excess rainwater into the pond.

9 Web-spinning spiders are welcome here all year round, catching small flying insect pests such as aphids and whitefly, and helping to keep their numbers down. Spiders make their homes in every nook and cranny, encouraged by a hands-off approach to over-zealous tidiness.

10 The two uppermost panes of glass at each end have been modified so they can be easily removed during spring and summer. These gaps act as 'escape hatches' for any insects passing through the greenhouse, such as honey and wild bees, hoverflies and butterflies, which always gravitate to the highest point. Encouraging insects into the greenhouse is vital for pollination and to keep a healthy balance between potential pests and their natural predators. Small birds which accidentally become trapped can also escape this way.

11 A fine wire-mesh cover over the outside of the louvre vent allows air to flow freely but prevents low-flying bumblebees from becoming trapped inside (especially in spring when the queens are searching for nesting sites).

12 Outside the doors and around the base of the greenhouse is a floriferous strip of simple, single and pollen/nectar-rich flowers which attract beneficial insects such as hoverflies, some of which fly inside. It also provides cover for frogs, toads, fledglings, and other wildlife.

13 During a scorching summer heatwave, leafy shoots of hazel are laid on the roof to create temporary shade (avoiding the need for plastic shade netting). After use they can be shredded into mulch.

14 Cordon tomatoes, supported by home-grown hazel stakes; aubergines and peppers are grown in soil beds.

15 Early potatoes and salad crops are grown in easy-reach soil beds.

16 Rainwater is fed to the crops at night via a length of curving repurposed copper pipe drilled with holes along its length. Water seeps out when it is connected to the water butt. Night-time watering, when it is cool and evaporation is minimal, makes best use of harvested water during prolonged hot spells.

17 A strip of orange and yellow single-flowered pot marigolds (*Calendula* and *Tagetes tenuifolia)* lure beneficial, aphid-eating hoverflies and other insects into the heart of the greenhouse.

18 The half in/half out pond connects the rain-free conditions in the greenhouse with the wider garden. Frogs and toads often spawn earlier in the 'in' half, where temperatures are slightly higher.

Above: Beauty and productivity entwine in this life-filled greenhouse where trailing nasturtiums (Tropaeolum majus) *scramble around the base of early-cropping sweetcorn plants. The ground-hugging nasturtiums cast shade which prevents weed seeds from germinating, and they also help stop the soil surface from drying out.*

Starting a food garden

A garden dedicated to growing food will be more successful if you start by drawing up an overall plan and then develop it in stages. This phased, evolving approach brings a gradual improvement to the soil, builds up a vibrant garden ecosystem, encourages you to perfect sowing and planting techniques with easy-to-grow crops, and allows time to identify the best spots for growing long-term crops, such as fruit.

Opposite, clockwise from top left: Fresh mangetout peas, like any other veganic food you grow yourself, comes with the reassurance that you know exactly what went into growing it. Brussels sprouts thrive in an open, sunny spot away from any shade. Red nasturtiums, orange and yellow pot marigolds (Calendula officinalis) *and blue borage are all edible annual flowers which will add beauty to your food garden. This sun-soaked slate wall radiates heat at night making it ideal for growing warmth-loving outdoor cordon tomatoes.*

FOOD YOU CAN TRUST

The joy of growing veganic food in your own garden or allotment is that you know exactly how the plants you ultimately eat have been grown – from the moment you sowed the seeds or planted some plug plants, to the moment they reach your plate. You know exactly what kind of compost (potting mix) they have been sown/raised in, and how the soil they are grown in has been treated and improved.

Most organically-grown plant-based food is still grown using animal manures and slaughterhouse byproducts. Only by buying food certified as 'vegan-organic' or 'stockfree', or by growing your own vegetables, salads, herbs and fruits veganically, can you be absolutely certain that the food you eat has not involved any animal inputs.

ASSESSING YOUR GARDEN

In a new or existing garden where you have decided to start growing food, the first step is to look at what is already there. It helps to sketch out a plan of your garden and record basic measurements, such as how wide and long it is. You can then mark the areas covered by paving or paths, the layout and shape of existing beds or borders, where fences are, and the position of any trees or a shed. Use a tape measure to make the plan as accurate as possible, but do not worry if some measurements are approximate – you can modify your plans as the garden evolves. If you can, live with a new garden for a year before making any major changes. This will allow you to see exactly what plants might already be there – spring-flowering bulbs, for example, will not be obvious until spring – and give any initial ideas time to develop.

SUN AND SHADE

It is important to identify those parts of the garden which receive most sun and those which remain in shade. Sheltered sunny fences can be used to grow warmth-loving fruits, while compost bins and sheds can go in the shadier spots. Taking photographs regularly is a simple way to record where the sun falls. On a bright day, preferably in summer when the sun is high in the sky (midday is ideal) take photographs from different points in your garden, including ones from any upstairs windows and from each corner of the plot. When you have a good idea of where the sunny and shady spots are, add this information to the plan.

STARTING A FOOD GARDEN

The garden plan shown in the following pages shows the gradual transformation of an ordinary back garden (7m x 10m/23ft x 33ft) into an abundant food garden over a five-year period. Veganic principles are followed at all times; no chemical weedkillers or pesticides are used; a dynamic garden ecosystem is encouraged; and wherever possible existing materials are repurposed and/or recycled.

It pays to start small when you first set out to make a food garden. Concentrating your efforts on modest areas, nurturing and tending to the crops grown, and then enjoying the success of being able to harvest and eat them, will boost your confidence as your garden evolves.

SOWING SEEDS OUTDOORS

Never sow when the soil is wet, frozen or sticks to your boots. Vegetables are usually sown outdoors from spring, when the soil feels warm to the touch, through to autumn.

Most vegetable seeds can be sown in a narrow, v-shaped groove, also called a drill. The depth of the groove depends on the seed size – smaller seeds are sown in shallower grooves and vice versa. In this garden, all of the outdoor sowings will eventually be made in no-dig raised beds 1.2m (4ft) wide, by working from the paths. The tip of a trowel blade, a short stick or even your finger will also form good grooves. If you are sowing many short rows, a home-made wooden former is quick and simple to use. It also acts as a guide to how far apart and how deep to sow seeds (or space out young plants) and is shown in the sequence below. Large seeds can be sown in individual, evenly-spaced holes made with a dibber or trowel.

If seeds have been sown close together in a groove, some of the seedlings will need

Left: *Squashes and pumpkins need a sheltered, sunny spot in your food garden. Where growing space is limited, choose compact bush rather than trailing varieties.*

Opposite, bottom right: *Food crops can also be grown in a series of easy-to-access raised beds. These are made from oak sleepers, which have not been treated with chemical preservatives.*

Sowing seeds in a soil groove

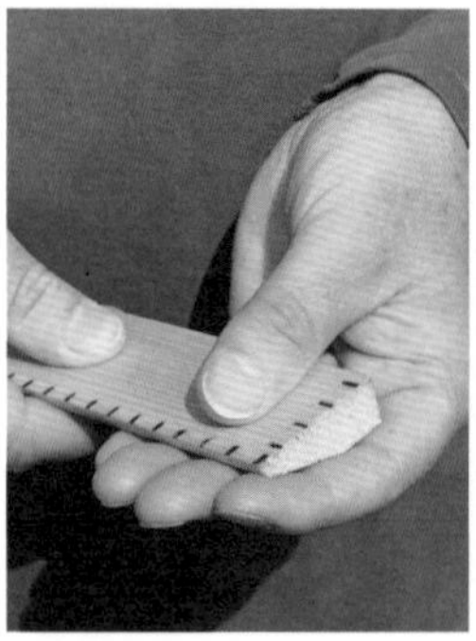

1 Use a piece of door frame that is narrower along one edge to make a simple wooden soil groove or drill former. Mark 1cm (½in) divisions along the edges.

2 To make a soil groove, press the wooden former into the surface of soft, level soil and rock it from side to side. Use the guide marks to check the depth.

3 If the soil is dry, water the bottom of the V-shape groove. This gives quicker seed germination and encourages the seedling roots down into the soil.

4 To sow seeds at the correct spacing (check the seed packet), lay the wooden former along the groove and sow the seeds. These are 3cm (1¼in) apart.

5 Label the row with the name and date, then float your fingers over the surface to draw loose soil into the drill to cover the seeds. Do not firm the soil down.

removing to give the others room to grow. Water the soil first and then gently uproot or nip off every other seedling, so those remaining are just touching. Several such thinning-out stages might be necessary depending on the type of vegetable and the recommended plant spacings.

PLANTING VEGETABLES

Vegetables can be planted, depending on the type of crop, from spring, when the soil is workable and warm, right through to autumn. Check planting distances for each crop before you start.

Young vegetable plants grown in pots, multi-cell trays or coir plugs should have a dense mass of fast-growing roots by planting time; this is called the root-ball. To check how well developed it is, gently tap a plant out of its pot, or ease one from its cell. The pale roots should just be starting to grow against the inside of the pot or cell.

The roots should hold the compost together. If only a few roots are visible and the compost falls away, put the plant back in its pot and grow

STARTER OR PLUG PLANTS

Unpack and water young starter or plug plants on arrival.

Plant each mini root-ball in a hole and firm in with your fingers.

Young vegetable plants grown in small individual cells of compost are known as starter or plug plants. They are a convenient choice if you do not have the facilities (or time) to raise plants from seed. Mail order is the commonest way of obtaining them; look for those from an organically-accredited grower and check they are using vegan-friendly peat-free compost to raise them. Starter plants are planted on arrival, and root disturbance is minimal. Water any dry plugs and put them in a shaded spot. Plant into small holes made with your finger or a dibber, firm them down gently and then water thoroughly. If you cannot plant immediately, grow them on in pots of peat-free compost and transplant later.

Planting a pot-grown vegetable

1 Water the plant first (this is a sweet pepper). Make a planting hole to take the root-ball, place it in the hole and check it is level with the surrounding soil.

2 Push the loose soil back around the root-ball and gently firm it down using your fingertips. Put in any sticks or other plant supports.

3 Draw some of the soil away from the base of the plant to form a shallow depression, then fill it with water so it soaks straight down around the roots.

Above left: Rainbow chard is a fast-growing, leafy vegetable that crops prolifically throughout the summer.

Above middle: Soft fruits such as raspberries are easy to grow, but will need protection from blackbirds and other garden birds. A wire mesh cage is the most effective method and avoids the use of plastic netting.

Above right: Growing your own allows you to grow crops which are rarely seen in shops – such as white currants.

it on for a few more weeks. If a thick dense mass of roots are circling the pot, the plant needs either planting immediately (after gently teasing the outermost roots loose first) or moving into a larger pot. Plants that run out of root room will stop growing and can take longer to establish after planting. When roots appear through the sides and base of biodegradable paper or coir pots, they are ready to plant. The pot is not removed – leaving the roots intact and undisturbed – and eventually rots down into the soil (although this process can sometimes take several years for thicker pots made from tough coir fibres bound together with natural latex).

Always water the plants thoroughly before planting out, preferably by giving them a thorough soaking the night before. If the compost feels dry and sticks to the pot or cell, the plant feels light in weight or it is wilting – or all three – first soak the root-ball(s) in a bucket or similar container of water, immersing it until no more air bubbles appear.

TRANSPLANTING VEGETABLES

Vegetable plants, such as lettuces, which are sown outdoors, then lifted when young and replanted where they will grown until harvesting, are called transplants. Root crops are not usually transplanted. Transplant vegetables when it is cool and overcast. Water them first, loosen the soil around the roots and carefully lift them out. Make a planting hole just big enough for the roots, push soil around them, gently firm and water in thoroughly. The leaves often wilt in the sun – this is normal until new roots grow.

HARDENING OFF

Plants grown under cover need acclimatising to the cooler and more exposed conditions outdoors by hardening off. Do this by standing the pots outdoors during the day and bringing them back indoors at night for a period of about 10 days. Towards the end of the period, unless frost is forecast, they can be left out day and night. Crops grown in a greenhouse or polytunnel do not need hardening off.

First pickings – Year 1

The first year is spent assessing the garden, finding out what the soil is like, identifying sunny/shady spots and drawing up an overall, phased plan. A start is made on growing some food by planting quick-growing summer crops in various containers on the paved area, and in the existing borders, which have been cleared of weeds and other unwanted plants. The soil has been improved by working in some locally-sourced green waste compost made without any animal inputs. From now on the soil will be treated as no-dig, and will be disturbed as little as possible.

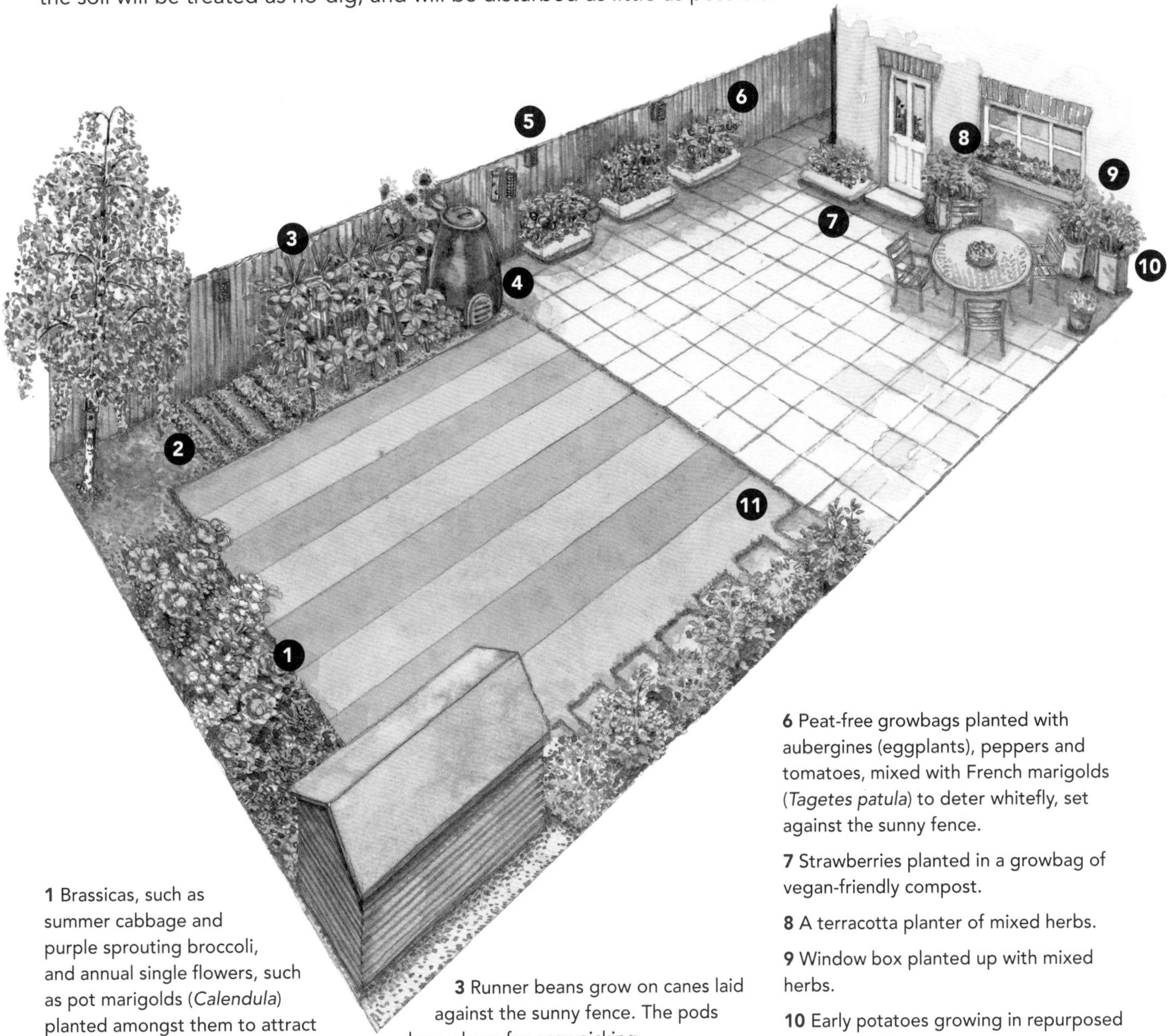

1 Brassicas, such as summer cabbage and purple sprouting broccoli, and annual single flowers, such as pot marigolds (*Calendula*) planted amongst them to attract beneficial bugs such as hoverflies.

2 Leafy and fast-growing cut-and-come-again salad crops sown direct in soil grooves. Organically-certified seeds are used.

3 Runner beans grow on canes laid against the sunny fence. The pods hang down for easy picking.

4 Lidded plastic bin used for wormposting (page 138).

5 Nest boxes to attract pollinating wild solitary bees.

6 Peat-free growbags planted with aubergines (eggplants), peppers and tomatoes, mixed with French marigolds (*Tagetes patula*) to deter whitefly, set against the sunny fence.

7 Strawberries planted in a growbag of vegan-friendly compost.

8 A terracotta planter of mixed herbs.

9 Window box planted up with mixed herbs.

10 Early potatoes growing in repurposed compost sacks.

11 The existing lawn will gradually be turned into beds for growing food. There is no need now for energy-intensive mowing.

Filling with promise – Year 3

By the third summer the lawn has gone, bringing an end to energy-intensive and polluting lawn mowing. The paved area has been reduced in size, with the lifted slabs being reused as permanent paths. The heavily compacted ground below the slabs has been loosened and lifted using a garden fork, and has been improved using vegan-friendly green waste compost delivered in bulk by the local recycling centre. Large stones and builders' rubble have been dug out and used as hardcore beneath the new central path. A pre-loved, reconditioned and sun-powered greenhouse has been added. The first raised beds are producing fresh veganic food for the household.

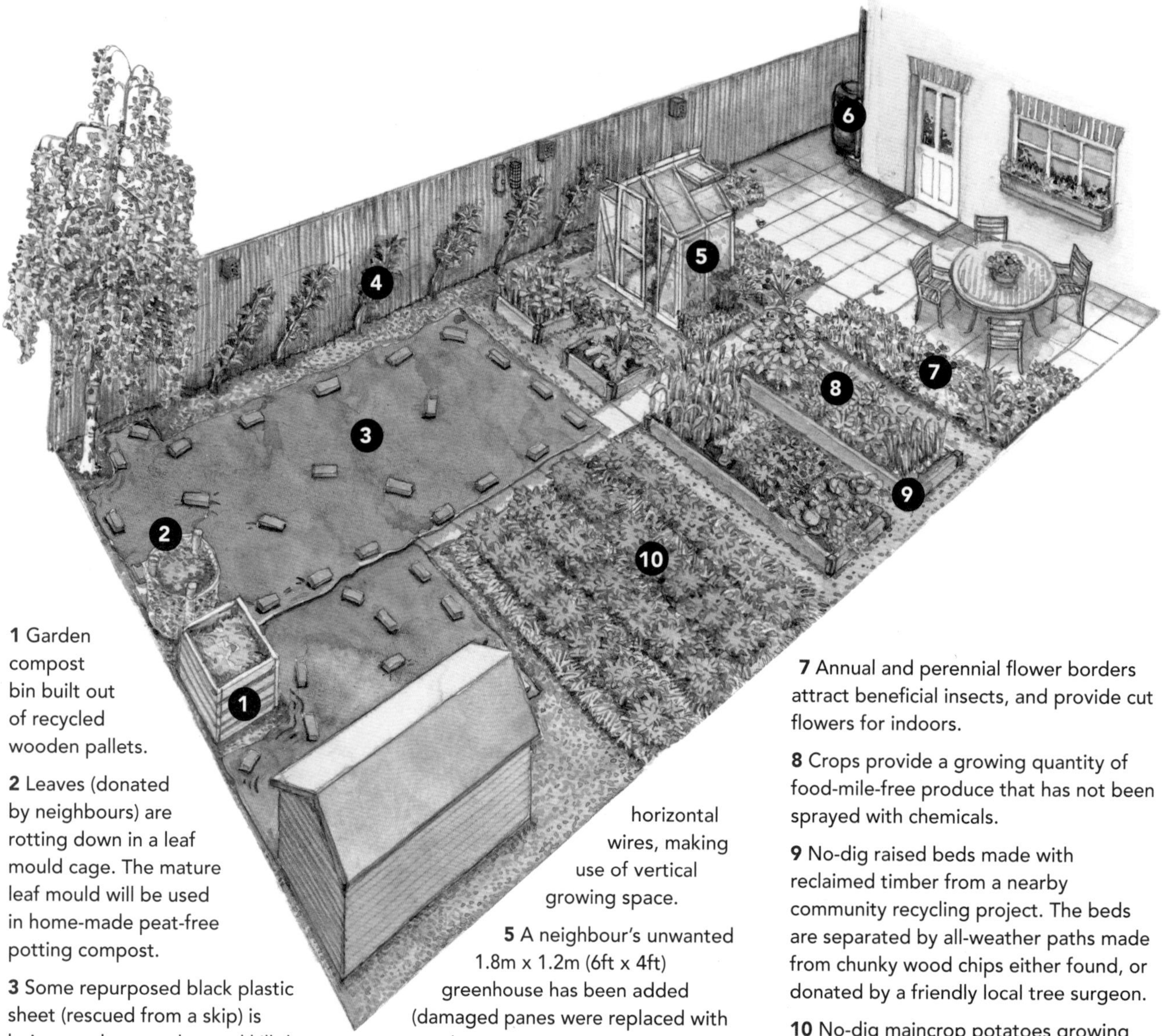

1 Garden compost bin built out of recycled wooden pallets.

2 Leaves (donated by neighbours) are rotting down in a leaf mould cage. The mature leaf mould will be used in home-made peat-free potting compost.

3 Some repurposed black plastic sheet (rescued from a skip) is being used to smother and kill the remaining lawn.

4 On the sunny fence, one year-old cordon fruit trees are trained at a 45-degree angle and supported by taut horizontal wires, making use of vertical growing space.

5 A neighbour's unwanted 1.8m x 1.2m (6ft x 4ft) greenhouse has been added (damaged panes were replaced with new glass). Tomatoes, underplanted with whitefly-deterring French marigolds, crop in the greenhouse.

6 Water butt fed by a rainwater diverter fitted to the downpipe.

7 Annual and perennial flower borders attract beneficial insects, and provide cut flowers for indoors.

8 Crops provide a growing quantity of food-mile-free produce that has not been sprayed with chemicals.

9 No-dig raised beds made with reclaimed timber from a nearby community recycling project. The beds are separated by all-weather paths made from chunky wood chips either found, or donated by a friendly local tree surgeon.

10 No-dig maincrop potatoes growing through a heavy mulch of overlapping cardboard sheets covered with green wood chips (delivered for free by a local tree surgeon) which has been laid over the remaining lawn.

Veganic abundance – Year 5

The structure of the garden is now complete and includes a wire mesh cage to protect the fruits from birds, more raised beds, a wildlife pond and a log pile to attract wildlife. The compost-making capacity has been increased with an extra bin (a third could be added). Fresh, ultra-local and veganic food is being harvested from the garden all year round, helping to reduce the household's overall environmental footprint.

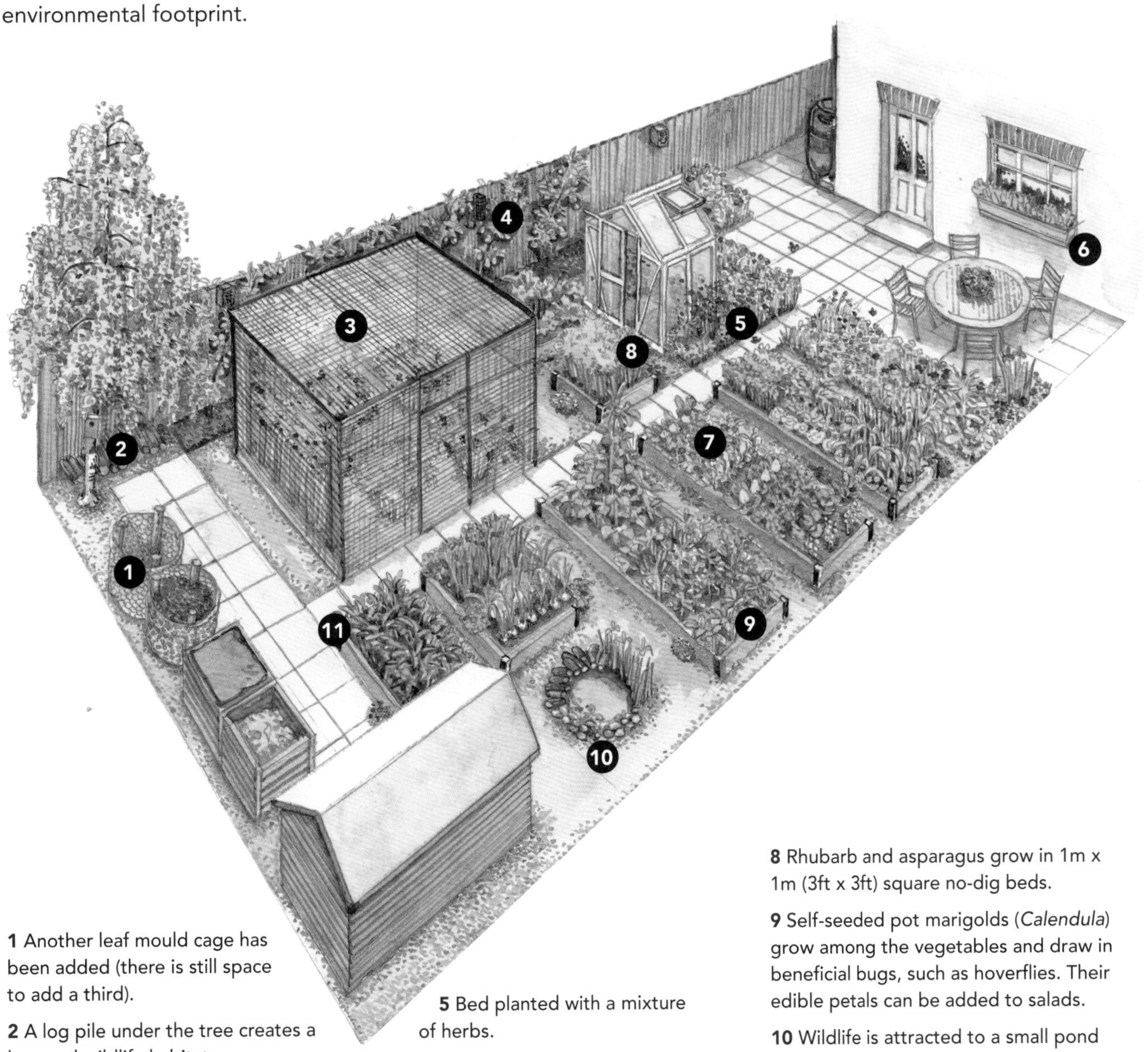

1 Another leaf mould cage has been added (there is still space to add a third).

2 A log pile under the tree creates a bug and wildlife habitat.

3 Black, red and white currants, and raspberries are grown in a 2m x 2m (7ft x 7ft) fruit cage covered with galvanised wire mesh. The cage is tall enough to allow easy access.

4 Cordon fruit trees are cropping heavily.

5 Bed planted with a mixture of herbs.

6 Up off the ground, fast-growing summer salad leaves are safer from slugs in the window box. In autumn it is planted with oriental greens such as mizuna and pak choi.

7 Blocks of annual vegetables are rotated each year.

8 Rhubarb and asparagus grow in 1m x 1m (3ft x 3ft) square no-dig beds.

9 Self-seeded pot marigolds (*Calendula*) grow among the vegetables and draw in beneficial bugs, such as hoverflies. Their edible petals can be added to salads.

10 Wildlife is attracted to a small pond 50cm (20in) in diameter. Frogs, toads and newts breed here in spring, helping boost the garden's population. Birds, mammals and insects drink at the pond's margins.

11 Comfrey produces material for turning into a nutrient-rich liquid soil tonic, and fresh 'greens' for the compost bin.

Sun-powered soil

This chapter describes what soil is, shows the different types, and explains how to nourish your own soil using plants powered by free and renewable sunshine. The no-dig approach, used in conjunction with a sheet mulch, is illustrated in detail, and there are tips for growing no-dig vegetables. How to make garden compost is clearly set out, along with all you need to know about 'wormposting'. Using green wood chips to enrich and invigorate soil is shown in detail. There is hands-on information on making leaf mould from fallen leaves, deploying mulches, using a shredder to make your own mulch, sowing living mulches, harnessing the goodness in seaweed, and making your own soil tonics from plants.

***Left:** Sunlight is what makes our plants grow. In a veganic garden we use renewable solar energy captured and stored by plants to build healthy soil brimming with life.*

Know your soil

Knowing which kind of soil you have and understanding its characteristics is crucial to your veganic garden's success. The soil in an established garden or allotment – which has potentially been cultivated for many years – might be very different to that found on a new housing development. By treating soil with respect and working with its strengths, it will eventually reward you with a plot that is both beautiful and bountiful.

Above: In this soil the distinction between fertile darker topsoil, where most plant roots are found, and paler, less fertile subsoil, is clear.

WHAT IS SOIL?

Complex and always evolving, soil, formed over millions of years, is a mixture of mineral particles weathered and worn from rocks; organic matter (animal and vegetable remains) in the various stages of decay; air, and water. All are essential to support plant life. The soil ecosystem is also home to a multitude of micro-organisms – algae, bacteria and fungi – together with insects, earthworms, and larger animals, such as moles. Soil provides anchorage for plant roots and it is the medium through which fine root hairs absorb water and nutrients. Veganic gardeners constantly nurture and improve soil, to encourage both the life found within it and the plants we grow in it to flourish.

Most soils are divided into distinct layers which are visible when you dig down through them. Topsoil is the darkest layer, contains lots of humus, and has the greatest concentration of soil life. Its depth can range from 5cm (2in) to 1.8m (6ft). Deeper topsoils mean more space for plants to grow and take up water and nutrients. Subsoil is usually lighter in colour because it has little or no humus and fewer plant roots. Subsoil sometimes sits on bedrock, from which the soil

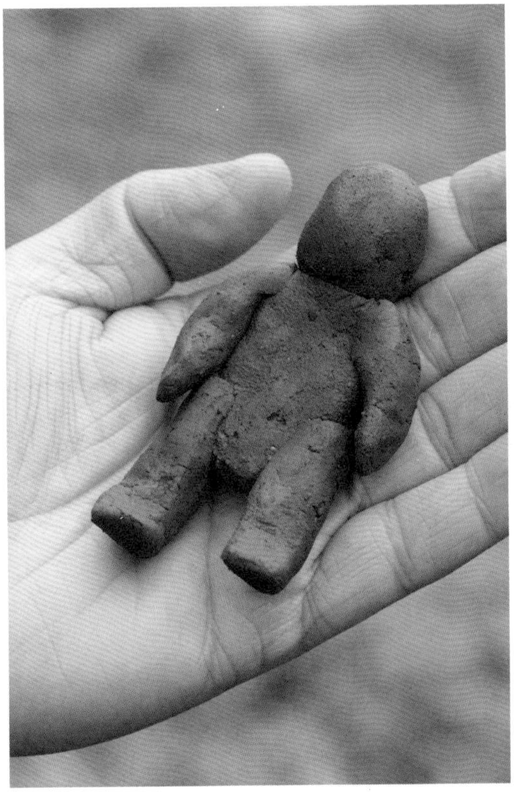

Far left: Clay soils are cold and heavy when wet but develop deep, distinctive cracks when they start to dry out.

Left: Sticky soil which is easy to mould into shapes is almost certainly clay, which is nutrient-rich and will grow a wide range of different plants.

above is derived. Digging a hole approximately 60cm (24in) deep will allow you to examine your own garden's unique soil profile.

PRE-LOVED OR VIRGIN SOIL?

Soil which has been cultivated for many years or even decades before you became its custodian is likely to be in good condition, especially following regular additions of organic matter. Pre-loved soil will usually be dark and easy to work with the tines of a garden fork; long-cultivated allotments or community gardens tend to have particularly deep and rich topsoils. Soil which has already been improved in this way – probably through regular digging and the addition of manure – can be converted to a 'no-dig' system straight away.

In contrast, the soil in a brand-new or 'virgin' garden is often unimproved, contains builders' rubble, is compacted from building work, and in need of improvement. It may need to be thoroughly dug or forked over and broken up first, to remove debris, rubble and any tough, woody weeds such as brambles, before switching to a no-dig approach. In a new garden it is worth digging a hole to see what if any topsoil exists, because it is sometimes removed during construction work. A lack of distinct horizontal layers in the cut-away soil, a pale colour, and an absence of plant roots indicates that you are dealing with largely subsoil. It can take several years to improve the fertility of raw subsoil by using a combination of organic matter added as garden or green waste compost, green wood chips, and by sowing living mulches.

KNOWING YOUR SOIL TYPE

Soil can be divided up into six broad types: sand, clay, silt, chalk, peat and loam (see overleaf). Each has its own set of qualities and characteristics, and its pros and cons. Deciding which soil type you have will help you work with it and nurture it in the most effective way.

How to identify your soil type

To find out your soil type, take a handful of soil from your garden and wet it until it is moist but not mud-like. How the soil responds to some basic tests will reveal what type of soil you have.

SAND

Contains particles between 0.2mm and 2mm in size. Dry, light and often pale, sandy soils are free-draining and always hungry, and need regular applications of organic matter. They warm up quickly in spring and suit early sowings.

How it feels: coarse and gritty when rubbed between the fingers and does not stick to them. Barely forms a loose and crumbling ball when rolled in the hand.

CLAY

Made up of tiny particles under 0.002mm in size. Clay soils are often dark, drain poorly, and are cold and heavy. However, they are rich in plant nutrients and can grow a wide range of plants.

How it feels: sticky when wet and hard when dry, often cracking in the sun. Can be rolled into a perfect ball, and will stain your hands. Sticks to boots in wet weather.

SILT

Comprised of particles between 0.002mm and 0.02mm in size. Heavy rain damages silt soils, leading to a hard surface crust or 'cap' when they dry out. Silt soil can be cold and slow to warm up. It is easily improved with organic matter.

How it feels: neither gritty nor sticky, but smooth and silky when rubbed between the fingers. A disc of moist silt will easily retain a thumbprint.

CHALK

Pale or dark soil with obvious stones, lumps of chalk or flints (or a mixture) and often looks thin and 'hungry'. Chalk soils are often shallow, free-draining and need plenty of organic matter to improve them. They contain lots of lime, have a high pH, and are suited to growing lime-loving plants (known as calcicoles).
How it feels: gritty and rough due to stones and chalky lumps, which are pale inside.

PEAT

Made up largely of decomposed mosses, sedges and other bog plants, peat soil is dark brown or almost black (sometimes grey) in colour and is naturally rich in organic matter. Gardens with peat soils are uncommon. They are have a low pH, making them suitable for growing acid-loving (ericaceous) plants. They can easily become waterlogged.
How it feels: soft and spongy, it will ooze brown water when a handful is squeezed.

LOAM

Most soils are made up of a varying mixture of sand, clay and silt known as loam. If there is a higher proportion of sand present, the soil is a 'sandy loam', which will be lighter and fast-draining. A high clay content results in a heavier and slower-draining 'clay loam'. Garden soil near rivers is commonly 'silty loam' due to the high proportion of silt deposited on flood plains.

Loams make ideal no-dig garden soils that are easy to lightly cultivate and rich in plant nutrients. They can be improved further when nourished regularly with organic matter, to produce a dark, rich topsoil filled with soil life. Loams are usually dark in colour due to an abundance of carbon-storing humus.
How it feels: soft and crumb-like; loam tends not to compact or become smeared if squeezed, but keeps an open texture.

Nourishing your soil

Gradually building up the amount of organic matter in your no-dig soil over time improves it and will reward you with more resilient, problem-free and productive plants. Nurturing soil has wider benefits for our natural world: dark, loamy soils with an open, crumb-like structure, and which have a dynamic and thriving ecosystem, lock up and store some atmospheric carbon, helping to reduce global heating.

Above: *Composted bracken is a potash-rich, vegan-friendly and renewable soil improver that is ideal for use on heavy soils.*

THE IMPORTANCE OF ORGANIC MATTER

In a veganic garden, organic matter is primarily the rotted down remains of plants. When added to any soil, it helps to glue together tiny mineral fragments to form crumbs and creates a good soil structure. As organic matter is broken down further, by earthworms and soil micro-organisms, it eventually forms humus – a stable form of soil carbon which gives the majority of soils their dark brown-black colour. By locking carbon into your soil, you can help reduce the atmospheric build-up of carbon dioxide, the primary driver of climate breakdown. Biochar can also be used to store carbon in soil.

Organic matter breaks up heavy clay soil, making it faster-draining and quicker to warm up in spring. Adding it to a lighter, fast-draining sandy soil improves its structure and helps it retain water and nutrients. Soil improved with organic matter is rich in microbial life, releases nutrients gradually to plants as and when they need them, and encourages strong, healthy pest- and disease-resistant growth.

Soils enriched with organic matter readily absorb water and retain it for longer. Even in urban areas, gardens with deep, healthy soil and densely planted with a range of different plants have a role to play in mitigating the effects of increasingly common extreme weather events, such as flash flooding. By absorbing and holding on to rainwater, our gardens can help to slow its run-off, easing the sudden pressure on local drainage networks.

VEGANIC SOIL IMPROVERS

Organic matter used for soil improvement can come from garden-made or locally-sourced green waste compost or leaf mould, green wood chips, wormpost, digestate, living mulches (green manures), and seaweed. Fresh or rotted animal manures (or materials containing them or any slaughterhouse byproducts) are not suitable for a veganic garden.

Mature garden compost can be used straight from your heap or bin. Bought-in green waste compost is made from garden waste composted at high temperatures to kill weed seeds and pathogens (check it is made from 100% plant waste). It can be a cost-effective way of quickly improving your soil if home-made garden compost is in short supply, especially where you are creating a new garden from scratch. Composted bracken is another nutrient-rich soil improver which also helps make heavy clay soil more workable.

WHAT IS BIOCHAR?

Biochar is a kind of charcoal used as a soil conditioner or for adding to sowing and potting composts (soil mixes). It improves fertility and buries carbon, helping to reduce global heating. Biochar is porous, absorbs water, increases the availability of plant nutrients and encourages beneficial soil micro-organisms. When woody plants (such as trees) grow, they absorb carbon dioxide from the air and store it in their tissues as carbon. When dry wood is burned without oxygen present, much of the carbon is left as stable biochar. Mixed with soil or compost, biochar does not decompose and so its carbon remains stored away indefinitely. Although the best ways of using biochar to store carbon are still being explored, its soil-enhancing properties have been appreciated by gardeners for thousands of years.

ACID OR ALKALINE?

Knowing the pH of your soil will help you decide what plants to grow – and which might struggle. The acidity or alkalinity of soil is determined by its lime content, which is measured in units of pH on a scale of 1 to 14. Neutral soil has a pH of 7; anything above that is alkaline and anything below it, acid. Most vegetables and other food plants thrive in soil with a pH of about 6.5, although there are exceptions. Blueberries, for example, need an acid soil (pH below 6.5), so in a garden where the soil is alkaline, they should be grown in pots of peat-free ericaceous compost.

SIMPLE PH TEST KIT

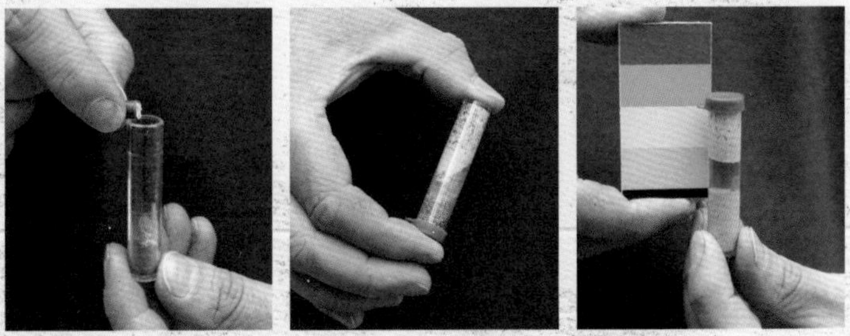

1 Add the soil sample and reactant to cooled boiled water in a test tube.

2 Secure the cap and throughly mix the contents of the tube together.

3 Compare with the colour chart; this soil is noticeably acid.

You can test your soil's pH using a simple home test kit. If you need a more detailed analysis – to tell you what key plant nutrients your soil contains, or might be lacking – it is better to send a sample to a soil testing service (this will provide a more accurate analysis than using a DIY test kit).

Raising the pH of soil, by using lime spread over no-dig soil in spring, is a relatively straightforward process. Lowering the pH is best achieved through regular and liberal additions of garden compost and other organic matter.

USING SOIL IMPROVERS

In a no-dig system (see overleaf), organic matter is spread over the surface of the soil without digging it in. Earthworms will pull some of it down into the topsoil, and microbes break it down further until it becomes dark humus. Green wood chips (page 142) are worked into the top 5–7.5cm (2–3in) of the soil, where they stimulate soil microbial life. Digestate used as a mulch will both nourish the soil and stop weed seeds from germinating.

Use soil improver generously and often, especially if your soil is initially poor – such as when you are starting a new garden with very little topsoil – and plants are not growing strongly. Organic matter encourages a thriving soil ecosystem, which is shown by an increasing number of earthworms and other soil life. If your soil is already dark, crumbly and the plants are growing well, you can use improvers such as garden compost more sparingly, focusing them on the areas where plants are not growing so well.

Soil improvers can play a dual role by also acting as a weed-suppressing mulch spread over the soil surface, where they will rot down and be incorporated by earthworms and other soil organisms. Weed-free digestate is an easy-to-use and nutrient-rich mulch.

Below: Veganic gardens use the soil-building power of plants to grow more plants.

No digging required

Nature does not constantly disrupt the soil in the way that traditional gardening wisdom urges; we are implored to dig soil annually, sometimes several spade-depths deep, at the same time adding animal manures to improve its fertility. Veganic gardening favours the no-dig approach, which mimics natural processes to help nourish and sustain life-filled soil. Going no-dig is a nature-friendly way to grow plants – and less work.

Above: In the author's no-dig garden, green wood chips are used to both invigorate soil microbial life and as an attractive and long-lived weed-stopping mulch.

NATURE DOES NOT DIG

Nature does not dig – gardeners do. Disturbed soil in nature is almost always a relatively rare and short-lived phenomenon – such as when a tree blows over, or there is a landslip. When this happens, wild plants quickly move to heal the tear in the earth's 'skin' because in nature, bare soil is an ecological no-no.

The first sign of the healing process is usually a green flush of tiny seedlings germinating on the bare soil, which sprout from dormant seeds. These quickly grow into mature plants and bare, exposed soil rapidly disappears. Plant roots quickly bind the disturbed soil together, stabilising it, and creating conditions for other wild plants to establish.

When we regularly dig or fork over (or rotavate) topsoil, we are deliberately cutting into the earth's living skin, triggering the healing process to start all over again, often on an annual basis. To the gardener's eye, the first phase of that healing is an explosion in the number of weeds – which then require effort to curtail them.

The life of the soil is disrupted in other ways when we tear into it with a spade.

• Soil life can be harmed and killed when it is suddenly exposed to sunlight; earthworms quickly burrow back into the soil when unearthed. Digging or forking soil lays waste to an entire subterranean ecosystem; a single teaspoon of soil is home to 10,000 different species of microbe.

• The extensive network of fine fungal hyphae that live throughout the soil, and which form symbiotic relationships with plant roots –

helping them to find and absorb plant nutrients and water – is physically broken up by repeated soil cultivation.

• Animals which live permanently in the soil – or those which enter it to hibernate in winter – are disturbed and exposed to predators by digging. Birds which pluck earthworms from freshly-turned soil (or seagulls which flock to recently ploughed fields) enjoy an artificial feast which depletes the soil ecosystem of one of its most vital inhabitants.

• Soil structure can be damaged, especially when soil is dug in autumn and winter and then left exposed to rain, frost and snow. The interwoven matrix of earthworm burrows, pores, and channels left by decayed roots is shattered when soil is dug up and smashed into smaller lumps. This natural network helps soils to breathe, by allowing air into them, and to drain without becoming waterlogged. Despite digging being routinely recommended as a way of 'improving' soil, it can have the opposite effect in practice.

• Adding animal manures, slaughterhouse byproducts and synthetic fertilisers to soil during or after digging overdoses it with nutrients harmful to microbial life.

• When dark, carbon-rich humus derived from organic matter is exposed to the air, it releases its carbon into the air. Digging soil turns it from being a carbon sink to a source of atmospheric carbon dioxide, the main gas which drives climate breakdown.

WHAT IS NO-DIG GARDENING?

No-dig gardening starts the moment you retire your spade, and use a garden fork only for minimal and shallow soil cultivation (such as incorporating green wood chips). Soil disturbance ends and its fragile ecosystem begins to recover.

Instead of adding organic matter to the soil by burying it using a spade, no-dig gardening relies on life largely unseen to 'dig' it in by incorporating it for us, slowly and naturally, but without disrupting the soil. In nature, dead plant matter – such as autumn leaves in woodland – falls to the ground, where it is slowly broken down and becomes part of the soil.

In a veganic garden, we mimic and supercharge that natural process: we make compost from plants and use it to nourish the life in the soil, which in turn nourishes the plants we choose to grow.

Above left: Natural woodland does not 'dig'. Leaves and other plant material falling to the ground are broken down and incorporated by soil organisms.

Above right: No-dig allotments can be just as productive as those which are regularly dug over.

How no-dig soil works

When we stop digging, forking over, or rotavating soil, its fragile and damaged underground ecosystem quickly begins to heal. Once disruption ends and it settles down, soil life soon begins to return in abundance. The illustration opposite shows how a once frequently-dug (and manured) soil – which has recently become overrun with weeds – quickly regains its natural equilibrium over a period of 24 months.

Clockwise from top: No-dig can be adopted all around a veganic garden, including in permanently planted beds and borders. Insect-boosting perennial flowers such as giant inula (Inula magnifica) thrive in rich, undisturbed soil. Populations of large and slow-moving earthworms soon increase when disruption of their habitat through digging ceases.

CLEARING THE WEEDS (right)

At the start, in autumn, while the soil is still warm, a deep mulch is used to kill the weeds (see 'Sheet mulching', overleaf). This helps to kick-start the soil's recovery.

1 This sheet mulch is made up of several layers of thick, overlapping cardboard covered with a 5cm (2in) deep layer of fresh and weedkiller-free lawn mowings to weigh them down.

2 Starved of light, the chopped-up weeds beneath the cardboard quickly turn yellow and begin to rot away. No weed seeds can germinate in the darkness.

3 The roots of the cut-down weeds remain in the soil. Those of annual weeds will die in a few weeks. This dandelion tap-root will reshoot, but will be killed due to lack of light.

4 Annual digging has left the soil solid and dense. Only a few earthworms (or their burrows) are present.

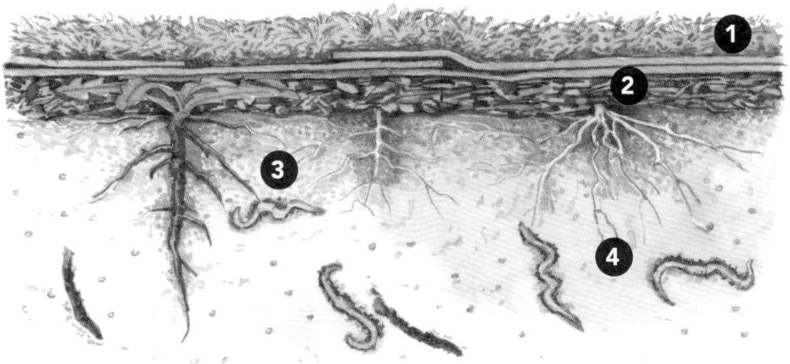

SOIL LIFE BOUNCES BACK (left)

After 6–12 months the sheet mulch has done its job and all but the most persistent weeds are dead. The cessation of digging has triggered an ecosystem recovery.

5 The mulch layer and the weeds it was smothering have rotted away to leave a dark and friable layer of organic matter on the soil surface.

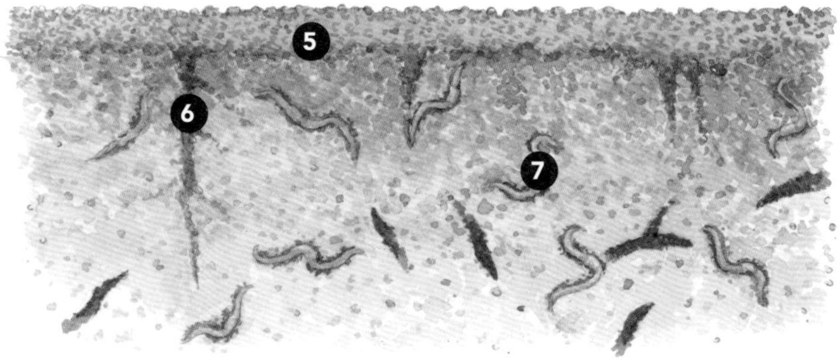

6 Weed roots, including the dandelion, have decayed into the soil. Because the soil is now undisturbed, weed seeds are not brought to the surface where they can germinate.

7 A growing number of earthworms are pulling some of the decomposed mulch down into their expanding network of burrows. Other soil life is flourishing, much of it unseen to the naked eye. Pale fungal mycelia now thread their way through the soil.

NO-DIG ABUNDANCE (below left)

Two years on, the soil's ecosystem is restored, it teems with life, and it is being used to grow a year-round abundance of food crops.

8 To nourish and sustain the soil, it is mulched in spring with a 2.5–5cm (1–2in) deep layer of mature garden or local green waste compost. Green wood chips could also be used.

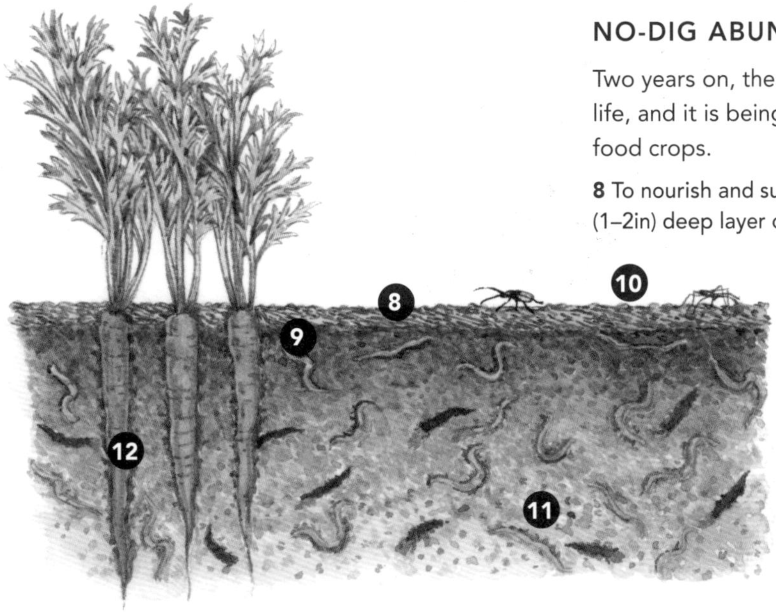

9 Soil microbes break the compost down, gradually releasing its nutrients to plants.

10 Wolf spiders and ground beetles hunt on the dry, warm surface of the mulch.

11 A now-flourishing earthworm population is busy pulling decaying compost into its numerous burrows.

12 Pulling up carrots sown into the now-friable soil will cause only minimal soil disturbance.

Sheet mulching

Clearing an overgrown garden or allotment of weeds without resorting to energy-intensive and potentially polluting chemical weedkillers usually involves a lot of hard work. Sheet mulching offers a simpler, easier and nature-friendly solution which can be used on a small or large area. Its greatest advantage is that it allows us to start growing no-dig vegetable crops at the same time as clearing an overgrown plot.

Opposite: *Six months after being sheet mulched, this previously neglected allotment is now a productive food garden laid out as a series of 1.2m (4ft) wide beds, separated by 45cm (18in) wide all-weather paths.*

Below: *Cabbages planted straight into a sheet mulched bed 1.2m (4ft) wide. Pest-eating wolf spiders (*Pardosa amentata*) hunt among the straw layer.*

WHAT IS SHEET MULCHING?

A sheet mulch is similar to other mulches (see 'Mulch magic', page 150) but is more heavyweight in the way it works. It is used to clear whole areas of all but the most stubborn perennial weeds. Sheet mulches are thick and heavy, and are made of layers of different materials laid one on top of the other on the ground, as shown in the sequence overleaf. This use of deep mulch is sometimes called 'lasagne gardening'. Some sheet mulch materials smother and kill existing weeds, while others also help to nourish the soil and prevent weed seeds from germinating.

HOW A SHEET MULCH WORKS

Laying the thick mulch layer instantly arrests weed growth by cutting off light, killing annuals and weakening any perennials with spreading or deep tap roots. Stubborn weeds are easy to remove if they break through the mulch – see page 120. Although it takes time and effort, sheet mulching is far quicker and easier than digging over large areas and removing individual weeds manually.

As the mulch gradually settles on to the soil, the layers of organic mulching materials, together with any dead weeds, start to rot down. Microbial soil life and earthworm activity increases beneath the mulch and the covered soil is less prone to drying out.

The best times to sheet mulch are in autumn, or mid- to late spring, when the soil is warm and weeds are just starting to grow. Never mulch during winter when the soil is cold or frozen – it could keep the soil temperature low for many months, hindering plant growth.

PLANTING THROUGH THE MULCH

Once the mulch is in place you have two choices: either leave the area undisturbed for the next 6–12 months, or plant through it with suitable vegetable crops to create an instant vegetable garden. Although the soil will not have

been cultivated or improved, unless it is heavily compacted it will still grow good crops.

Compacted soils might need loosening before you sow or plant into them. Do this by pushing a garden fork (to the depth of its tines) into moist soil at roughly 15cm (6in) intervals, and then ease the tines upwards, until the soil heaves and cracks at the surface – but do not lift it and turn it over. This relieves compaction, allows in air, while leaving the fragile soil ecosystem intact.

If you decide to grow crops through the mulch, this is a good time to mark out any permanent beds and paths. You then tread only on the paths, preventing soil compaction where plants are grown. Crops can also be planted in rows, although this will compact the soil across the whole area that has been mulched.

To plant, use a trowel to dig down to the soil surface, loosen it and mix it with some of the organic matter from the mulch. You can also add some garden compost or similar vegan-friendly soil improver. Pot-grown vegetable plants are then planted into the pockets of soil and the mulch is drawn back, but without burying the plants. Potatoes are an easy crop to grow in a sheet mulch – see 'No-dig vegetables', overleaf. Whether or not you choose to grow crops straight after mulching, 6–12 months later the soil should be largely weed-free. You can then loosen and ease out any persistent weeds with deep roots, level any uneven ground, and switch to no-dig.

Some short-term soil disturbance is inevitable when planting perennial and larger food-bearing plants, such as asparagus, or fruit trees and bushes. These need bigger planting holes to accommodate their roots, especially if they are bought bare-rooted. Once planted, these kinds of long-lived crops will be in the ground for many years, automatically becoming part of an overall no-dig approach.

SOWING SEEDS

Sowing smaller seeds is difficult because seedlings are easily overwhelmed by the mulch materials (which birds will often flick about as they hunt for food), but you can sow larger seeds such as those of runner beans by scraping back the mulch layer first and making a hole in the soil and sowing into it.

To sow smaller seeds, especially those of root crops such as carrots, it is better to set aside an unmulched, relatively weed-free area, and then sow seeds direct. Mulch can gradually be added as the young plants grow larger and their leaves are held well above the mulch layer.

OUSTING TOUGH WEEDS

Some tough, mostly perennial weeds such as dandelions, shown left, are not always killed outright by a sheet mulch and can eventually push up through it. To remove them individually, part the mulch, loosen them using a fork and lift out as much root as possible. If they regrow, repeat the process.

After several months, any dense patches of persistent weeds, such as field bindweed (*Convolvulus arvensis*), will become obvious. To tackle them, scrape the area clear of mulch and fork over and loosen the soil, removing as many of the weed roots as possible. This inevitably disrupts the soil in the short term, but is the only pragmatic option for removing troublesome weeds. The mulch layer can then be relaid, as deep as you can make it, or the area can be planted with a weed-suppressing crop such as potatoes, which cast deep shade below their dense canopy of leaves.

How to lay a sheet mulch

1 Cut down and chop up any weeds using a sickle, or, for larger areas, a hook or scythe. Dig out any tough, woody weeds such as bramble (*Rubus fruticosus* agg.).

2 Collect enough large sheets of cardboard to cover the area, and remove any plastic tape. Lay the sheets so their edges are overlapping by at least 30cm (12in).

3 To anchor the light-excluding cardboard layer, spread a 10–15cm (4–6in) deep layer of organic matter (this is local green waste compost) over the sheets.

4 Add a top layer of old straw roughly 15cm (6in) deep. In summer, fresh (guaranteed weedkiller-free) lawn mowings can be used as a topping, or in autumn, fallen leaves.

5 These maincrop 'Desiree' potatoes were grown by pushing the seed potatoes under the mulch layer, and covering them with newspaper and straw. They are harvested as needed.

No-dig vegetables

Growing vegetables, fruits and herbs in a no-dig garden requires no special techniques and only basic tools to succeed. It is a gentler and kinder way of gardening, because we are not regularly upending an entire living ecosystem – the soil – through digging or rotavating. Crops are easy to sow and plant, straightforward to look after, and simple to harvest, while soil disturbance is kept to a minimum.

Above left: Root crops such as beetroot are easy to harvest by gently pulling them up.

Above right: A stainless steel fork is useful for some no-dig jobs, such as lightly working compost into the soil surface.

PUT AWAY THE SPADE

In a food garden or allotment which has been cleared of perennial weeds, and where any heavily compacted soil has been loosened and opened up, tools such as the spade become largely redundant. A spade can still be useful for moving garden or green waste compost, leaf mould, green wood chips and mulches around, but you will not need one for digging once you have transitioned to no-dig.

One of the most useful no-dig tools is the garden fork. It can be used to incorporate compost and/or green wood chips into the soil surface, although even this is not essential if they are being used primarily as a mulch. A hand-held hoe for nipping out odd weeds, and a trowel or wooden dibber, are also useful for making planting holes.

Gardeners who use copper tools claim their plants are less prone to damage by slugs and snails, and that copper does not disturb the soil's natural magnetic fields (which iron tools do). You might want to test out the theory.

SOWING AND PLANTING

Seed sowing and planting out young plants in a no-dig garden is straightforward. To sow smaller seeds, such as radish, a wooden soil groove (drill) former can be used to form a v-shaped groove in the soil surface (after parting any mulch first), into which the seeds are sown. Larger seeds, such as those of runner beans, can be sown into individual holes made with your finger, or a dibber or trowel.

You can also use your fingers to make curving grooves, or patterns of holes in the soil, to sow

Opposite: Edible crops and pollinator-friendly flowers, such as these self-sown orange pot marigolds (Calendula officinalis), growing together in a thriving no-dig food garden.

Right: Leafy vegetable crops such as rainbow chard thrive in no-dig soil, which is rich in moisture-holding organic matter.

Far right: A trowel is useful for planting, or for sowing large seeds. Some gardeners find using copper tools (like this one) at planting time helps to reduce damage to crops from slugs and snails.

into; crops do not have to be grown in straight rows. Planting out pot-grown or young starter or plug plants is easy in no-dig soil because it stays looser and more open, and is not compacted. The root-balls of plants should always be watered thoroughly before planting. Then part any mulch and use a trowel or dibber (or your fingers) to make appropriately-sized planting holes. Check the top of the root-ball is level with the soil, gently firm it down, pour water around the plant to settle it in, and draw back any mulch around it.

EASY HARVESTING

Harvesting no-dig crops is straightforward and less work. There is always some soil disturbance involved in harvesting your produce, but the aim is to minimise it.

On lighter, sandy soils, deep-growing root crops such as carrots and parsnips can simply be pulled up. On heavier clay soils, loosen the soil around and beneath them first using a garden fork, then grab their leaves and slowly ease them from the ground. Any holes will soon close and fill as the soil settles. Crops with roots or bulbs that grow largely above the soil, such as beetroot and onions respectively, can be pulled straight up.

CLIMATE-FRIENDLY

LEAVE ROOTS TO ROT

At the end of its productive life, almost any crop not grown for its harvestable roots can be cut off at soil level and its roots left in the ground to rot away. Even tough roots soon start to decay, as microbial soil life breaks them down. As decay progresses, they become food for earthworms and many other soil-dwelling organisms.

By not pulling roots up, the soil's fragile ecosystem remains undisturbed, and they add valuable humus, increasing soil carbon. The roots of legumes – plants in the pea family, Fabaceae – house bacteria in their root nodules, which grab nitrogen from the air. When these rot down, they slowly release it again, and it is available for hungry leafy crops such as cabbages. Leaving roots in situ has other benefits. The spaces left by decaying roots become channels that allow air and water to easily pass into the soil. This makes no-dig gardening especially valuable for absorbing the large amounts of rain that now fall during extreme weather events, driven by climate breakdown.

No-dig gardens and allotments, with their high levels of organic matter, and their more open and stable water-absorbing properties, can play a useful role in alleviating localised flooding, especially in urban areas.

Growing potatoes without digging

The effort involved in growing potatoes traditionally – by first planting them in the soil and then earthing them up (mounding soil around them) as they grow, is avoided by the no-dig approach. Growing them is easier and there is no need to disturb the soil to gather the tubers, or to harvest them all at once.

1 Prepare your seed potatoes by 'chitting' them for several weeks in a cool, bright, frost-free place. Plant them in early to mid-spring when the 'chits' are 2.5cm (1in) long.

2 Spread a 2.5–5cm (1–2in) deep and even layer of mature garden or green waste compost over the surface of the no-dig soil (do not work it in).

3 Space the tubers (chits uppermost) evenly over the soil, 30cm (12in) apart. This variety, 'Rocket', is grown for its immature 'new' potatoes which can be harvested from early summer.

4 Spread full thickness, overlapping sheets of newspaper over the tubers, and then soak them thoroughly. This layer helps keep the young potatoes in darkness as they develop.

5 Cover the newspaper with a 10–15cm (4–6in) deep layer of mulch. Used here is spoiled hay; straw, weedkiller-free lawn mowings or green wood chips are also suitable.

6 Leafy shoots will push up through the damp paper/mulch layer. Potatoes are frost-sensitive, so cover the emerging young shoots with mulch on cold and clear nights.

7 Young tubers form on the soil below the paper/mulch layer (part it to check their progress). Harvest what you need, then cover the rest up to keep growing.

Above left: Anything that once lived can be turned into compost, including these old bird's nests cleaned from nesting boxes in spring.

Above right: Adding nutrient-rich comfrey (Symphytum) leaves as a 'green' (page 132) to your compost mix helps stimulate unseen microbial life.

Compost, compost, compost

Turning freely available and valuable ultra-local resources that we usually think of as waste into garden compost benefits both your garden and our wider natural world. Setting up your own compost cycle helps to relieve pressure on landfill and reduce emissions of the greenhouse gases contributing to climate breakdown, while creating a rich and nourishing soil improver that boosts soil biodiversity and encourages strong and healthy plants.

WHAT IS COMPOSTING?

Making garden compost is simply encouraging the breakdown (rotting) of once-living materials until they form a crumbly, dark brown material which is used to improve your no-dig soil. This process is carried out by more obvious creatures, such as composting worms and bugs which eat decaying plants (detritivores), and by mostly unseen bacteria, fungi and other soil organisms. Veganic gardens and allotments rely on fertility derived from plants, including garden compost, because we do not use commercial animal manures or fertilisers made from slaughterhouse or other byproducts.

Composting materials come from various sources. In a veganic garden they might be weeds, grass mowings, soft and leafy hedge trimmings, food crop remains, sappy green wood chips, comfrey leaves or stinging nettle shoots, or fallen leaves which are turned into leaf mould. Household materials include vegetable and fruit peelings, loose tea or plastic-free teabags, coffee grounds, shredded paper, used paper towel, cardboard and plastic-free food packaging. Even cloth made from natural and biodegradable plant-derived materials, such as cotton, will slowly rot down.

Veganic gardeners following a plant-based diet ensures that food waste can safely be composted. If you have only a small garden, and can't fit in large heaps, wormposting (see pages 138–141) is an easy way to deal with kitchen/cooked and household waste, by getting compost worms to help.

If something will rot, it can usually be turned into garden compost. Non-living materials such as glass, plastic or metal are not compostable and should be recycled at the kerbside or at

your local recycling centre. The 'holy grail' of composting is to make as much from your degradable refuse as you can.

BENEFITS TO OUR NATURAL WORLD

Transporting garden and household waste requires fuel to truck it either to landfill sites (large holes in the ground) or to air-polluting incineration plants, while bonfires cause both annoyance and widespread air pollution. Composting waste where it is produced requires minimal transport, other than by wheelbarrow, does not pollute, and so has a small gardening footprint.

Although waste separation and recycling is improving, large volumes of garden and household waste are still sent to landfill sites. When once-living and biodegradable materials are buried and compressed, they will rot, but because air (oxygen) is absent, they produce methane, which is a potent greenhouse gas helping to drive climate breakdown. Well-aerated compost heaps and bins generate minimal if any methane.

Making garden compost utilises our valuable resources, improves your soil, locks some carbon away in it, and causes little or no environmental harm in the process.

LARGE-SCALE COMPOSTING

If you cannot make your own compost, perhaps through lack of space, any garden or kitchen waste should be left out for collection, or taken to your nearest green waste collection site. At a large-scale composting facility, the materials are chopped up and mixed together, then arranged in elongated hot heaps or 'windrows', which reach high temperatures. This speeds up the composting process and kills any weed seeds, pests or diseases. The resulting compost is sieved and used as a soil improver or mulch. Green waste compost is often the most readily available source of organic matter in urban areas. If you can be certain it is produced free of any animal inputs (manures or pet or food waste), and is made entirely of composted plant waste, buying it stimulates the ongoing recycling of local garden waste.

HOME COMPOSTING

Garden, kitchen and household waste which is turned into compost in your garden or allotment has a tiny gardening footprint. You can make your compost in a cool and slow way (page 130), or hot and fast (page 134). The method you choose will depend on the composting materials and the time, space and energy you have.

Above left: Fungi are just one group of organisms which play a key role in breaking down raw materials into nutrient-rich garden compost. Here pale fungal mycelium is spreading through a heap.

Above right: Many councils turn locally-collected garden waste into soil improver in large-scale composting facilities, then supply it to gardeners. Check that it is made from plants and that it is not contaminated by fragments of plastic.

The garden compost cycle

Your own garden and home is a rich source of raw materials for making garden compost. Here you can see how composting materials (the inputs, shown in blue), as well as the resulting compost (the outputs, in green), flow into and around your garden (together with any neighbouring ones), and some of the ways in which they can be used. Compost is made here, cool and slow, all year round, in a lidded wooden compost bin with three separate bays.

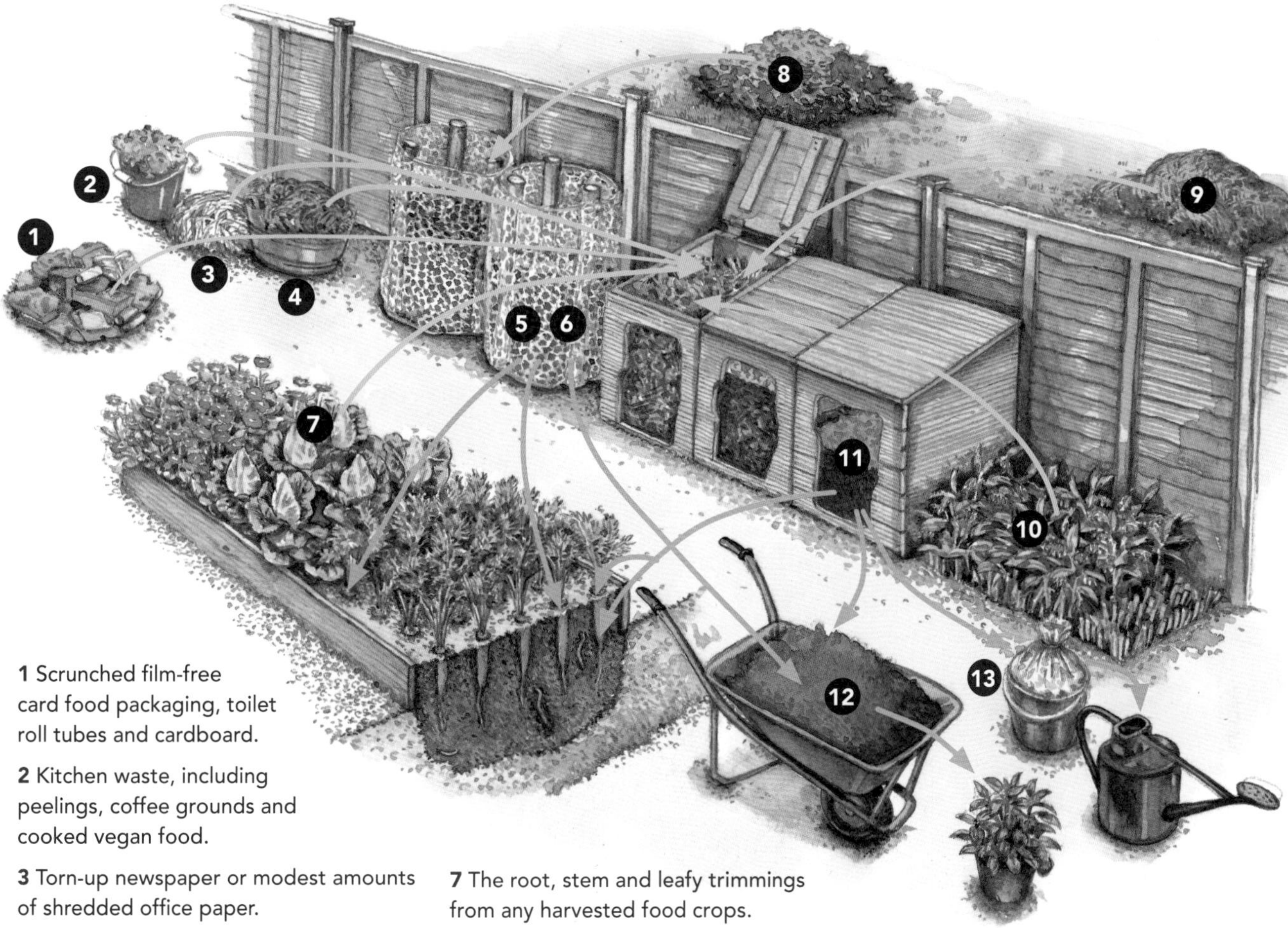

1 Scrunched film-free card food packaging, toilet roll tubes and cardboard.

2 Kitchen waste, including peelings, coffee grounds and cooked vegan food.

3 Torn-up newspaper or modest amounts of shredded office paper.

4 Garden waste, including weeds, soft prunings and faded bedding plants.

5 Use coarse, part-rotted leaf mould as a mulch and soil improver for raised no-dig vegetable beds.

6 Add sieved leaf mould that is two to three years old to home-made peat-free potting compost. During sieving, remove any stones or twigs, along with any tree seeds, such as acorns.

7 The root, stem and leafy trimmings from any harvested food crops.

8 Collect autumn leaves from your own or a neighbour's garden, for making leaf mould.

9 Lawn mowings donated by a neighbour; check that no weedkiller has been used. Use mowings when they are still green and fresh, and easy to mix with other materials.

10 Comfrey produces green leaves for adding to your compost bin and can be cut repeatedly during summer. Chopping them up first makes them easier to mix with other composting materials.

11 Mature garden compost improves all soil types.

12 Mix sieved garden compost 50:50 with leaf mould to make a home-made peat-free compost.

13 Soak a hessian (burlap) sack of garden compost in water overnight to make 'compost tea', then dilute it and use immediately as a soil/plant tonic.

Opposite, clockwise from top: *A two-bay compost bin made of reclaimed timber. Every scrap of plant material can be added to a cool compost bin. Turn fallen leaves into leaf mould (page 147) as part of your veganic garden's overall compost cycle.*

Making compost: cool and slow

'Cool' composting is easy and straightforward, requiring only modest physical effort but plenty of time. Depending on the size of your garden, all you need is the space for one or more compost heaps or bins. These can be made cheaply from wooden pallets, or you can buy bins made of timber or recycled plastic. You also need a steady supply of composting materials known as 'greens' and 'browns'.

Opposite: *A basic cool composting system made of galvanised fencing formed into a 1.2m (4ft) diameter cage lined on the inside with a layer of dead bracken fronds. The stinging nettles (Urtica urens) growing around the base can be cut several times during summer and added as 'greens' to the composting mix.*

Below: *In this cool bin, fresh composting materials are simply added to the top, but no mixing takes place. The level slowly falls as the materials rot down.*

WHAT IS COOL AND SLOW COMPOSTING?

Adding a mixture of once-living materials little and often to a compost heap or bin, where they rot down slowly over 6–12 months (or longer), is known as cool composting. The composting materials are added regularly, in modest amounts and are not turned or disturbed. The contents of the heap or bin does not usually heat up, although it might become warm at times. Fresh materials are added to the top of the heap or bin and they are gradually broken down by larger soil organisms such as compost worms, other small invertebrates, and by soil micro-organisms which move into the bin from the soil. In a veganic garden we only add plant-derived materials.

As the contents of a heap or bin gradually rot down, its level falls and you can add more materials to the top. This happens faster in summer, when it is warmer, and slows down or stops during winter (it will continue to slowly sink during mild winters). Any composting worms in your heap or bin will burrow into its depths during prolonged cold spells, returning when temperatures rise. The fully decomposed materials eventually accumulate at the base.

HEAPS OR BINS?

You can make cool compost by simply mounding materials up in either a round or square heap. As a minimum, aim for 1.2–1.5m (4–5ft) wide. A disadvantage of heaps is that the sides tend to dry out and rot down very slowly. You can overcome this by covering a heap with an old cotton sheet to help keep it moist, which also prevents nutrients from washing out. Pre-used plastic sheet can also be used, but be sure to recycle it before it becomes brittle.

A simple recycled cylindrical plastic compost bin with a lid is ideal for cool composting. In a bin the composting process is contained, is less prone to drying out, and most of what you add turns into garden compost. Standing the bin on a sheet of 6mm (¼in) galvanised wire mesh stops small mammals from burrowing up into it from the soil below. Bins with a hinged/removable hatch at the base allow mature compost to be accessed without having to remove the whole bin first. Two (or more) bins make composting easier because when one is full, you can start filling the next. Bins standing in the sun warm up quickly and help accelerate the composting process.

Single or multi-bay wooden compost bins can be purchased, or home-made using wooden pallets or other reclaimed timber. If you know where a new bed will eventually be made,

'GREENS' AND 'BROWNS'

'GREENS':

- Vegetable, fruit (tear citrus skins into small pieces) and mushroom peelings, banana skins. Avoid plastic labels.
- Loose tea leaves and plastic-free, biodegradable teabags and coffee grounds.
- Weed leaves, stems and roots (excluding tough perennials unless they have been killed first – page 78).
- Chopped-up stinging nettles and comfrey leaves.
- Soft hedge trimmings, sappy green wood chips (page 142) and faded cut flowers.
- Fresh lawn mowings that have not been treated with hormone weedkiller.

'BROWNS':

- Woody shredded prunings and evergreen hedge clippings.
- Scrunched cereal or pizza boxes, and other plastic-film-free card food packaging.
- Spoiled straw and hay (preferably organic).
- Tough (chopped/shredded) stems of weeds, herbaceous plants and vegetables.
- Torn-up newspaper, scrunched envelopes (remove plastic windows first).
- Occasional handfuls of moist autumn leaves.
- Brown cardboard with any plastic tape removed.
- Kitchen roll or toilet roll tubes.

build the bin there; when it has broken down the compost can be spread over the area to be cultivated. Corrugated iron sheeting and loosely-stacked bricks also make useful bins. Galvanised stock fencing, lined with layers of thick, rottable cardboard, is easy to make into a circular bin supported by wooden stakes.

BALANCE 'GREENS' AND 'BROWNS'

For any composting to work well, the materials you use must be a balanced mixture of 'greens' and 'browns' (examples are shown in the panel).

'Greens' are softer, sappier materials containing water (they are not always green in colour). They help to kick-start the composting process by providing food for micro-organisms. 'Browns' are tougher, drier materials that break down more slowly and help to absorb any excess moisture.

As a general rule, try to add a 50:50 mix of greens and browns every time you add fresh material to a bin or heap. Do not worry if the proportions vary occasionally, but avoid adding too many greens (such as lawn mowings) at once, or they will form a slimy, bad-smelling mass. Scrunching browns, such as paper and card, by crushing them into a loose ball, introduces air and keeps the mixture open.

Sprinkling a handful of soil or rotted leaf mould into the mix every few weeks inoculates it with microbial life and encourages the composting process.

CHECK ON MOISTURE

Dry materials will not rot down. Kitchen waste can be mixed with paper or card and moistened before they are added. When adding a lot of dry plant material, spray it over with water first and soak any tough and dry 'browns', such as cardboard, in water first.

Compost bins are prone to waterlogging, whereas heaps tend to be drier. Never soak the contents of a bin, or leave the lid off during rain. Waterlogged bins turn slimy, smell and do not break down. If the contents become soggy, loosen the top layers with a fork and remove the lid on fine breezy days to allow them to dry out.

WHAT NOT TO COMPOST

Cool composting does not kill the seeds of weeds, or destroy some plant diseases. The tougher weeds such as docks can be drowned first (page 81), and then added to a heap or bin, but large amounts are better dealt with in a hot heap (see overleaf). Badly diseased plants can go into a kerbside green/garden waste recycling bin. Cooked vegan food scraps from the kitchen are better composted by wormposting – see page 138.

Certain product packaging is marked as 'compostable', but check which composting route it is suitable for. Materials intended for large-scale municipal composting will only break down at sustained high temperatures, so add them to a kerbside collection with garden waste you cannot compost yourself, as they will only semi-rot in a garden-scale heap or bin, and turn gooey. Packaging marked as suitable for home composting will rot down completely in a heap or bin.

Left: *A sheet of galvanised wire mesh allows soil life access to the contents of your cool composting bin, while keeping out any small mammals.*

Do not compost the lint from washing machine and tumble-dryer filters; this is made of tiny fibres, some of which will be soil-polluting microplastics. Vacuum cleaner fluff – unless you have only natural, plant-derived floor coverings – should not be composted for the same reason.

Never add materials which will not rot, such as glass, plastic or tin cans, but recycle them responsibly instead.

Cool composting in a bin

1 'Greens' and 'browns' from the kitchen and elsewhere are mixed together before tipping them into this recycled plastic compost bin. Wet them if they are dry, to give the rotting process a kick-start.

2 Keep plenty of air in your composting mix by scrunching pieces of cardboard and plastic-film-free food packaging into loose balls first.

3 When it is full, ease the bin off. The still-to-rot material can be used to kick-start an empty bin, leaving dark mature compost behind.

Making compost: hot and fast

'Hot' composting is a quick way of making garden compost. It requires forward planning, a good deal of physical effort, generous quantities of suitable composting materials, and ample space. In a sizeable garden or on an allotment it is a useful way of turning large amounts of material into rich and usable compost in just a few months. Hot compost can be made anytime from spring through to autumn.

Above left: *Leafy rosebay willowherb (*Chamaenerion angustifolium*) being chopped up into manageable chunks prior to building a 'hot' heap.*

Above right: *Leafy summer hazel prunings are ideal for adding some 'greens' to a hot composting mix, but shred them first.*

WHAT IS HOT AND FAST COMPOSTING?

Combining large amounts of composting materials together all in one go stimulates an explosion of microbial activity, producing a heap which quickly heats up inside, usually within a few days. When it shows sign of cooling, the heap is then turned/loosened and the materials are mixed up together, wetting them if necessary. This process is repeated until high temperatures are no longer reached. (A new heap can be started up nearby in the meantime.) The building of a heap is shown in the sequence overleaf. A hot heap passes through three distinct phases:

WARMING UP

Mesophilic (warmth-loving) micro-organisms kick-start the composting process, causing the heap to warm up in the days after it is first built.

MAXIMUM HEATING

When the temperature inside the heap reaches 40°C (104°F), thermophilic (heat-loving) micro-organisms take over, predominantly *Bacillus* bacteria. During this phase plant matter is rapidly broken down, it smells 'earthy', fungi and moulds are visible on it, and steam rises from heaps, especially at night. The heap is too hot for larger animals to enter it.

COOLING OFF

Once the heap has been turned several times and no longer gets hot inside, mesophilic micro-organisms take over as it cools down. These continue the slow breakdown of the now maturing compost. Worms and larger animals will gradually move into the heap, and toadstools might sprout on it. The longer you allow it to mature, the more crumbly and decomposed the compost becomes.

PREPARING YOUR MATERIALS

A fast-heating heap relies on having a good, roughly equal mixture of 'greens' and 'browns' (see previous page) all ready to mix together. Cut and stack any weeds, long grass, or leafy hedge trimmings, and shred any woody material in advance, so that they are ready in separate piles in the location where you are planning to build your heap. Water is needed to wet the mix, and a bucketful of leaf mould, garden compost or soil works as a natural microbial activator that kick-starts the process.

BUILD BIG HEAPS

Making your initial heap large is key to successful hot compost-making. It will heat up faster and then stay at a high temperature for longer – larger heaps generally need turning less often. Hot heaps should be a minimum of 1m (3ft) wide and deep or they will struggle to heat up sufficiently. The ideal-sized heap is 1.5–1.8m (5–6ft) wide and deep (any taller and the heap will be prone to toppling over as it sinks).

Build the heap on level ground, preferably soil, allowing plenty of space so you can turn and mix the ingredients, aerating them, and so that you can build another heap next to it. The next turning/mixing returns the heap to its original spot. Each successive heap is smaller than the last as the materials break down.

TEMPERATURE CHECK

The heap's temperature can be taken using a soil thermometer, or you can do a rule of thumb test by pushing a metal rod into the heart of your heap and leaving it for 10 minutes. If the rod feels warm, the heap is either in the early warm-up phase, or it may need turning again. If the rod is too hot to touch, the heap is in its thermophilic phase and its temperature is at maximum. Reaching 40–60°C (104–160°F) in the centre of the heap kills weed seeds and the roots of tough perennial weeds. The rod will feel less hot and eventually only warm as the heap enter its final mesophilic stage.

Above: Large compost heaps heat up quickly and cool down slowly, helping speed up the composting process. This heap is in the cooling-off stage.

'HOT' COMPOST BINS

Plastic compost bins are available which encourage their contents to reach high temperatures. They have an insulated outer casing, which traps heat inside the bin, speeding up the composting process. Some are designed to constantly feed air through the mixture of materials, and may be fitted with a thermometer. They can be used for turning modest quantities of kitchen, household and garden waste into usable compost in approximately a month; removable hatches allow compost to be harvested from the base of the bin. Hot bins do not have to sit directly on soil, so can be useful where there is only hard surfacing. Dark brown nutrient-rich leachate can be collected from some bins, diluted with water and used as a soil tonic and growth stimulant.

Above: *Steam will rise from a hot heap, especially at night.*

Hot composting in a large heap

1 Gather your composting materials. For this heap a large pile of freshly-cut weeds supply the 'greens' and organic straw provides the 'browns'.

2 Use a 15cm (6in) deep layer of straw to start the heap by making a circular base 1.5m (5ft) across (square/rectangular heaps also work).

3 Spray the straw, and each subsequent layer of 'greens' and 'browns', lightly with water to help kick-start microbial life in the heap.

4 Add an even 15cm (6in) deep layer of chopped-up weeds, gently tamping them down so that the heap maintains its shape without collapsing.

5 Sprinkle mature leaf mould over each successive layer. This introduces microbial life to the heap, especially those bacteria which break down plant matter.

6 Gradually build the heap up, using alternating layers of 'greens' and 'browns', adding mature leaf mould and wetting each layer as you go along.

7 Heavy rain can waterlog the finished heap and stop it heating up, so cover it with a circle of repurposed waterproof sheet held in place with log sections.

8 The heap sinks as it heats up. Drive in a metal rod: if it is too hot to touch after 10 minutes, the composting process is under way.

9 When the initial heap cools, loosen and turn the partly-rotted mixture, and build another alongside. Turn and rebuild the heap two or three times.

10 Move green and unrotted material from the outside of the initial heap into the centre of the next one, and spray it with water.

11 After being turned several times, the final resulting heap will no longer heat up. Cover it to keep out rain and leave it to mature.

12 Three to six months later the matured compost is dark, crumbly and ready to use around your garden. Keep it covered until you need it.

Wonderful wormposting

By respecting all living things, the veganic approach avoids the deliberate exploitation of all animals – including worms. In a wormery, compost worms are effectively farmed and held captive, cut-off from the rest of the natural world. Veganic gardeners can still call on the amazing ability of worms to transform their household waste into nutrient-rich compost, but without relying on the confines of a wormery. Welcome to wormposting.

WORMS + COMPOSTING = WORMPOSTING

Making compost with worms using a sealed wormery is called vermicomposting. In a wormery, the worms are provided with everything they need to eat, reproduce and survive (often a long list of purchased must-haves). Because they are kept captive, they are at risk if things go wrong; if the contents of the wormery dry out, get too wet, or too hot – or freeze solid – the worms will perish.

Wormposting combines the transformative power of worms with composting. It takes a different 'free range' approach, allowing us to work with the worms, rather than keeping them captive. In a wormposting bin, the worms are free to come and go as they please, because they always have access to the soil below. This is crucial in extremely hot and cold spells, when worms will move deep into the contents of the bin (in freezing spells they may exit it altogether, returning when the temperature rises). The bin drains freely and cannot become waterlogged (although the contents need to be kept moist).

Worms live and reproduce, often rapidly, in the bin, while they eat their way through the raw materials we give them. Their droppings (wormcasts) are charged with plant nutrients, growth stimulants and microbes which encourage healthy plants. The mature wormpost they give us can be used to feed garden soil, make compost 'tea', or be used as part of home-made peat-free potting compost.

CLIMATE-FRIENDLY

LOVE WORMS, HATE LANDFILL

By turning our assorted kitchen and household waste into rich soil food, wormposting stops it going to landfill (also avoiding the emissions caused by transporting it there). Buried and rotting in the ground, in anaerobic (oxygen-free) conditions, organic materials produce methane, a powerful greenhouse gas that is contributing to our climate emergency.

Instead, working with worms, we can slowly and easily create a supply of dark, friable wormpost (below). As with other kinds of home-made compost, when wormpost is incorporated (by earthworms) into undisturbed, no-dig garden soil, it decomposes further, eventually forming humus, a dark brown/black organic material that helps to lock carbon into your soil.

TYPES OF WORM

Wormposting relies on encouraging fast-moving *compost* worms to enter the bin. Unlike larger and more sluggish earthworms, smaller compost worms are red or orange in colour, with paler stripes. *Eisenia fetida*, the tiger or brandling worm, is one of the commonest.

If you cannot find any compost worms a month after setting your bin up, relocate a few handfuls of decaying compost from a neighbour's garden (check there are worms in it first), or look for them in leaf litter (decaying leaves will help to kick-start decomposition in your bin). Avoid buying farmed worms.

GETTING STARTED

Your worms will eat almost anything that is organic in origin. Aim for an equal mix of 'greens' and 'browns' (page 132): fruit and vegetable scraps/peelings/skins, tea leaves and coffee grounds, scrunched-up plastic-free card packaging, non-glossy paper and cardboard (check there is no thin plastic 'skin'), sappy

Opposite: Tiger worms (Eisenia fetida) *can eat their own weight in decaying vegetable matter each day, turning it into dark, nutrient-rich wormpost.*

Above, clockwise from top left: *Carefully set free any worms which gather around the inside of the bin. Compost worms are smaller, move faster and are more brightly coloured than earthworms. Kick-start wormposting with a fresh layer of 'greens' and 'browns'.*

prunings, annual weeds (without seed heads), dead leaves, flowers, and small amounts of cooked vegan food.

To kick-start your bin, add a 15cm (6in) deep layer to the base, moisten it, and wait for the worms to move in from the soil below. Add more waste (mix it together well first) as and when you have it. In hot weather the bin's contents can be sprayed over with water to keep everything moist. If you remove the lid and find worms are massed around the bin's rim, carefully wash them on to the soil with water. This can be a sign of a population explosion. To allow some of the worms to move out, prop the bin's lid open overnight (or leave it off if no rain is forecast) to allow them to crawl out. Listen carefully and you can hear them moving about!

Worms eat waste quickly, so the contents of the bin are constantly sinking, especially in summer, slowing down in winter. It can take many months until the bin is full. When the contents reach the top of the bin, add a 'finishing' layer of grass mowings or old part-rotted leaves, replace the lid and leave it for another 6–18 months. The worms will eat whatever is left, before burrowing down and back into the soil. Repeat the process with another bin ready alongside.

HARVESTING YOUR WORMPOST

Remove the bin to reveal the wormpost. If worms are still around, heap batches of the wormpost into a cone-shaped mound on a sheet; the worms will quickly burrow away from the light, allowing you to skim off the wormpost until only a small amount sheltering the worms is left (add it to your active bin). The wormpost is now ready to use, or can be stored in bags. If you want to add it to home-made potting compost, sieve it first.

How wormposting works

This slice through a simple wormposting bin (this one is almost full) shows how a mixture of everyday household waste is transformed into rich wormpost.

1 Simple cylindrical compost bin made of recycled plastic.

2 Push-on lid.

3 Soil surface.

4 Mixed fresh material is added to the bin at the top, which the worms invade as it begins to rot down. Fungi soon begin feeding on organic matter – which might produce toadstools.

5 Deeper in the bin, more worms are eating their way through the decomposing waste, which is now becoming unrecognisable. Moulds, fungi and other decomposers are busy here, too.

6 Near the bottom of the bin, the waste has been turned into dense, dark and crumbly wormpost. Fewer worms are found here, with most moving up to feed on the fresher material above.

7 Compost worms are free to come and go as they please, moving between the soil and the contents of the bin.

8 The bin sits on a sheet of 6mm (¼in) galvanised mesh to stop rodents (but not worms) from burrowing up into the bin (it is turned up at the edges so there are no gaps).

Using green wood chips

Making your own garden compost takes time and effort, and it is hard to make enough for all your needs, especially when it comes to improving no-dig soil. But there is another abundant and easy-to-use, constantly renewing material which veganic gardeners can utilise. Green wood chips will quickly enrich even poor soil, injecting this vital underground ecosystem with an explosion of beneficial life.

Opposite: *Here in the author's no-dig garden in spring, dandelions, blue cammasias and a spiny teasel (*Dipsacus fullonum*) grow through a fresh layer of green wood chips (these are willow) used as mulch on top of a layer of fresh seaweed.*

HOME-GROWN SOIL FOOD

Green wood chips (also known as chipped or ramial branch wood) are made from the small- to medium-sized twigs and branches – those growing closest to the light – of any actively-growing deciduous shrubs and trees. Oak (*Quercus*), sycamore (*Acer*), willow (*Salix*), hazel (*Corylus*), and ash (*Fraxinus*) are all suitable for chip-making, as are any prunings from ornamental shrubs. Conifer chips from larch (*Larix*), pine (*Pinus*) and spruce (*Picea*) can be used, but always use them in a mix with deciduous tree/shrub chips, using no more than 20% by volume. Avoid using cedar (*Cedrus*) wood chips.

Any woody prunings up to 7cm (2.75in) in diameter can be used to make green wood chips, by passing them through a powered shredder. The resulting handfuls of sweet-smelling, green, soft and sappy chips are packed with amino acids, enzymes, proteins, sugars and minerals, and contain the highest concentrations of the main plant foods. Adding these chips to your soil triggers an explosion of biological life, as soil fungi, moulds and other micro-organisms start to feast on them.

Below, left to right: *Fresh and sappy green wood chips as they appear straight from the shredder, and then 3–6 months after being buried in the soil. The pale filaments of mycelium belong to soil-dwelling fungi which coat the darkening chips, breaking them down and releasing plant foods.*

TOO MANY CHIPS?

If you have more wood chips than you can use, they can be stored in a heap; it will heat up rapidly as microbial life starts to break the sappy chips down, steam will rise from it, and it will feel hot if you dig into it. Once the heap cools down, it will be colonised by various fungi which will coat the decomposing chips in pale mycelium, breaking them down even further. Several weeks later, flushes of toadstools – the spore-dispersing fruiting bodies of certain fungi – will appear over the heap.

The brown and part-rotted chips will now have a distinct 'mushroomy' smell. They can be used in home-made sowing and potting compost (pages 42–45), or as a mulch.

SOURCING YOUR WOOD CHIPS

Green wood chips can be made from prunings and hedge trimmings from your own garden, or those gleaned from friends, neighbours or a local tree surgeon. You can cultivate fast-growing shrubs, such as hazel and willow, for specifically turning into chips. Wood chips made from evergreen shrubs such as laurel (*Prunus*) and rhododendron, which can have an adverse effect on soil, are best used for making paths, as are chips from thorny shrubs such as hawthorn (*Crataegus*) or blackthorn (*Prunus spinosa*).

The pale heaps of tough, woody chips (made from branches over 7cm (2.75in) in diameter) found on roadsides are not suitable for adding to soil, as the wood in these harder chips can 'steal' nitrogen from the soil, adversely affecting other plants. However they are ideal for surface mulching, for using as hard-wearing paths, or for adding, in small amounts, to a compost heap where they will slowly break down.

GETTING STARTED

Boosting your soil's fertility and structure with green wood chips is easy and you will begin to see results in just a few months. This technique can be applied to any bare soil, whether it has been dug over regularly, or left fallow for a time. The soil must be clear of weeds at the start, especially any deep-rooted perennials.

The chips can be added at any time when the soil is workable. Incorporating them in autumn allows soil life to slowly start breaking them down before sowing and growing kicks off the following spring. Chips can also be added in to soil beds inside a greenhouse or polytunnel, but need to be kept moist for soil life to thrive.

Above: *Hazel (Corylus avellana) is ideal for making green wood chips.*

Left: *Fresh wood chips can be worked into the soil surface with a fork.*

Below: *Flushes of small toadstools appear as green wood chips are broken down by soil fungi.*

CLIMATE-FRIENDLY

GARDEN CARBON STASH

Trees and shrubs absorb carbon dioxide from the air as they grow, locking it away in their tissues. This drawdown of carbon by plants is one of the 'natural climate solutions' we gardeners can deploy to remove carbon from our atmosphere and to help stem the worst effects of global climate breakdown.

When we add green wood chips to our soil, on a small or a large scale, we are not only improving it for our plants and crops and the biological life found there, but we are also stashing away the carbon stored in the chips. As the chips moulder and decay, they eventually form crumbly, brown-black and long-lived humus, a very stable form of carbon, some of which stays locked away in your no-dig soil. It helps soil to hold on to moisture and plant nutrients, is key in improving its structure, and in promoting all-round soil health. Regularly adding more chips helps to lock away more carbon over time, turning your garden or allotment into a carbon stash.

How to use green wood chips

Even well-tended soil that has been improved over many years, through regular additions of organic matter, experiences a rush of beneficial, reinvigorating life when wood chips are added. Here you can see how a frequently cultivated but relatively poor unimproved soil, with few earthworms and little other signs of soil life, is transformed into a vibrant, interconnected underground ecosystem in just two years. Digging ceases and there is only minimal cultivation of the soil surface.

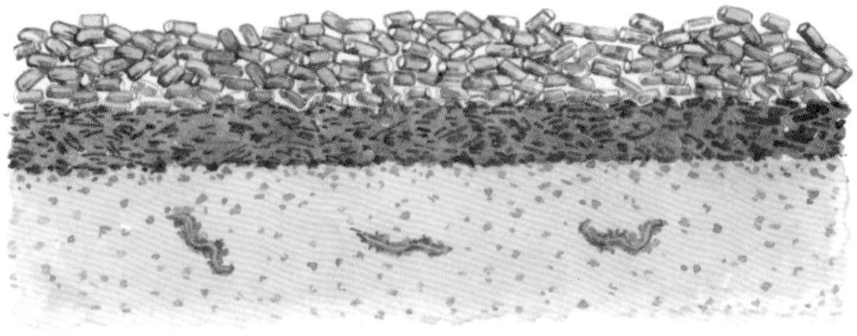

1 Start by spreading a 2.5cm (1in) deep layer of well-rotted leaf mould over the soil surface. This inoculates the soil with beneficial microbes which kick-start the breakdown of the green wood chips. At this stage, earthworms are sparse.

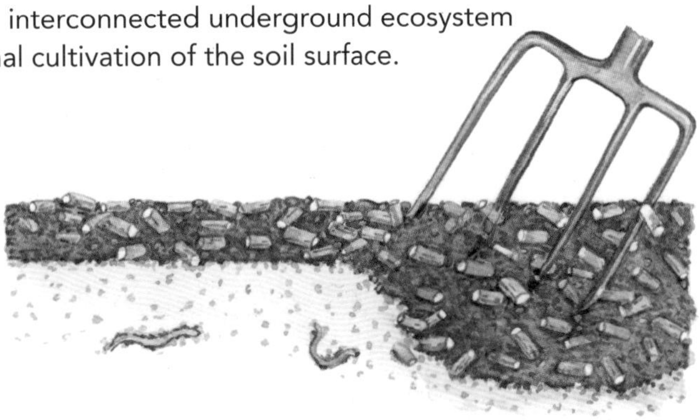

2 Use a garden fork to mix the leaf mould and wood chips into the top 5–7.5cm (2–3in) of the soil (they do not need to be buried any deeper). Incorporate them thoroughly, until the chips disappear.

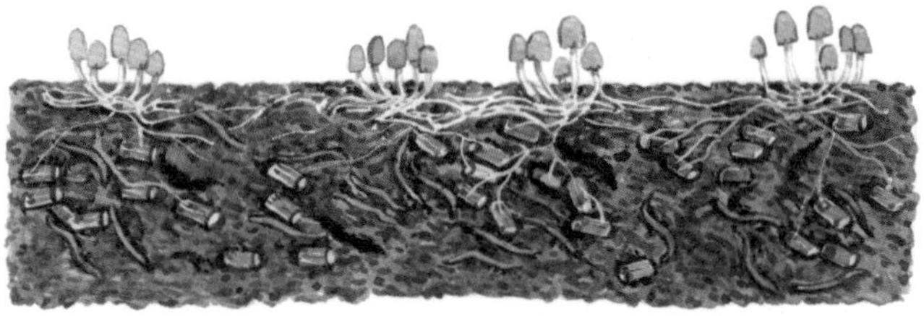

3 After 3–6 months, the wood chips are beginning to decay as soil life breaks them down, releasing their nutrients to the soil. Pale fungal mycelium grows in and around the chips and flushes of small toadstools appear periodically.

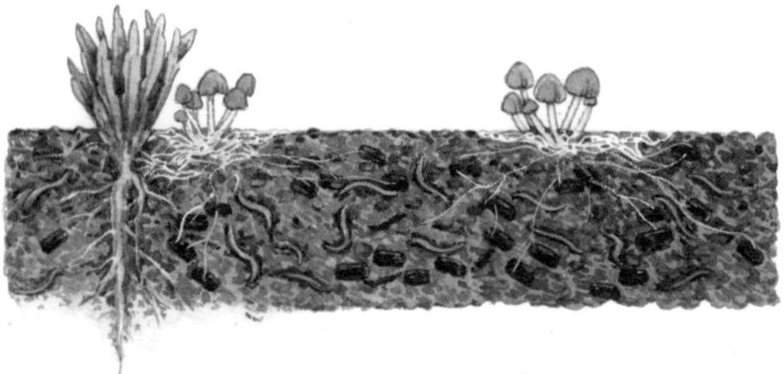

4 After 12 months, the wood chips are still breaking down, enriching the now darkening soil. A network of pale fungal mycelium intermingles with any plant roots, boosting their growth. Soil fauna is now increasingly abundant.

5 After about 2 years the wood chips are forming dark and crumbly carbon-storing humus. Flushes of toadstools still appear and earthworms (and their burrows) are plentiful, especially near the undisturbed surface. More fresh green chips can be gently worked in to lock away more carbon.

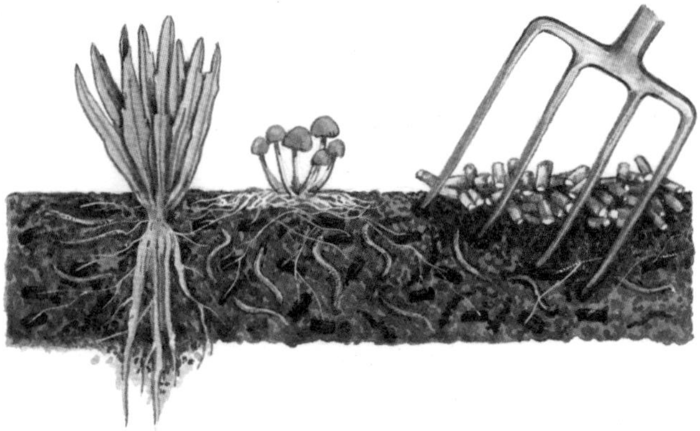

Falling assets

Simple to obtain, leaf mould is a type of garden compost made from the fallen and decayed leaves of deciduous trees and shrubs. Apart from some muscle power required to rake up and gather the leaves, nature and time do most of the hard work of transforming them into dark, soil-enriching organic matter. Easy to make, leaf mould is of value all around your veganic garden.

WHAT IS LEAF MOULD?

Falling leaves are a free asset that rains down on our gardens annually each autumn. In nature, dead leaves rot down beneath trees, enriching the soil. As gardeners, we effectively divert fallen leaves from where they naturally fall to a suitable collection point. Stored *en masse* in one place, the leaves are slowly broken down by microbes, fungi, worms, and other detritivores (bugs that feed on decaying organic matter derived from plants). Later on, we return their goodness by using the resulting leaf mould around the garden. Locally-sourced leaves, slowly decaying in a corner of your garden, incur no gardening footprint at all; they require no transport, processing or packaging.

Dead leaves do not need high temperatures to break down, but they do need to be kept moist to keep the mouldering process going. The softest parts of leaves rot away first, and when breakdown is complete, and the original leaves are unrecognisable, you are left with a dark and spongy crumb-like material (largely free of any weed seeds). It takes from 1–3 years for most leaves to be transformed into leaf mould; the longer you can wait, the finer and more crumbly it becomes.

Leaves from deciduous plants (which drop their leaves each autumn) are the best ones to turn into leaf mould. Tougher leaves, such as horse chestnut (*Aesculus* spp.) and sycamore (*Acer pseudoplatanus*), will break down in time, but shredding them hastens their decay. Conifer

Left: Leaves are a free and annually renewing resource.

Right, top to bottom: *Dry leaves are easier to collect (on still days) and lighter to move around. A builder's bag in a wheelbarrow will hold a large volume.*

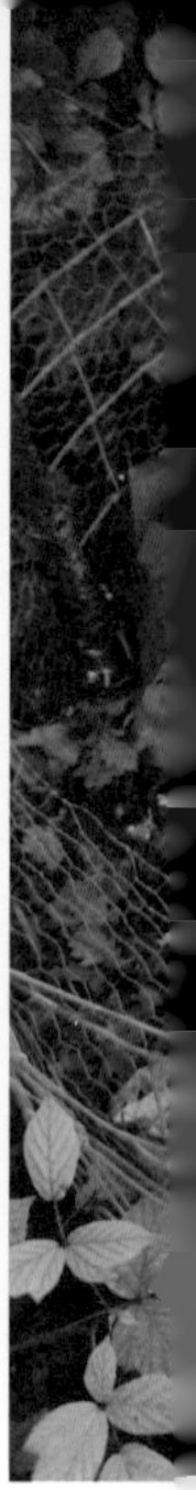

Above, left to right: The author's leaf mould cages are 1.8m (6ft) in diameter. Leaf mould matures slowly over several years, becoming a wildlife habitat in its own right. Flattened cardboard boxes help keep mouldering leaves moist as they slowly rot down themselves. Sieve crumbly, mature leaf mould to remove stones and use in a home-made peat-free compost mix (page 45).

needles and evergreen leaves are also better shredded into smaller pieces first, and added to a cool/hot compost heap.

GATHERING LEAVES

Lawns, paths, driveways, roadsides and roof gutters all yield fallen leaves. In towns and cities, avoid collecting leaves from busy roadsides because they might be contaminated with vehicle pollutants and/or litter. Avoid animal faeces when gathering leaves in parks. Neighbours can be a rich source of leaves – especially if you help collect them.

A spring-tine rake, with long wire tines, is ideal for raking leaves into heaps on a still day. A simple leaf grabber can be made out of two pieces of thin, flat wood; holding a piece in each hand extends your overall 'grab', allowing you to pick up more leaves than you could using just your hands. Gathered leaves are easily transported in a large builder's bag, set in a wheelbarrow.

MAKING LEAF MOULD

The easiest way to make leaf mould is by piling leaves up in a mound in an unused corner of the garden (such as in the deep shade beneath a tree). Make sure they are moist, then cover them with sheets of hessian, or old cotton sheets weighed down with stones or logs to stop them blowing about. Compostable jute sacks filled with leaves can be stacked together (the jute rots down with the leaves). A large polypropylene builder's bag can be filled with leaves and left to rot down (tie its corners together first). To stop the bag degrading, put it in a spot away from direct sunlight.

Simple cages made of wire mesh fixed between four wooden posts are a neat way of stopping gathered leaves blowing about (the mesh allows air into the mass of decomposing leaves). Cages need to be at least 1m (3ft) square and 1m (3ft) deep to work effectively; if you have large quantities of leaves, build bigger cages. Circular cages work equally well. Having two or three cages side by side means that when one batch of leaf mould is ready, it can be emptied out and then filled up with fresh leaves.

Mounds or cages of leaves will sometimes become warm, or even hot, inside for a few days after being gathered; steam may plume from them during cold weather. Small insects, drawn to the warmth, will be feasted on by insect-eating birds. Once any heat subsides, microbial

life begins to break the leaves down, and flushes of toadstools might appear, showing that fungi are present too.

USING LEAF MOULD

Although mature 2– to 3–year-old leaf mould contains few plant foods, it is a valuable soil improver, adding large amounts of organic matter to your no-dig beds. It boosts soil microbial life, especially when you are incorporating green wood chips at the same time. Leaf mould helps lighter, sandy soils hold on to moisture, and opens up heavier soils. A 2.5cm (1in) deep layer can be spread over no-dig beds in spring, where it will be incorporated by earthworms and other organisms.

Mature, sieved leaf mould can be used in home-made peat-free sowing and potting compost; a 50:50 mix of leaf mould and mature wormpost is a good basic mix (page 45). It can be added to a bought-in compost or soil mix to make it go further.

Part-decayed 1- to 2-year-old leaf mould (where some leaves are still visible) can be used as a 2.5–5cm (1–2in) deep mulch around vegetables, flowers and plants growing in borders or in large pots.

Using rot-away leaf sacks

1 Woven leaf mould sacks made from biodegradable jute fibre allow air and moisture to reach the leaves, and rot down with them. Pack them tight with moist leaves, straight after rain.

2 Tie a knot in the bag when it is full. Check the weight of the bag as you fill it; large amounts of damp leaves can be heavy to lift.

3 Choose a suitable spot for stacking your bagged leaves, and pack the bags tightly together. The jute rots in a few months and you will not be able to move them.

Mulch magic

Using mulch in your veganic garden will reduce water use, improve your no-dig soil, curtail the spread of weeds, boost your plot's wildlife, save you time, and give your beds, borders and pots an attractive finish. Mulching is easy, instantly effective, will help shrink your gardening footprint, and has long-lasting benefits. There are different types of vegan-friendly mulch, some of which are abundant, local and cost-free.

Opposite: *Using mulch is easy and its benefits are instant. These wood chips will keep this border free of weeds and keep the soil moist. They slowly rot down over time, adding organic matter.*

WHAT IS A MULCH?

A mulch is any material that is laid on the surface of the soil, either in the garden, in a greenhouse or polytunnel, or in pots. Mulches can be made from natural organic materials (meaning they are derived from living organisms), such as grass clippings, leaf mould, tree bark, shredded woody stems, straw/hay, found wood chips, bracken, seaweed, jute/hemp fibre, or paper and cardboard (made from wood pulp). These mulches are all biodegradable (and renewable), meaning they will eventually all rot down harmlessly into the soil.

Synthetic mulches such as black plastic and porous 'weed fabric' are non-biodegradable and do not rot down, although they will eventually degrade in sunlight and break up into polluting microplastics. Synthetic mulches are also made from oil, a non-renewable resource, via polluting, energy-intensive manufacturing processes, which increase your gardening footprint if you use them – as do using mulches made from other synthetic fibres, such as polypropylene.

Inorganic mulches such as stones, slates, rocks, bricks or broken paving do not decay and can be reused indefinitely. Animal-derived mulches, such as those made from seashells (a byproduct of the shellfish industry) or wool-based materials are not suitable for a veganic garden.

GROWING YOUR OWN

Although mulch is easily made by shredding woody garden waste, some plants can be grown intentionally to turn into ultra-local and annually renewable mulching material. *Miscanthus* x *giganteus*, a perennial, clump-forming hardy ornamental grass growing 3m (10ft) tall, which is used as a foliage and screen plant in gardens, is also used as an effective mulch in agriculture. *Miscanthus* maximises vertical growing space, and passing its faded stems through a shredder (page 154) produces useful quantities of fresh mulch, year after year.

Below right: *Shredded stems of* Miscanthus *produce a tough and long-lasting multipurpose veganic mulch.*

CLIMATE-FRIENDLY

MULCH MILES

Mulches sourced locally to your garden will have the smallest gardening footprint. A wheelbarrow full of wood chips collected from a neighbour's garden a few minutes away uses much less energy than mulching material transported many miles by vehicle (or delivered by courier), which uses fossil fuel, contributes to air pollution, and will possibly arrive in potentially non-recyclable packaging.

Letting your neighbours know you need any woody prunings to make into mulch will encourage donations, and will reduce the footprint of their own gardens, by removing the need for garden waste to be trucked away (using fossil fuel energy) to a municipal composting site. You can always return the favour by sharing the mulch you make.

An electric-powered shredder (above) will quickly and easily turn any woody materials, including tough perennial plant stems, into ultra-local, multipurpose mulch for your garden.

Clockwise from above: Reclaimed blue slate chips are an attractive and long-lasting inorganic mulch that help to set off plants in a border. Fast-moving wolf spiders (Pardosa spp.) love to hunt in dry, sun-warmed mulches such as straw. Adult ground beetles (Carabidae) will prey at night on slugs, cutworms and leatherjackets (the larvae of crane flies, Tipula spp.).

USING MULCH

Mulching keeps the soil in the same condition as it was when the mulch was laid. If you need to remove perennial weeds or loosen heavily compacted ground, do this before mulching. With a no-dig approach (page 114), an organic mulch becomes incorporated (quickly or slowly, depending on the material used) into the soil surface as it decays and is pulled underground by earthworms.

The thickness of a mulch depends on the material you use. Denser mulches such as grass clippings or seaweed can be 2.5–5cm (1–2in) deep, while straw can be up to 15cm (6in) as it quickly settles. Generally a thicker mulch is more beneficial in terms of suppressing weeds and retaining moisture. Borders of ornamental plants can be mulched whenever material is available. In a food garden, mulch can follow on whenever sowing/planting takes place.

Late spring onwards and autumn are optimum times to mulch larger areas, when the soil is moist and warm. Avoid adding mulch in winter, when the ground is cold, frozen and/or snow-covered, or it will delay the soil warming up the following spring.

BENEFITS OF MULCHING

• Weed seeds buried under a light-excluding mulch cannot germinate. A thick mulch laid over small annual weed seedlings smothers them (it will not suppress established perennial weeds, which can push through it).
• During heavy, pounding rain, a mulch protects the surface structure of the soil, stopping a hard crust from forming.
• Soil life flourishes below a mulch, protected from the sun. Earthworms will pull organic mulch underground, where it decays.
• As they rot, natural mulches such as seaweed enrich the soil with organic matter, which releases nutrients slowly (in symbiosis with fungal mycorrhizae) to the plant roots.
• Mulch stops the soil surface from losing moisture through evaporation.
• Dry, loose mulches such as straw and wood chips create habitat for beneficial garden predators such as ground and rove beetles (which eat slugs), and hunting spiders. Straw also makes an attractive, ephemeral path.
• Spreading a straw mulch below the ripening fruits of outdoor bush tomatoes and strawberries keeps them mud-free.

MULCH IN ACTION

Mulches bring benefits to all parts of a veganic garden. Using a mulch helps to insulate soil (and plant roots) from temperature extremes, keeping it cooler in summer and warmer in winter. Attractive and vegan-friendly mulches such as slate chips, wood bark or seaweed make a useful foil for ornamental plants.

Use a 2.5–5cm (1–2in) deep layer of organic mulch to smother just-germinated weed seedlings. This is semi-rotted leaf mould.

Flat pieces of reclaimed slate laid over the surface of this peat-free compost stop it drying out as moisture evaporates from the surface, while allowing water to seep through the gaps.

Straw laid as a thick mulch around these Brussels sprouts creates both a temporary mud-free path, and a safe habitat for predatory beetles and quick-moving hunting spiders to move about in.

Cardboard, weighed down with stones, is useful as a temporary mulch to cover bare soil. It keeps the soil moist and cuts off the light, preventing weed seeds from germinating.

Recycled paper mulch, or six-sheet newspaper or cardboard can be laid over the soil surface and young plants inserted through holes. It soon starts to rot, and will compost.

Fresh, plastic-pollution-free seaweed is effective at suppressing weeds and enriches the soil as it breaks down, improving its crumbly structure and adding valuable plant nutrients.

Shredded chips of non-thorny trees and shrubs make a useful pot-top mulch (shown here on pots of spring-flowering bulbs). Afterwards, the chips can be added to existing mulch in beds and borders, or they can be mixed into a compost heap or bin.

Shredders and chippers

Nurturing your veganic plot requires relatively few tools and items of machinery, but one piece of kit to consider is a motorised electric shredder (or chipper). This lets you transform even tough, thorny and bulky woody material (which might otherwise leave your garden as cumbersome 'green waste') into a manageable and valuable resource. It produces mulch, soil-building green wood chips, and raw material for composting, year-round. Always use them carefully, in strict accordance with the manufacturer's instructions.

> **SAFETY NOTE**
>
> Study the machine instructions before use. Always keep fingers clear of moving parts when the shredder is in operation, and avoid loose clothing such as scarves. If the machine becomes blocked, switch off the power and unplug it first.

SHREDDER BASICS

A shredder – also known as a chipper – is a machine which chops tough and thick woody prunings, thick dead stems of perennial plants, tough-stemmed weeds such as brambles, or thick stems of vegetable crops such as Brussels sprouts, into smaller, easier-to-manage pieces. These shreddings can be used as a mulch (page 150), or they can become part of your composting mix (pages 126–137). Shredding softer woody material produces green wood chips, used to build and enrich no-dig garden or allotment soil (page 145).

'Quiet' shredders are ideal for garden use and work by cutting and chopping woody stems into coarse chunks, emitting a low rumble. Other shredders – which generate an annoying, high-pitched noise when in use – smash stems against a fast-moving blade and produce thinner, finer fragments. Running a quiet shredder on green, renewable electricity (rather than fossil fuel) lessens your garden's environmental footprint.

Shredding is easy: stems up to around 4.5cm (1.7in) in diameter are fed manually into a hopper, which pulls them into the cutting mechanism, where they are chopped up. Any thicker branches could be turned into a wildlife-friendly log pile (page 173).

Sturdy gloves and face/ear protection are essential kit when using a shredder. The machine should always be connected to the power supply via a device giving protection from electrical shocks. Check the mechanism cuts the stems cleanly, making the shreddings easier to spread as a mulch, or add to a compost bin or heap.

A quality shredder will give many years of service, and is a useful piece of equipment for co-purchasing and then sharing with others; not everyone is likely to need to use it on the same day, and someone may offer to do regular communal shredding sessions.

USING A SHREDDER

Always work on a hard, even surface, during dry weather. Quiet cut-and-chop shredders usually include an integral collection box which stores the shreddings (as a safety measure, some models will not operate when the box is removed for emptying). Working on a cotton/canvas sheet contains any debris produced when filling the hopper. Familiarise yourself with the operation of the machine, and always switch it off if it becomes temporarily blocked.

Shred dry prunings by feeding them into the machine's hopper (keeping your fingers well clear of it, at all times). When the prunings are grabbed by the cutting mechanism, it will pull them into the machine (beware of long prunings whipping around as they are pulled in). Feed in thicker stems one at a time; thinner prunings can be bunched together.

When the collection box is full the shreddings can be used straight away as mulch, or piled up ready for composting.

Soft, sappy plant stems do not shred well, will clog the machine with 'mush' and are better chopped up using a spade and added straight to a compost heap or bin. Avoid shredding roots as soil and any stones clinging to them will damage the machine's cutting mechanism.

DEPLOYING YOUR SHREDDINGS

A shredder turns lengthy, awkward pieces of tough, woody material into smaller usable chunks far quicker than using hand tools such a secateurs or loppers. Once you have a supply of fresh shreddings, you can:

• Spread them as instant mulch around the garden straightaway, or store them for use later.
• Use any green wood chips (made from thinner, sappier woody shoots) to nourish your soil and lock away carbon (page 142).
• Make or top-up existing paths with thick and tough woody chips.
• Add fresh shreddings to your compost-making. If you are planning to build a 'hot' compost heap (page 136), shred the material in advance so it is ready to mix with other composting ingredients.
• Put any shreddings with thorns/spines aside, for long-term composting – see below.

*Opposite, clockwise from left: Smaller cut-and-chop shredders produce thick and chunky shreddings. High-speed (noisier) shredders turn woody stems into finer fragments. Tough stems of rosebay willowherb (*Chamaenerion angustifolium*); when shredded, they can make a mulch or be composted.*

THORNY SOLUTION

The prunings of roses, raspberry canes, shrubs such as holly, some spiky hedging plants, and woody weeds such as bramble (below), are armed with thorns and spines, which need careful handling. These kinds of 'problem' prunings exit our gardens when we put them out for collection for municipal composting, or worse, when they are burnt in air-polluting bonfires. A quiet shredder turns prunings into a valuable resource, resulting in zero garden 'waste'.

Thorny and spiny prunings need treating differently, and should be kept separate from other materials after shredding. Thorny prunings are not suitable for mulching in any areas where you will be sowing or planting (although they could be spread over the soil beneath a hedge). Nor can they be used for cool/hot composting, because the thorns/spines take a long time to rot down. Given time they will turn into a useful mulch, but need storing in a separate, extra-long-term cool compost heap, for up to 3 years (perhaps longer) first, in an out-of-the-way part of the garden. Wet the fresh shreddings before heaping them up, then cover them with an old cotton sheet (or similar), and keep them moist. Mixing the heap up twice a year, and working the less-rotted outer layer deeper into the centre, then soaking it again, will speed up decomposition.

Spines and thorns gradually become blunted as the shreddings decay. Test progress by carefully squeezing a handful of the shreddings; if you can still feel (and see) thorns/spines, the heap needs to be left longer. When it is dark brown and crumbly, the rotted shreddings can be sieved to remove lingering thorns/spines, then used either as mulch, or in a home-made peat-free potting compost (see page 45).

Living mulches

Living mulches – also called green manures or cover crops – are low-work plants we grow in a no-dig veganic garden to capture sunlight energy to turn into soil-enriching organic matter. They offer other benefits, including protecting bare soil, grabbing nitrogen from the air, suppressing weeds, and providing forage for beneficial pollinating insects. Afterwards they can also be used for making garden compost.

WHAT IS A LIVING MULCH?

Sometimes called 'cover crops' because they are grown (from seed) as a living blanket over otherwise bare earth, living mulches are plants grown specifically for enriching and building soil, rather than for their ornamental or edible value (although some are beautiful). 'Green manures' is a misnomer; these plants have nothing at all to do with animal manures, other than the fact they are also used to boost the fertility of soils and are suitable for veganic growing.

Living mulches can be sown on both small and large areas outdoors, or in a greenhouse or polytunnel. They can be used in food gardens once a crop has been harvested and cleared, or anywhere in a new and evolving garden, including in beds and borders that will eventually be planted with ornamental plants. The length of time you grow them varies. Fast-growing mustard (*Sinapsis alba*) can be chopped down after only 2–3 weeks, while alfalfa (*Medicago sativa*) can be sown on a still-to-be-laid-out part of your plot as a perennial living mulch. Alfalfa's deep roots improve the soil, its dense growth smothers out weeds, and it can be cut several times during summer and used either as fresh mulch, or as nutrient-rich 'greens' for composting (page 132).

All living mulches help improve and build soil, and have other interlocking benefits:

Right: *Fiddleneck can be sown from spring to autumn as a living mulch on any bare ground. Rich in pollen and nectar, it flowers over several weeks and is foraged by bees, hoverflies and other pollinating insects. It is a prolific self-seeder.*

• Some living mulches can 'grab' nitrogen from the air, releasing it later for use by leafy, nitrogen-hungry crops such as cabbages.
• Hardy and overwintering living mulches hold on to plant nutrients which would otherwise be leached from the soil by winter rain. When they decay after being chopped down, these nutrients become available for other plants.
• A blanket of living mulch protects the soil surface from damage by heavy, pounding rain, especially during winter.
• Deep-rooted plants such as buckwheat (*Fagopyrum esculentum*) 'pull' nutrients up from deep in the soil, releasing them, as their roots, stems and leaves decay, for follow-on plants and crops to utilise.
• Alfalfa and other long-lived plants can be cut in summer and used as a leafy mulch, or used as 'greens' for composting.
• Dense living mulches smother out weed seedlings and stop seeds germinating.
• Some have flowers that attract beneficial insects (if you let them bloom). Buckwheat, fiddleneck (*Phacelia tanacetifolia*), field beans (*Vicia faba*) and clovers (*Trifolium* spp.) are all a rich source of forage for wild bees and many other beneficial insects.

NITROGEN GRABBERS

Living mulches from the pea family (Leguminosae/Fabaceae) form pale nodules on their roots, housing bacteria which can grab and 'fix' nitrogen from the air. When the plant is eventually chopped down, the severed roots rot down, releasing the nitrogen they have grabbed and making it available for follow-on plants to use. This avoids the need to use synthetic nitrogen fertiliser. Winter tares (*Vicia sativa*) and field beans are tough, hardy and deep-rooted autumn-sown living mulches. After chopping and mulching them in spring, the ground can be planted with leafy, nitrogen-hungry crops such as cabbages and other brassicas. Alfalfa, clovers and trefoil (*Medicago lupulina*) are also effective nitrogen grabbers.

CLIMATE-FRIENDLY

SOIL FROM SUNSHINE

Living mulches use renewable sunlight energy and carbon dioxide from the air to build roots, stems, leaves and flowers. When they are eventually chopped up and rot down into the soil, they add valuable organic matter, which is decayed further by soil life to become dark, carbon-rich humus. By soaking up carbon when they are growing, living mulches allow gardeners to 'lock' that same carbon away in their soil, making a modest but useful contribution to slowing climate breakdown. Adopting and maintaining a no-dig approach, where the soil is rarely disturbed, means some carbon is held safely in our soils, helping plants to grow indefinitely.

CHOOSING WHAT TO GROW

Sowing small 'test' patches of a range of living mulches will reveal those likely to succeed in your own garden or allotment; it is also worth seeing what other gardeners have success with.

Seeds of living mulches are sown either in soil grooves (drills) or broadcast over the ground and lightly raked in. Big field bean seeds can be pushed into the soil one at a time. Taller-growing vegetables such as runner beans can be undersown with red clover (*Trifolium pratense*), or trefoil, after the crop is planted. Courgettes (zucchini) can be undersown with red clover, which is left to grow as an overwintering living mulch once the courgette harvest ends and the plants are removed. Field beans, grazing rye and winter tares are sown in autumn/early winter. Alfalfa, fiddleneck, mustard, red clover and trefoil are sown in spring/summer. Buckwheat must be sown after the risk of frost.

'CHOP AND MULCH' METHOD

In a regularly cultivated garden, living mulches are usually chopped up and buried in the soil by digging. The no-dig approach is gentler: chopped-up plant material is simply left on the soil surface and covered with a 2.5–5cm (1–2in) deep mulching layer, where it is decomposed by soil life, including earthworms which pull decaying organic matter underground. Below the surface, the roots of living mulches also decay, providing food for an array of soil organisms, and leaving behind channels which allow air and water to move through the soil, improving drainage and aeration.

Living mulches are best chopped and mulched while they are still soft and sappy, not tough and woody. Once a mulch has been cut down allow 3–4 weeks before you attempt to sow seeds or put young plants in the same piece of ground.

*Below, clockwise from left: The nodules on these field bean roots will release nitrogen as they decompose. Mustard seedlings form a green carpet a few days after sowing. Chopped stems of forage rape (*Brassica napus*) being mulched. Buckwheat quickly forms a dense and leafy weed-smothering canopy.*

Left: *Living mulch seedlings, from far left: summer-sown buckwheat, overwintering grazing rye (Secale cereale), versatile mustard, and autumn-sown winter tares.*

Chop-and-mulch mustard

Mustard is a quick-growing mulch producing generous quantities of soil-building organic matter in just a few weeks. It is easy to sow, during spring/summer, and simple to chop and mulch (the same technique is used for other living mulches).

1 The top 2.5cm (1in) of soil is loosened, mustard seeds are scattered over it evenly, and are then worked in using a rake (or just your fingers on small areas).

2 Mustard germinates in only a few days in warm soil and soon forms a dense and leafy living mulch. Aim to chop it down before it produces buds and flowers.

3 Use shears (or a hand-held sickle) to chop the sappy stems into short sections that form a thick and even layer of fresh green mulch on the soil surface.

4 Cover the wilted mustard with a 2.5cm (1in) deep layer of leaf mould or fresh/composted green wood chips. The chopped tops and roots will rot down.

Sea food

Seaweed is an important, renewable source of animal-free fertility for your veganic garden, being rich in natural substances that encourage strong, healthy plants. If your plot is near the sea, fresh seaweed is usually abundant, easy to collect (if allowed) and can be used straight away. Seaweed's benefits can also be employed in gardens and allotments far from the sea by using it in dried or liquid form.

Above: *Sustainably-sourced seaweed meal is used as a veganic soil improver.*

FERTILITY FROM THE SEA

Seaweeds are not true plants but plant-like forms of 'macroalgae', which live submerged in the sea and are integral parts of our marine ecosystems. The commonest seaweeds to use in our gardens are those which have grown permanently attached to rocks, and which are washed up on beaches following storms which tear them free from their anchors. Two of the familiar seaweeds we collect are bladderwrack (*Fucus* spp.), with branching fronds dotted with air-filled 'bladders', and kelp (*Laminaria* spp.) with its long and flat brown fronds.

Seaweeds are rich in nitrogen, phosphate, potassium and magnesium, plus many other minerals, trace elements (needed by plants in tiny amounts), vitamins, amino acids, natural hormones (which stimulate plant growth), carbohydrates and alginates, which increase soil microbial activity. When we add seaweed to our garden soil, or use it to make plant tonics, these nutrients are released for plants to utilise. Fresh or dried seaweed will improve soil's structure, and helps lighter, sandy soils to retain moisture.

Products containing seaweed include dried and crushed meal, and filtered liquid extracts. These

Above, left to right: Only collect loose seaweed from a beach's strand line. Seaweed is easy to spread as a dark, nutrient-rich border mulch. Bladderwrack is plentiful and adds fertility to garden and allotment soil.

are made using seaweed which is harvested sustainably (so it regrows after cutting). 'Seaweed extract' is included in some liquid plant foods and peat-free composts. Always study suppliers' ethical/environmental policies, checking that products have been sustainably obtained and made without added animal byproducts. So-called 'calcified seaweed' is not suitable for veganic gardening because it is made from coral-like algae, harvested from temperate seas by dredging, which can harm marine ecosystems.

COLLECTING FRESH SEAWEED

If you live near the coast, seaweed is a multipurpose and local source of fertility for your garden or allotment. Never cut seaweed from rocks (or from loose stones or boulders), or gather it from shorelines of special conservation status. Loose seaweed is abundant following autumn/winter storms; always shake it well first to allow beach wildlife such as sand hoppers (sand fleas) to depart. Fresh seaweed taken from the strand line is ideal, and will have a low salt content which will not damage plants; dry weed found at the top of the beach will have a higher salt content and is best avoided.

Wear gloves when seaweed-collecting, and avoid taking it from near sewage or industrial outlets, or major storm drains, to avoid potential

CLIMATE-FRIENDLY

SINKING CARBON

As they grow, seaweeds absorb large amounts of the carbon dioxide dissolved in seawater, which is then stored when they die and their remains sink, helping form sediment on the undisturbed seabed.

Ongoing research is exploring exactly how much so-called 'blue carbon' seaweeds can absorb and then lock away. As veganic gardeners we can also help sequester some of this blue carbon in our own soil by using seaweed, which slowly breaks down, alongside other organic matter, into wonderful carbon-rich humus.

Opposite, clockwise from top left: *Kelp makes dense, weed-blocking mulch. Check and clear fresh seaweed of any plastic pollution and spread it on soil straight away, before it decomposes. The pale and dry seaweed crumbs (shown left), turn darker and expand in size after they have absorbed water.*

contamination. Fresh seaweed has a strong 'seaside' smell, which fades after several weeks.

USING SEAWEED

All plants benefit from seaweed, and it can be used in different ways:

• As mulch – fresh seaweed is free of weeds seeds, pests and diseases. It is easy to spread in a 2.5–5cm (1–2in) deep layer over the soil, and is an excellent weed-stopper. In time it will rot down, turn dark and crumbly, and be pulled gradually into the soil by earthworms. Its dark green/brown tinge acts as an attractive foil to many ornamental plants in garden borders. In summer, hunting spiders might dash over its crisp, dry surface.

PLASTIC IN SEAWEED

The downside of collecting fresh seaweed is that it will be marred by plastic pollution. Remnants of commercial fishing lines and nets, plus complete or fragmented everyday plastic items (plus numerous other items) now contaminate all of our seas and oceans, and inevitably become mixed in freshly-stranded seaweed.

No one wants to deliberately import plastic into their garden, but seaweed is a rich and natural source of fertility. As gardeners, a visit to a local beach can be multifunctional: we can harvest soil-building fertility while collecting and disposing of marine litter at the same time – a win-win for our natural world. Some of this plastic will find its way into your garden (black fishing line is impossible to see among dark fronds), but you can remove it when seaweed eventually rots down and leaves its plastic stowaways behind.

• Crushed/shredded – dried and crisp seaweed fronds can be turned into coarse crumbs by spreading them out over a hard surface, or putting them inside a bag, and then crushing them underfoot. The resulting crumbs are easy to scatter over the surface of no-dig beds, or to add alongside green wood chips. Dried seaweed fronds can also be passed through a shredder (page 154), to chop them up into a more usable form (check they are not attached to pebbles/sea shells, which could damage the cutting mechanism).

• Root/foliar tonics – diluted with water, concentrated liquid seaweed is watered around the roots of plants and/or sprayed over both sides of their leaves. Liquid tonics are the fastest-acting way of imparting seaweed's benefits to plants, especially those which have suffered any kind of check to their growth. You can make your own liquid tonic by steeping seaweed (fresh or dried) in water – see opposite.

• For compost-making – a pile of fresh seaweed will break down into a smelly, gelatinous mass, but it can be added sparingly to cool or hot compost heaps (pages 130–137), by mixing it thoroughly with other ingredients first, where it will help to stimulate microbial life. Dried seaweed crumbs can be used in the same way. Modest amounts of these can be added to a wormposting bin (page 138).

• Potting mix booster – finely-milled dried seaweed can be added to home-made potting mixes to add some nutrients and boost growth. Err on the side of caution: adding too much can result in overly-wet compost that damages roots. As a guide, thoroughly mix a teaspoonful of seaweed meal into each bucketful of home-made compost.

• Added to pots – a thin layer of fresh seaweed laid below a rootball when a plant is potted on into a larger pot will slowly rot down, helping nourish the plant for several months.

• Natural moisture retainer – crumbs of dried seaweed can be mixed with potting compost used in containers and hanging baskets to help hold on to moisture and stop it drying out so quickly in hot spells.

Making seaweed tonic

Fresh seaweed can be used to make your own all-purpose liquid plant tonic, below. When prepared, dilute 1 part tonic to 10 parts water. Apply it around roots, or use it as a foliar spray on dull days.

1 Fill a hessian sack with fresh, plastic-free seaweed.

2 Tie off the sack and steep it in a bucket of rainwater.

3 When the 'brew' turns dark brown, it is ready to use.

Sustaining your plants

Like us, plants need feeding as they grow. In a veganic garden we do not use synthetic or animal-derived fertilisers to feed plants – our goal is to improve and nourish our no-dig soil so that it provides everything a plant needs for strong and healthy growth. But we do sometimes need to help them along by producing low-impact, plant-boosting tonics and teas, using plants and garden compost.

Opposite, clockwise from top left: Liquid tonic made from potassium-rich comfrey helps heavily-fruiting crops, such as this tomato 'Tigerella' to keep cropping throughout the summer. Always dilute home-made plant tonics before use. Foliar sprays are a direct way of giving plants a fast-acting tonic; overcast days or during the evening are the best times to spray, to avoid scorched leaves.

Below left: Comfrey pellets are made from the leaves of comfrey and are rich in NPK, trace elements and natural plant-growth hormones.

Below right: Alfalfa pellets (sometime combined with comfrey and seaweed) are valuable for stimulating the soil ecosystem.

WHY FEED PLANTS?

When seeds first germinate, a small reserve of food helps them produce their first roots and seed leaves (cotyledons). As they grow, plants draw water and nutrients from the soil or compost and use energy from the sun, and carbon dioxide from the air, to build roots, stems, leaves, flowers and fruits.

The three main plant nutrients are nitrogen (N) for leaves; phosphorous or phosphate (P) for roots; and potassium or potash (K) for flowers and fruits. These nutrients are often referred to as NPK. Most plant foods contain all three, in varying amounts, sometimes with other nutrients such as calcium, magnesium or iron, and with trace elements (micronutrients), which plants only need in small amounts. Synthetic fertilisers are designed to feed plants directly via their roots. Being highly soluble, they can have a detrimental effect on soil life.

If you use purchased plant foods, choose those that are organically-certified and contain no animal byproducts. Pelleted comfrey and alfalfa are both vegan-friendly, rich in plant nutrients and help stimulate plant growth.

SOIL AS A GO-BETWEEN

In a veganic garden the aim is to provide all of the key nutrients that plants need by nurturing the soil, using it as a kind of intermediary: we feed and nourish the soil, not the plants themselves. We achieve this by adding organic matter derived from plants, as garden or green waste compost, green wood chips, seaweed, or by growing living mulches (or by using a combination of them all).

This takes time and our plants sometimes need a helping hand. In a new garden, for example, you might be starting from scratch with soil in a poor and unimproved condition, in which plants are struggling to flourish. Plants in containers of peat-free potting compost will need extra nutrients after 4–6 weeks, once the supply in the compost runs out. Plants constrained in even a large pot will eventually become hungry and this could stall their growth – they can visibly stop growing – if they run short of essential plant foods. Equally, over-feeding by applying too much and/or too often can damage roots. As a general guide, feeding plants diluted tonics weekly (or purchased liquid feeds applied at the recommended rate) should give good results. Outdoor crops which have struggled to establish themselves and grow – perhaps during extreme weather, such as an unseasonal drought, or a spell of dull, wet and cool summer weather – can benefit from a pick-me-up to get them growing strongly again.

We can easily make our own nutrient-rich plant tonics using plants we already have growing, a bucket, water, and a few weeks of fermentation. Garden compost can also be used to make a tea rich in beneficial micro-organisms (see panel overleaf).

Above: Every veganic garden needs a patch of comfrey to turn into tonic.

Opposite top: Perennial stinging nettles can be cut and fermented several times from spring onwards.

HOME-GROWN PLANT TONICS

Comfrey (*Symphytum*) and stinging nettle (*Urtica dioica*) are both valuable and easily-grown plants for turning into tonics. Comfrey is rich in potassium and especially useful for flowering and fruiting plants. It can also be used in pelleted form. To extract the goodness from comfrey leaves, fill a large bucket with fresh chopped leaves, pack them down, weigh them down with a brick, and cover to exclude rain. In a few weeks the comfrey will blacken and break down, and a brown liquid collects in the bucket, which is poured out. Use the pungent concentrate (it stores well in a sealed container) by diluting it 1 part concentrate with 10 parts of water. Apply it to the soil around plants or use it as a foliar spray. The rotted leaves can be composted.

Nettles are also rich in plant nutrients and grow abundantly, making them a free and useful alternative tonic while you are establishing your own comfrey plants. Nettles are rich in nitrogen and a good tonic for leafy crops.

BREWING COMPOST TEA

Soaking mature garden compost in water infuses the latter with plant nutrients and micro-organisms found naturally in soil. When it is watered on to soil around plants, or sprayed over their leaves (spray it on to both sides of the leaf), the compost tea has a beneficial probiotic effect.

To make a tea, put some garden compost in a hessian sack (or an old cotton pillowcase) and steep it overnight in a bucket or butt of water. The following day, swirl it around. Use the dark tea neat, or dilute 50:50 with water.

DIGESTATE LIQUID

This nutrient-rich fertiliser is a byproduct of the anaerobic digestion system that produces biogas (used to generate 'green' electricity), which is formed from chopped-up maize crops broken down by added bacteria. The fibrous digestate can be bought and used as mulch and for making home-made potting compost (page 45), and as a smelly liquid which is rich in NPK and other nutrients. The liquid is entirely natural in origin, free of synthetic fertilisers, and does not harm soil life when diluted and used as a tonic. Only digestate liquid made entirely from plants is suitable for a veganic garden.

HOW TO USE TONICS

Liquid tonics are especially useful for plants in containers but can also be used to feed those growing in soil. Always dilute them first: 1 part tonic to 10 (or more) parts of water. Never use tonics on dry, wilting plants, or you could damage their roots; water the plants thoroughly first and use the tonic when they have recovered.

Plants can also absorb nutrients through their leaves. Foliar spraying is an effective way to give any plants which are growing slowly, or showing signs of leaf yellowing, a fast-acting tonic which also improves their general health. Water or spray the entire leaf surface, top and underside, at least once a week.

Making nettle liquid feed

1 Chop fresh nettle (*Urtica dioica*) stems into a bucket. Pack them down tight and cover with water.

2 Place a heavy flat stone over the bucket to weigh the nettles down (and keep out rain) and leave for 2–4 weeks.

3 The resulting strong-smelling green-brown slurry (wear gloves) is rich in plant nutrients. It can be strained through a cotton cloth.

4 Make up a solution of 1 part nettle concentrate to 10 of water, then use it to soak the soil around your established plants.

Welcoming nature in

This chapter is infused with ideas intended to enrich your garden or allotment with wildlife. Veganic gardening respects nature and allows it to flourish. The value of different types of bugs in the garden, and their place in its ecosystem, is explored, and step-by-step sequences show how to build bug hotels. There are tips on choosing flowers to boost your garden's pollinators plus advice on using dandelions to benefit bumblebees, and you are urged to encourage pest-eating garden spiders. Practical advice is given on adding a wildlife pond, letting parts of your plot go wild, growing fuss-free self-seeding plants, and allowing your lawn to grow long and free to attract beneficial wildlife.

Left: *Hoverfly on a borage (Borago officinalis) flower. Hoverflies are among the veganic gardener's most treasured wild allies because their larvae eat sap-sucking aphids.*

No-kill zone

Veganic gardens are strict no-kill zones where all forms of life are respected, and nature is welcomed as our greatest ally. Encouraging a rich diversity of species is key to avoiding many of the problems that can affect our plants, especially pests. The guiding ethic of veganic gardening is to create conditions in which a vibrant, biologically alive and self-balancing ecosystem – where wild species freely and harmoniously coexist together – flourishes amongst the plants we want to grow.

Above left: Tagetes tenuifolia *is an easy to grow half-hardy annual which produces pollen- and nectar-rich flowers throughout summer. It is a favourite plant of refuelling hoverflies.*

Above middle: Perennial flowers such as Echinacea *'White Swan' bloom over a long period, attracting bees and other insects to your garden.*

CHECKS AND BALANCES

Veganic growing diverges from straightforward organic gardening in a significant way: we do not intervene directly to kill pests or treat plant diseases by using pesticides – organic or otherwise. Instead, veganic gardening focuses on nurturing and maintaining soil health in order to grow strong and healthy plants, which are inherently less vulnerable to pest and disease problems. It also relies heavily on a simple 'checks and balances' approach.

Plant pests are usually only a serious problem when the ecosystem of your garden tips out of balance. Many of our plants, especially edible crops, are extremely attractive to some species, notably insects, as a source of food. When we plant our crops, they become part of the living fabric of the garden – and other species take an interest in them. Where a thriving, balanced mix of insects is present, any potential pests will be kept in check by their respective predators, most commonly other insects and birds. A few pests always briefly find their way to your plants, but they are unlikely to do significant harm.

WILD THINGS

Garden wildlife – mammals, birds, reptiles, amphibians, insects, spiders and other invertebrates, together with earthworms and other soil life – all have a vital role to play in a

thriving veganic garden. They are all part of a living and interconnected web of life providing us with natural checks and balances.

The challenge for the gardener is in creating a garden that is as diverse as possible, which incorporates the maximum number of different habitats, or habitats within habitats:a wildlife pond, for instance, is an individual and unique aquatic habitat that sits within a garden's or allotment's wider ecosystem.

Wherever we provide a suitable home for nature, wild species soon move in. In areas of intense agricultural activity, urban gardens are becoming increasingly important sanctuaries for wild species large and small. Adding as many different habitats as possible to your garden will help bring it to life; the following are some which are proven to be the most beneficial:

Long grass: Letting all or part of your lawn grow long and wild reduces pollution (air and noise), while encouraging wildflowers and insects.

Wildlife pond: Even a small fish-free pond puts a self-contained aquatic ecosystem at the heart of your garden, boosting numbers of slug-eating frogs, toads and newts.

Trees and shrubs: Bird, insect and spider numbers are all boosted by trees and shrubs in the garden. Choose plant species that provide both pollen and nectar in spring, then fruit in autumn. Leaves from deciduous trees can be turned into leaf mould (a microbial habitat in its own right).

Compost heap: Hundreds of different species live in compost heaps which are built on the soil

Above right: *A retaining wall made partly from logs creates nooks and crannies for wildlife.*

Below: *Boost your garden's ecosystem with a small pond.*

Right: *Common wasps (Vespula vulgaris) are veganic gardening allies because they prey on aphids and caterpillars, and are important pollinators. This wasp is collecting wood pulp from a sweet chestnut fence paling to use in spring nest-building.*

and left open around their base. Small mammals such as hedgehogs, and reptiles such as slow worms, will often set up home and sometimes breed there.

Log pile: Mimicking a dead, decaying tree, a log pile provides shelter for lizards, slow worms, frogs and toads, and invertebrates such as ground and rove beetles, slugs, snails, earthworms, spiders, solitary wasps, centipedes, millipedes and woodlice. Hedgehogs like to shelter during daytime in a larger pile with plenty of dry hollows.

Mixed species hedge: Birds use hedges for shelter, nesting and food, and small mammals travel below them. A mixture of evergreen and deciduous species, which includes flowers and autumn fruits, attracts the most wildlife.

Drystone walls: Crevices in mortar-free walls are an ideal habitat for lizards, which bask, alongside butterflies, on the sun-warmed stones. Self-seeding plants such as Welsh poppies (*Meconopsis cambrica*) will grow in the cracks, while solitary bees will nest there.

CLIMATE-FRIENDLY

POLLUTION-FREE BUGS

Coaxing nature into your veganic garden, allotment or greenhouse makes perfect sense, and is inherently climate-friendly. Bringing a diverse array of species into our gardens, by providing habitats and food sources, means we do not need to rely on resource- and energy-hungry pesticides to kill the organisms we do not want there in damaging numbers. There is no need to spray oil-derived and potentially polluting insecticides to control aphids when we can grow simple nectar- and pollen-rich flowers, such as pot marigolds (*Calendula officinalis*), to attract the insects which feed on them.

As an example, an adult hoverfly can lay up to 100 of its tiny pale, pill-like eggs (top right) among colonies of aphids, and the ugly, lumbering larvae (bottom right) which hatch from them can devour around 50 aphids each (5,000 aphids per egg-laying female). They do this for free, incurring none of the emissions associated with the manufacture, packaging and transport of chemical pesticides. Research shows that adult hoverflies will only lay their eggs on plants which they can 'smell' are giving off the right signal.

Building a log pile

3 Place a thick, stumpy log in the centre of the hole and then fill in around it with loose dry leaves and twigs, to provide ground shelter for wildlife.

1 Gather a selection of logs of different lengths and thicknesses. These are 30–45cm (12–18in) long. You can use a mix of older, part-rotted, as well as fresh wood.

2 Site the log pile in an out of the way spot in the garden. First make a shallow hole 30–45cm (12–18in) across and up to 15cm (6in) deep.

4 Arrange the first layer of logs so they rest on the first one set in the hole, and radiate out and sit on the surrounding ground.

5 Add more logs and gradually build up the pile. Thinner logs can be pushed into larger spaces, but leave plenty of gaps for wildlife to move in.

6 Top the pile off with some thin log rounds. The whole pile will slowly sink as the wood rots; add fresh logs by simply laying them against it.

Bank on bugs

Bugs – insects and other invertebrates – are the veganic gardener's most important natural allies. Familiar insects such as wild bees and honeybees pollinate flowers and improve crop yields, while hoverflies are important predators of pests such as aphids. But there is an array of other bugs, many of which are too small or too inconspicuous for us normally to notice, which live and reproduce in a healthy, balanced garden or allotment.

Below: A seven-spot ladybird (Coccinella septempunctata) hunting for aphids on a lily flower. Ladybirds are predatory bugs which are commonly seen on garden plants, and their larvae also eat aphids.

WHERE DO BUGS LIVE?

We tend to think of bugs as fast-moving, airborne insects which attract our attention because they are eye-catching (butterflies, dragonflies), noisy (bumblebees, hoverflies) a nuisance (flies, mosquitoes and midges), or capable of stinging (social wasps). We observe most bugs during daylight hours, even though our gardens are buzzing with them at night. But there are many more bugs we simply do not notice, because of their small size, because they do not fly, are not showy, or they stay well hidden among plants.

Different groups of bugs inhabit different parts of our gardens depending on their role in its ecosystem. They can be divided into three main 'bug groups'.

POLLINATING BUGS

Pollination is when the pollen of one flower is transferred to another of the same species, fertilisation occurs, and the plant produces seeds. These seeds form inside pods (e.g. runner beans, peas) or fruits (e.g. apples, tomatoes). Without insect 'pollinators' many plants would fail to produce the crops we grow in a food garden. Most crops rely on pollinating insects, with a few, such as cereals, relying on the wind to move their pollen around. In a veganic garden we want to encourage as many pollinators as possible, not just to carry pollen between flowers, but also to help keep pests in check. Hoverflies, for example, are multi-tasking insects whose adults pollinate flowers, while their larvae feed on aphids.

Pollinators feed on pollen and nectar and use it for rearing their young. They also become food for other insects, and for birds, bats and other animals. We can encourage a healthy and varied pollinator population by filling our growing spaces with a diverse mix of nectar- and pollen-rich flowering plants (pages 183–85) from a variety of countries and regions. Tilting the balance toward plants which are native or near-native to your own country and hemisphere is advantageous, but you should also try to include some 'exotic' plants from a different hemisphere, which provide nectar/pollen for insects later in the growing season.

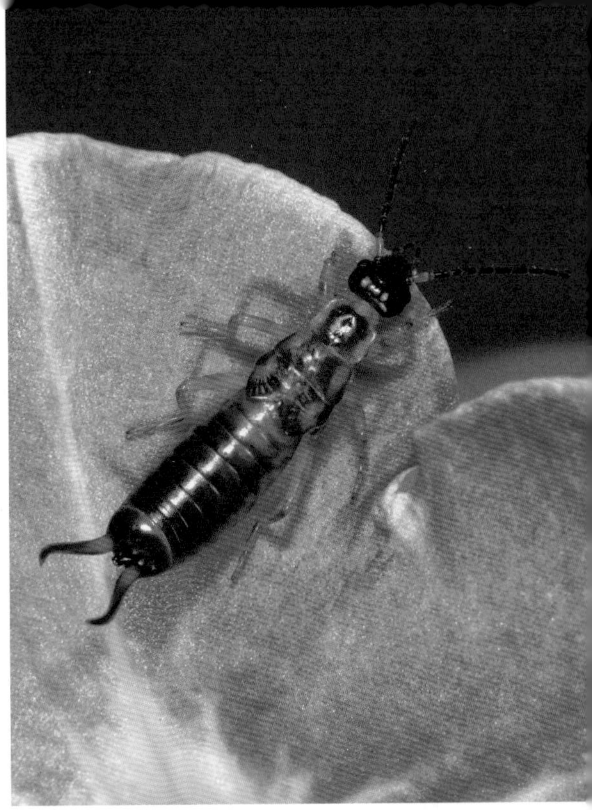

Clockwise from top left: *Harvestman* (Opilones). *Earwig. Two-spot ladybird* (Adalia bipunctata). *Large cabbage white butterfly* (Pieris brassicae) *caterpillars. Ground beetle* (Carabidae). *Pill woodlouse* (Armadilidium vulgare). *Centipede* (Lithobius forficatus). *millipede* (Julidae).

PLANT-DWELLING BUGS

These are bugs which live on plants and eat either living or rotting plant material. For instance caterpillars (the larvae of butterflies and moths) feed on live, sappy leaves and shoots or roots, while springtails (*Collembola*) eat algae on leaves and the fungal moulds which form when leaves decay. Plant-dwelling bugs are divided into:

Herbivores: The bugs most likely to damage our growing plants. Some have chewing mouthparts, such as caterpillars and some beetles, e.g. the scarlet or red lily beetle (*Lilioceris lilii*), while others have sap-sucking mouthparts, such as aphids and capsid bugs. Most herbivores will feed on a wide range of plants.

Predators: This is an important group because they eat other bugs, especially troublesome herbivores, and help keep pests in check. The group includes predatory beetles such as ladybirds or ladybugs, true bugs, spiders and tiny parasitoid wasps.

Detritivores: These feed on decomposing matter of plant or animal origin, fungi and algae, and play an important role in the recycling of dead material. They include springtails, woodlice and certain beetles.

Omnivores: These are adaptable because they can eat plants and other bugs. They include the harvestman and common earwig (*Forficula auricularia*), which nibble and damage leaves and flower petals, but also devour aphids and other small insects.

To encourage plant-dwellers, try to include as many plants as possible that are native/near-native to your region. Including some plants, such as single-flowered dahlias, which persist later in the season when other plants are fading, also encourages them. The most important action you can take to boost plant-dwelling bugs in a garden or allotment is to include densely-planted schemes comprising a medley of different plants.

Left: This flower-filled bed along the base of a dense hedge creates a rich and diverse habitat which is attractive to all kinds of garden bug.

GROUND-DWELLING BUGS

The soil surface is a busy and living 'highway' for bugs, especially those that cannot fly, and is a key part of your garden's ecosystem. Ground-dwelling bugs include herbivores, predators, omnivores, and large populations of detritivores, such as woodlice and millipedes, which eat and recycle rotting vegetation (and the fungi and bacteria that feed on it). Many garden-friendly predators live on the soil surface, including hunting spiders, carnivorous ground and rove beetles, and centipedes, which eat slugs. All ground-living invertebrates can become a meal for other garden wildlife, such as hedgehogs, frogs, toads, slow worms, birds and small mammals, making them an essential part of the garden food chain.

Ground-living bugs thrive in gardens containing dense groups of plants, which cover the ground during the growing season (hunting spiders are an exception, as are ground-nesting bees, which prefer open gaps between individual plants). Choosing predominantly native/near-native plants, possibly in a 'bug bank', supports the widest range of ground-dwellers. Including some hardy exotic plants, especially those which stay evergreen year-round, also helps to boost their numbers. Evergreen shrubs also favour ground-dwellers, offering them shelter and protection in winter.

GARDENING FOR BUGS

Studies have shown that the greater the variety of plants in a garden, the richer the diversity of bugs it will support – whether they are pollinators, or plant- or ground-dwellers. When choosing plants to grow, follow these bug-boosting pointers:

- Include as many different plants which are native/near-native to your region as you can, perhaps in a 'bug bank' (see panel).
- As well as focusing on plants from your own hemisphere, consider including some exotics, which are proven to benefit pollinating insects. Growing exotics might mean fewer herbivores, but their late-season blooms will benefit pollinators, when native plants have faded.
- Aim for dense, lush planting that covers the ground, while leaving some sun-warmed gaps for hunting spiders and soil-nesting bees.
- Relax if you see some nibbled or eaten leaves; plants are unlikely to suffer serious harm.
- Avoid being too fastidious about tidiness; allow dead foliage and other debris to accumulate and rot down beneath plants, to encourage ground-dwelling bugs (and the wildlife that eats them).

Above: *A carpet of fallen and decaying leaves creates an ideal habitat for ground-dwelling bugs such as hunting spiders and slug-eating ground beetles and centipedes.*

BUG BANKS

One of the easiest and most effective ways of attracting a vibrant population of bugs to your veganic plot is to grow a 'bug bank'. This is essentially a wild strip, square or circle, 1m (3ft) or more across, where predominantly native plants such as stinging nettle (below) are allowed to grow. Any patch of unused, semi-wild ground, an area of lawn (which you stop mowing), part of an existing border, or the ground surrounding the base of a tree, or an old stump (page 197) can become a bug bank. If the range of plants is limited, enrich it by sowing wild flower seeds, or by planting young plug plants. It can also incorporate log piles (page 173) and/or a pond (page 192), providing habitat for other garden wildlife. A bug bank is especially valuable in urban areas, where your own garden or allotment might be surrounded by neat, tidy, bug-deficient plots.

Building bug hotels

Lots of nectar- and pollen-rich flowers will draw pollinators and other bugs to your garden or allotment, and you can encourage them to stay there by providing places for them to build their nests, and to shelter during winter. 'Bug hotels' are easy to make to your own unique design from scrap timber and other found, cost-free materials. The more hotels you add, the more the bugs will benefit.

POTENTIAL GUESTS

Home-made hotels will attract a range of bug species. Among the most common are solitary bees, including the leaf cutter (*Megachile* spp.) and mason (*Osmia* spp.) bee. Rather than forming large colonies with a queen and many workers, solitary bees make individual nests for each of their larvae. Those that use hollow plant stems and holes in dead wood for nesting will be attracted to a purpose-built hotel. Some solitary bees nest in the crumbling mortar in brick walls, and will often use hotels if they are placed near them. Although they

SIGNS OF GUESTS

After filling a nest hole with food and laying a single egg, solitary bees and wasps will seal up the entrance with a mortar-like plug of either light-coloured mud or chewed plant material. Leaf-cutter bees use circles of fresh green leaves, such as rose leaves, to seal their nests (page 49). Hibernating insects hide away deep in holes and crevices during winter; do not be tempted to dismantle the hotel to check for their presence.

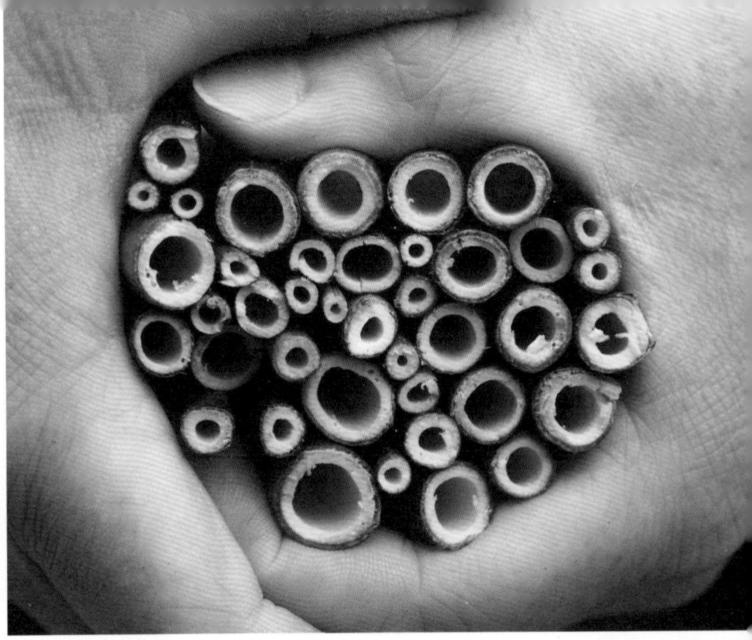

are less conspicuous than honey bees and noisier bumblebees (neither of which use bug hotels), solitary bees are pollinators of many garden food crops. Solitary wasps will also check into bug hotels, and lay a single egg in individual nests. These solo-living wasps are important gardening allies because they catch and paralyse aphids, caterpillars, flies and leafhoppers, which can become pests. Solitary wasps are smaller than larger social wasps (which do not use hotels) and are perfectly harmless.

Tree bumblebees (*Bombus hypnorum*) will sometimes co-opt an empty bird nest box, or a loft cavity accessible via a building's eaves. These bees do not use hotels, and are important garden pollinators.

HOTEL MANAGEMENT

Bug hotels need minimum care and should be disturbed as little as possible. However, to ensure the survival of still-sealed nests and any hibernating residents, move the hotel to shelter by mid to late autumn. Cardboard or plant stems will rot if they stay wet, rain can wash away nest seals, and woodpeckers and tits will peck at nests (although a fine wire mesh covering will help protect them).

Move hotels under the wide eaves of a building to protect them, or store them in a cold and dry shed or garage; avoid warm places, or bugs will emerge prematurely and perish. Always relocate hotels back to their previous spot in early spring, as temperatures start to rise.

Above, clockwise from left: Attractive bug/wildlife hotels can be built using different natural, found and repurposed materials. Wild solitary bees and wasps will build nests in hollow plant stems. Nest holes 10–15cm (4–6in) deep, drilled in a garden fence post.

Opposite: The upper section of this wooden log has been drilled all over with nesting holes and then placed among plants in a sunny border.

Making an insect hotel

This 'luxury' hotel, made entirely from found and cost-free materials, will attract not just solitary nesting insects and other garden bugs, but spiders as well. The key to success is to use a wide variety of mostly natural, plastic-free materials to create as many different niches, nooks and crannies as possible. Insect hotels can be any shape you choose: square, rectangular, circular, or even triangular.

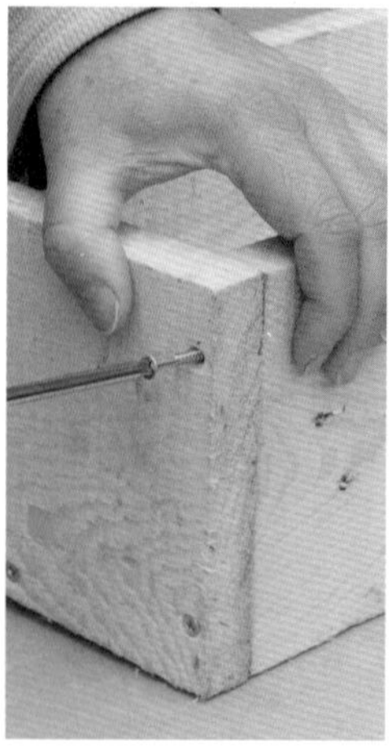

1 Make a rectangular box 60cm (24in) tall, 20cm (8in) wide and 15cm (6in) deep, using untreated pallet wood or similar scrap timber (do not treat it with a preservative). Leave one side open.

2 Collect together your materials: dry, hollow plant stems with different diameters; freshly cut log sections and wooden bee blocks, drilled with holes; and tin cans filled with rolls of corrugated cardboard.

3 Lay the box down and fill it out with the various materials, fitting them together randomly, and as snugly as you can. Then use individual stems to fill in any gaps between the larger components.

4 Fix the completed hotel securely to a sunny wall, fence or post, keeping it clear of any foliage, and so that its top is between 1.2m (4ft) and 1.8m (6ft) from the ground.

SIMPLE NESTING BLOCKS

A block of untreated wood at least 10–15cm (4–6in) square can easily be turned into a 'nesting block' for solitary wild bees and wasps.

The blocks found in untreated timber pallets are ideal. Drill holes at least 10cm (4in) deep (do not drill right through), in varying diameters between 4mm (⅛in) and 1cm (just under ½in) – but not larger – randomly over one side of the block. Prospective nesters prefer the entrances to be splinter-free, so smooth around the holes using sandpaper. Tap out any sawdust, then fix the block in a sunny spot a good height above the ground.

Can o' bees (or wasps)

A simple and cost-free nest 'box' can be made using a tin can and hollow plant stems, including home-grown bamboo. Remove any sharp edges and drill some drainage holes along one side of the can (this should be at the lowest point when the can is fixed in position). Making several boxes and positioning them around your garden will improve your chances of attracting nest-makers.

1 Fix the empty can securely to a wall, fence or post, choosing an open, sheltered spot that receives sunlight for most of the day.

2 Cut up dry and hollow plant stems, with hole sizes between 4mm (⅛in) and 1cm (just under ½in) in diameter, to fit inside the can.

3 Fill the can with the cut-to-size stems. Fill any remaining gaps carefully, ensuring the stems are packed in together tightly so they do not fall out.

4 If any stems work loose, just replace them. It may take a couple of seasons before solitary bees or wasps start to build their nests, so be patient.

Boosting pollinators

Packing your veganic garden with a mixture of different flowers, and focusing on those with simple, single and scented blooms which are rich in pollen and nectar, will boost its population of pollinators. The more of these beneficial insects you can attract, the healthier your garden's ecosystem will be. Aim to grow some plants which will be in flower during every season, even in winter.

CHOOSING PLANTS

Pollinators, primarily insects, visit flowers to gather nectar and pollen to feed both themselves and, in some cases, such as with bees, their offspring. Aim to plant a diverse mixture of annual and perennial plants, trees and shrubs that flower over many months, so that at least some are in flower all year round (see the suggestion list overleaf). Early and late flowers are especially valuable for pollinators. Oregon grape (*Mahonia aquifolium*) flowers in late winter and is a valuable food source for queen bumblebees emerging from hibernation, while ivy (*Hedera helix*) flowers in autumn and provides a vital energy top-up for butterflies before they hibernate for winter.

Simple, single and wherever possible scented flowers are preferred by pollinators; hybridised, complex 'double' blooms make it hard for insects to access pollen/nectar (if it is present at all). Avoid any 'pollen-free' varieties bred for human, not insect, convenience. Including plants with different flower shapes also encourages pollinator diversity; bumblebees visit the long, tubular flowers of foxgloves, while hoverflies prefer to forage on the flat, daisy-like heads of pot marigold (*Calendula officinalis*) which have only short tubes. Moths are pollinators, too, so grow some night-scented flowers such as annual flowering tobacco (*Nicotiana*) and climbing honeysuckle (*Lonicera*).

Pollinators find cultivated garden plants just as attractive as native ones, so try and fill your plot with a mixture of plants from your own hemisphere, and from other parts of the world. Include some exotic flowers, such as single dahlias, which will bloom until the first frosts. Some vegetables, such as runner beans and peas, are excellent sources of forage for all types of bee; their visits pollinate the flowers and trigger the pods to set.

Two plant families in particular are invaluable to pollinators: the Compositae or daisy family, and the Umbelliferae or umbel family. Plants in the daisy family typically have circular flowers comprising a central disc with an outer ring of petals. Pot marigold is one of the easiest to grow, is a prolific self-seeder, and is favoured by bees and hoverflies. Plants in the umbel family typically have flat heads made up of masses of small flowers held aloft on what resembles

Opposite top: *Helianthus 'Lemon Queen' flowers nonstop from midsummer to autumn and is a favourite with butterflies searching out nectar, such as this red admiral (Vanessa atalanta).*

Opposite bottom: *Wild plants such as hogweed (Heracleum sphondylium) help boost a veganic garden's pollinators. Its flat heads act as 'landing pads' for hoverflies and other beneficial insects.*

LET VEGETABLES BLOOM

Many common vegetables which have passed their best and are 'bolting' and starting to flower, are magnets for pollinators; overwintered crops are especially valuable for providing pollinator forage during spring. Brassicas such as cabbages, Brussels sprouts, land cress, red mustard, pak choi (below) and other oriental greens, all carry a profusion of long-lived, pollen- and nectar-rich flowers, which benefit bees of all types. Root crops such as carrots and parsnips amass their flowers in flat landing pad-type umbels, attracting all kinds of flying bugs, including hoverflies, while leek and onion flowers form round, densely-packed heads. You can grow an extra patch or row of pollinator-boosting crops just for their blooms.

YEAR-ROUND POLLINATORS

Listed here are just some of the many pollinator-boosting plants which provide flowers in every season. For a fuller list, see page 234.

SPRING

Berberis darwinii **S**
Crocus spp. **Bu**
Dandelion (*Taraxacum officinale*, see also overleaf) **P**
Flowering currant (*Ribes sanguineum*) **S**
Honesty (*Lunaria annua*) **B**
Horse chestnut (*Aesculus hippocastanum*) **T**
Lungwort (*Pulmonaria* spp.) **P**
Perennial wallflower (*Erysimum* varieties) **P**
Primrose (*Primula vulgaris*) **P**
Sicilian honey garlic (*Nectaroscordum siculum*) **Bu**
Skimmia japonica **S**
Welsh poppy (*Meconopsis cambrica*) **P**

SUMMER

Angelica (*Angelica archangelica*) **P**
Borage (*Borago officinalis*) **A**
Butterfly bush (*Buddleja davidii*) **S**
Coneflower (*Rudbeckia* spp.) **T**
Dahlia 'Bishop's Children' **B**
Hardy geranium (*Geranium x magnificum*) **P**
Helen's flower (*Helenium* spp.) **P**
Honeysuckle (*Lonicera periclymenum* varieties) **Cl**
Ox-eye daisy (*Leucanthemum vulgare*) **P**
Plume thistle (*Cirsium rivulare* 'Atropurpureum') **P**
Sunflower (*Helianthus annuus* varieties) **A**
Verbena bonariensis **P**

AUTUMN

Autumn crocus (*Colchicum* spp.) **Bu**
Autumn ox-eye (*Leucanthemella serotina*) **P**
Calico aster (*Symphyotrichum lateriflorum* var. horizontalis) **P**
Henry's lime (Tilia henryana) **T**
Japanese anemone (*Anemone x hybrida*) **P**
Leadwort (*Ceratostigma plumbaginoides*) **P**
New England aster (*Symphyotrichum novae-angliae* varieties) **P**
Oleaster (*Elaeagnus pungens*) **S**
Perennial sunflower (*Helianthus* 'Lemon Queen') **P**
Sage (*Salvia greggii* varieties.) **S**
Stonecrop (*Sedum*) (*Hylotelephium* 'Herbstfreude') **P**
Strawberry tree (*Arbutus unedo*) **S/T**

WINTER

Clematis cirrhosa **Cl**
Crocus spp. **Bu**
Laurustinus (*Viburnum tinus*) **S**
Mahonia spp. **S**
Musk willow (*Salix aegyptica*) **S/T**
Shrubby honeysuckle (*Lonicera x purpusii* 'Winter Beauty') **S**
Snowdrop (*Galanthus nivalis*) **Bu**
Sweet box (*Sarcococca confusa*) **S**
Winter aconite (*Eranthis hyemalis*) **Bu**
Winter-flowering hellebore (*Helleborus foetidus*) **P**

A: Annual **B**: Biennial **P**: Perennial
Bu: Bulb **S**: Shrub **T**: Tree **C**: Climber

Left: Peacock butterflies (Aglais io) flock to the pollen- and nectar-rich flowers of 'Bishop's Children' dahlias.

an umbrella. Sweet cicely (*Myrrhis odorata*) is a particularly useful perennial umbel providing many weeks of spring forage for pollinators, including hoverflies.

LOOK AND LEARN

One of the best ways to discover which plants are proving most attractive to pollinators in your area is to study the insect activity in action, in neighbouring gardens and allotments, in public gardens and parks, and also the sales benches of your local plant nurseries (where labels also often indicate whether a plant is favoured by pollinators). Start your nature observations in spring, when the warm, sunny days encourage insects to take to the wing. Noting those flowers which are – literally – generating the most 'buzz' due to the visits by foraging insects, helps you choose the best plants to grow for pollinators in your own garden.

Clockwise from top left: Pot marigolds have simple, single flowers. A bunch of pot marigolds, pink/purple cosmos (Cosmea) and white cornflowers soon attracts pollinators. Yellow and orange perennial coneflowers flower profusely in late summer.

Potting up dandelions

Despite being cast as unsightly, troublesome weeds by those selling chemical weedkillers, dandelions *(Taraxacum officinale)* are arguably the most beautiful and wildlife-enhancing plants you can include in your veganic garden. Trusting in nature, and allowing these adaptable wildflowers to share your growing space, they will soon begin to enrich your garden's living ecosystem. Growing them in pots allows their benefits to be brought into your greenhouse or polytunnel.

Opposite: *Each dandelion seedhead can carry up to 200 airborne seeds. A single plant can release up to 15,000 seeds, which germinate as soon as they land on soil.*

Below: *Allow wild-spirited dandelions to find their own niche in your veganic garden. This clump is at home growing at the edge of a bed filled with ornamental plants.*

WILD THINGS

Dandelions are wild perennial plants with deep tap roots and a circular rosette of long leaves which lay flat against the ground, and die back to a crown in winter. From spring until early autumn they produce flushes of round, bright yellow heads – each is comprised of up to 200 individual florets (small flowers). They are a rich source of pollen and nectar for various insects, especially in early spring when other food sources are scarce. The flowers close up in the evening and on dull, wet days. After they have faded, the blooms open up again on dry, sunny days to reveal a pale, fluffy orb of seeds (or 'clock'), each of which is attached to a silky 'parachute' (the pappus). Dislodged by the wind, the seeds are carried about on the air, travelling from a few metres up to several kilometres from the parent plant.

Dense thickets of dandelions are common along roadsides and on traffic islands, where their seeds are swirled into the air by passing vehicles. They can also colonise fields and meadows which are not routinely treated with weedkiller. Dandelions readily invade lawns, where their ground-hugging rosettes survive below a lawnmower's blades.

Leave dandelions to find their own niche in your garden. They soon establish themselves in more out-of-the-way, wilder, more unkempt patches, the edges of food garden beds, along paths, or in the cracks between paving, so long as it is an open, sunny spot. Aim to have a generous number of them scattered throughout your plot; the more dandelions your garden or allotment has, the more beneficial wildlife they will entice.

INSECT MAGNETS

Each dandelion floret has only a short 'tube', meaning that insects large and small can easily access its stores of pollen and nectar. A fully open flower will attract wild solitary and honey bees, and bumblebees, butterflies, beetles, true flies, adult hoverflies, ladybirds and lacewings, and social and solitary wasps. Many of these insects are important pollinators and predators, so luring them into your veganic garden is hugely beneficial for fruit and vegetable crops.

Hoverflies foraging on dandelion blooms will stay around your garden, laying their pill-shaped eggs among aphid colonies. After hatching, their larvae eat aphids, keeping them in check. Tiny adult parasitoid wasps, refuelling

*Above: Goldfinches (*Carduelis carduelis*) will sit on a lawn and strip open green, immature dandelion seedheads, devouring the seeds inside.*

TOO MANY DANDELIONS?

Dandelions are prolific and opportunistic self-seeders; given a chance their seeds will germinate quickly on any patch of bare soil. If you want to stop them shedding seeds, nip off the green seedheads when you see the tips of parachutes protruding, but before they open up, and compost or drown them – or leave them for seed-eating birds to feast on.

Seedlings are easy to pull up or hoe off, but more mature, established plants can be trickier to remove, and cutting their tops off stimulates them to sprout again from the severed roots. To remove dandelions whole, including their deep roots, loosen the (preferably moist) soil beneath them using a garden fork, then grip the crown of the plant, gently teasing it from the ground. If the roots still hold tight, loosen the soil some more, until the plant comes cleanly away; if you leave fragments of root behind, new shoots will sprout from them.

Uprooted dandelions can be potted up (see opposite), or buried in the centre of a cool or hot compost heap (pages 130–137), after laying them out to wilt and die in the sun for a few days beforehand. They can also be drowned in a bucket of water, along with other tough weeds, such as stinging nettles and docks, where they will rot down into a pungent liquid feed (page 81).

on dandelion flowers, will lay their eggs inside aphids and caterpillars, where their larvae devour them from within.

Queen bumblebees emerging from winter hibernation forage spring dandelion flowers for food as they establish new nests, and on warm spring days overwintered butterflies visit the blooms to feed on nectar. The offspring of both will visit dandelion flowers throughout the summer. Caterpillars of the garden tiger moth (*Arctia caja*) feed on dandelion foliage.

FOOD FOR BIRDS

If you leave dandelions to produce seedheads, wild birds will be drawn to your garden to feast on them. Bullfinch, goldfinch, house sparrow, linnet and siskin will all tear open the green, faded heads, removing the immature, developing seeds (while carefully discarding the parachutes). Voles and other small mammals will also eat dandelion seeds. Insectivorous birds such as flycatchers benefit from the boost in the insect population in your garden, themselves feeding on the bugs drawn to your dandelions.

Dandelions in pots

Growing dandelions in pots turns them into a movable feast. Potted plants can be coaxed into producing extra-early blooms by bringing them into an unheated greenhouse, polytunnel or sunny porch in late winter/early spring, or even by standing them against a warm, sunny wall. The extra protection encourages them to grow and flower more quickly than plants outdoors.

1 Dandelion seeds germinate quickly and easily in pots of peat-free compost – or you can pot up young seedlings straight from your garden.

2 Mature dandelion plants can be lifted and potted up at any time of year. Plant up to five tap-rooted crowns in a 15cm (6in) diameter pot.

3 Potted dandelions can be situated just inside/outside your greenhouse door to lure in wild beneficial insects, such as adult hoverflies.

4 On warm and sunny days, the first, extra-early spring flowers that open on your pot-grown dandelions provide valuable forage for noisy and low-flying queen bumblebees.

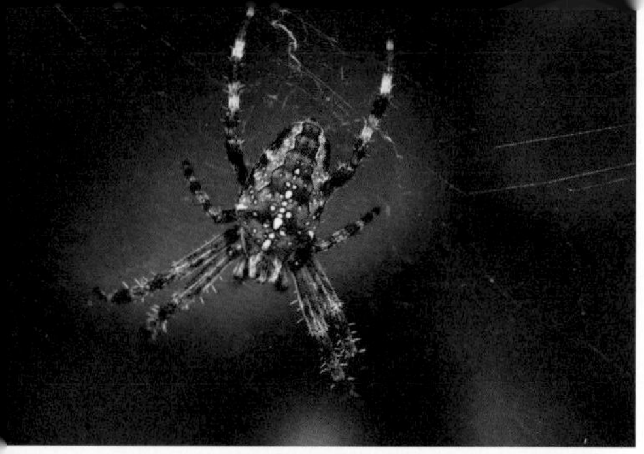

Love your spiders

Spiders play a vital yet overlooked role in a vibrant garden ecosystem. Together with beneficial insects, such as hoverflies, they help – with their sticky cobwebs and their voracious hunting – to curtail the activities of many bugs we consider to be pests. Spiders come in a array of sizes and colours, and will live and breed in all parts of a diverse, balanced garden. None of them will harm your plants – or you.

*Clockwise from top left: This pest-eating garden spider (*Araneus diadematus*) is common in gardens. Orb webs on* Verbena bonariensis *are revealed by early morning dew. Garden spiders spin their orb webs where they are most likely to catch flying insects. Tangle webs on curly kale leaves.*

ALLIES WITH EIGHT LEGS

Spiders have eight legs, and fangs they use to inject venom into their prey. In gardens, spiders fall into two broad groups: those which spin silken webs (the silk is also used for binding their prey, as a trip wire and abseiling line to escape predators), and those which roam and hunt freely over the ground. Spiders are found everywhere in a garden or allotment, both outdoors, or inside a greenhouse or polytunnel, where they can be active year-round. Some spiders have striking markings, but the majority are more muted in their colouring. Because spiders live silently compared to noisier and showier insects, such as bumblebees, they attract less attention, although they are still a key component of a healthy garden ecosystem.

Garden-inhabiting spiders vary in size, from tiny money spiders (they are reputed to bring you good fortune if they land on you) of the family *Linyphiidae*, just a few millimetres across, to house spiders (*Tegenaria* spp.) with a leg span of up to 12cm (5in), which live in garden sheds and lofts – and startle us when they venture indoors during autumn.

Spiders are indiscriminate predators, and will eat almost anything they trap in their webs or hunt down on the ground; do not be surprised to sometimes see 'good' insects, such as hoverflies, butterflies and moths, caught in a spider's web. Although they will prey on beneficial insects, the good they do by helping keep other bugs such as aphids and whitefly in check more than compensates.

As well as being predators, spiders are themselves food for birds, slow worms, frogs, toads, and other spiders. In winter, birds will peck under dry building eaves to feed on silky egg sacs, while long-tailed tits (*Aegithalos caudatus*) gather cobwebs to build their nests.

WEB-SPINNERS

Spiders spin different kinds of webs. Two-dimensional orb webs comprise strands of silk radiating out from the centre (resembling a bicycle wheel), overlaid with a spiral of sticky thread that catches prey. Orb-shaped webs tend to be vertical and are spun among plants where they have the greatest chance of catching flying insects. The spider either sits in wait in the centre of the web, or lies in wait among vegetation. When an insect flies into the web, the spider is attracted to the vibration, bites the insect to paralyse it, then wraps it in silk to feed on later. Orb webs range in size from just a few centimetres to 60–90cm (24–32in) across.

Sheet webs are made up of layers of horizontal, hammock-like silk sheets strung between the twigs of low-growing shrubs and among grasses. Airborne bugs either tumble into the web, or are knocked down into it when they collide with the tangle of threads above it. The spider runs out, attracted by vibrations, to secure its prey. Money spiders build sheet webs, then hang in wait below them.

Tangle webs comprise a messy tangle of threads and are often found covering flowerheads on ornamental plants in borders. Daddy-long-legs spiders (*Pholcus phalangioides*) are often found in greenhouses, where they catch flying pests (and also other spiders). False widow spiders (*Steatoda* spp.) spin their three-dimensional webs in garden sheds, cluttered greenhouses, among stones, and in walls and garden fences.

Funnel webs are shaped like a funnel, and are often seen in greenhouses among stacks of plant pots and trays. House spiders (*Tegenaria* spp.) spin large, closely woven, dusty sheets of silk which funnel into a tubular retreat at one end, where the spider lies in wait. Successive generations will refurbish the webs, increasing their size. When prey falls on to the web, the spider rushes out to claim it.

Autumn mornings, when webs are outlined by dew, mist droplets, or frost clinging to their threads, are when the spider population in your garden is fully revealed.

SPIDERS IN YOUR GREENHOUSE

Allowing spiders to live in a greenhouse (or polytunnel) might go against your instinct for tidiness, but they are invaluable in helping control the bugs which have the potential to become troublesome pests. Spiders tend to inhabit the nooks and crannies in a greenhouse, so they actually utilise otherwise unused space. Spider faeces – small dark or pale dots – is unsightly on glazing or shelving, but easily washes off and will not harm plants. There is no need to evict resident spiders if you need to clean greenhouse glazing, because they almost always spin their webs and live in recesses, or among plants, and do no harm. Using pesticides in a greenhouse will both poison spiders' prey, and kill them directly.

If you do need to relocate a spider – it might be spinning a web just where you walk everyday – do it carefully by gently brushing it into your hand, or into a container, and putting it on a plant outdoors. Never pick spiders up by grabbing their legs, which are easily damaged, with your fingers.

Above: Garden shrubs are a favourite haunt of orb web-spinning spiders.

GROUND-LEVEL HUNTERS

Some spiders do not spin webs but instead lead a roaming, nomadic existence on the ground, where they actively hunt down their prey. A no-dig veganic garden, where mulches are used extensively to avoid bare soil, is ideal habitat for fast-moving species, such as the wolf spider (*Pardosa amentata*). Dry, sun-warmed mulches (page 150), such as straw and wood or bark chips, create perfect hunting conditions – and somewhere to hide if the spiders themselves risk falling prey to birds or animals.

Wolf spiders will roam, camouflaged, over dry mulch, searching for and leaping on prey when they find it. On spring days they bask on sun-warmed stones. Although they do not climb to hunt, they will eat garden pests, such as aphids and caterpillars, which become dislodged and then fall to the ground. Keeping your garden mulched will encourage a healthy population of wolf spiders.

Just add water

Creating a modest-sized pond will inject a dynamic, self-contained aquatic ecosystem into the very heart of your veganic garden. Adding a small underwater world will dramatically increase the range of wildlife, big and small, helping to sustain a healthy and balanced garden ecosystem. Attractive, nature-friendly ponds, made from repurposed and/or recycled and often free materials, are simple and easy to make.

POND LIVES

Even a small pond will soon teem with all sorts of wildlife. Some species will spend their entire lifecycle submerged in the self-contained aquatic ecosystem. Others, such as frogs and toads, will visit a pond briefly, to breed, before returning to nearby habitats on land. Their tadpoles remain in a pond for the entirety of their juvenile life, then mature into froglets and toadlets, which depart the pond for land.

Many eye-catching insects are drawn to a pond: airborne adult dragonflies and damselflies catch and eat smaller flying insects which breed in ponds, and their own predatory larvae live there, too. Water beetles, water boatmen (backswimmers), alder flies, pond and water skaters, caddis fly and mayfly larvae are some of the other insect life found in ponds, along with leeches and water snails. Ponds increase the number of flying insects whose larvae live in water, which means more in-flight food for web-spinning spiders, adult damselflies and dragonflies, insectivorous birds such as swifts, swallows and flycatchers, and bats. Pond-rich gardens tend to have higher levels of biological diversity – there are simply more species living there – which in turn helps to enrich garden food chains.

Mammals, birds and insects such as wild and honey bees visit ponds to drink. Birds will bathe there, and some, such as house martins, will collect mud for nest-building.

ANY SIZE WILL DO

The overall size of a pond is not that important, and it does not need to be deep (if young children play in the garden, ensure ponds are made safe and secure). Water depth of around 30cm (12in) will suit most kinds of pond life, but it is vital to include some shallow edges to allow pond visitors to drink at the margins, and to climb out should they fall in accidentally. Deep, steep-sided ponds are intrinsically unfriendly to wildlife; adding large stones or cobbles creates shallows, while building a submerged 'staircase' allows animals to climb out. Making several small, easy-to-install ponds (using found/reclaimed, locally-sourced materials) throughout your garden or allotment can be more beneficial than a single large pond, because they spread their aquatic benefits far and wide. Small ponds can even be made inside a greenhouse or polytunnel (page 96).

STAY FISH-FREE

Fish (wild or domesticated) are best avoided as they will dominate the delicate ecosystem of a pond. They will eat almost all other types of aquatic life, from water fleas (*Daphnia*), to insect larvae and tadpoles, preventing these from achieving maturity and thus resulting in a duller pond lacking in biodiversity.

PLANTS FOR PONDS

In a pond, wildlife needs some shelter from predators, and a place to feed and breed, in for example, marginal plants grown around

Above: *Common frogs* (Rana temporaria) *will keep cool in a pond on hot summer days, then move around the garden at night, eating slugs and other pests. In winter frogs hibernate in the mud in ponds, or under any stones/logs placed around the margins.*

Opposite: *Several small, fish-free ponds scattered around your veganic garden will quickly become magnets for an array of wildlife and help enrich your garden's wider ecosystem. This pond is in a bed containing ornamental plants (see how to make it overleaf).*

GOOD OXYGENATING PLANTS:

Water starwort (*Callitriche stagnalis*)
Hornwort (*Ceratophyllum demersum*)
Water milfoil (*Myriophyllum spicatum*)
Water violet (*Hottonia palustris*)
Curled bindweed (*Potamogeton crispus*)
Water Crowfoot (*Ranunculus* spp.)

INVASIVE OXYGENATORS TO AVOID:

Water fern (*Azolla filiculoides*)
Australian swamp stonecrop (*Crassula helmsii*)
Floating pennywort (*Hydrocotyle ranunculoides*)
Water primrose (*Ludwigia grandiflora*)
Parrot's feather (*Myriophyllum aquaticum*)

the edge of a pond, either in the mud or in containers situated in the water. Tall-growing marginal plants such as bulrushes (*Typha* spp.) are ideal for allowing mature dragonfly nymphs to crawl up and out of the water, where they turn into adults.

'Oxygenators' are submerged plants that add oxygen to the water. They help keep the water clear and provide hiding and egg-laying places for various aquatic creatures. Every pond needs at least one oxygenator, but check that the plants you choose are not ecologically-invasive species, which can become damaging weeds (see left).

Right: In this shallow, recently-made wildlife pond, marginal plants have been planted in the mud around the edges.

Making a small wildlife pond

1 This repurposed, watertight plastic tub is 60cm (24in) wide and 30cm (12in) deep. Its red colour will soon be masked by algae (or apply eco-friendly paint first). The tub sits in a hole dug in a bed. A spirit level is used to check that the rim sits level with the surrounding soil, which is then backfilled around it and firmed.

2 To help any wildlife – from hedgehogs to ground beetles – that accidentally falls into the pond, build a flight of submerged 'escape steps' to one side, using bricks, stone or broken paving slabs. These steps will help wildlife to clamber out, and they also create nooks and crannies where pond-dwellers can shelter from any predators.

3 Check that the stone at the top of the 'steps' sits above water level; choose one that slopes away into the water, to allow birds and insects to drink. Pieces of lichen-encrusted slate are laid around the edge of the tub, disguising it with a 2.5–5cm (1–2in) overhang. Old bricks, roof tiles or even logs work equally well.

4 To maximise wildlife habitat, the slate is layered to create sheltered nooks and hollows. Frogs, newts and toads will hide in the dark, moist spaces next to the pond's edge, where it overflows during rain. In spring and summer the slate will heat up, tempting common lizards and slow worms to bask in the sun.

5 Fill the pond with rainwater from a water butt. If there is a fish-free pond nearby, a bucketful of water from there will inject your pond with instant life, helping kick-start its aquatic ecosystem. If you use tap water to fill your pond, it will take several days to 'purify' itself before wildlife starts to move in.

6 Hornwort taken from a fish-free pond has been added as an 'oxygenator'. Because this pond is only small, no marginal plants have been used as they could easily overwhelm it. Instead, the slate surround provides numerous cool and damp refuges for wildlife. Use rainwater (not tap water) to top up an established pond during dry spells.

7 A few months later the pond is alive with water fleas, and frogs are now regular visitors. Small leeches and water snails feed on the algae disguising the tub. Ants run over the slate and are eaten by lizards, which skitter in and out of the gaps. Duckweed (*Lemna* spp.) is growing on the water surface.

Letting-go gardening

By allowing some parts of your garden to break free of the usual gardening rules, and letting its wild, untamed spirit run free, you can enrich the diversity of wildlife found throughout your garden's ecosystem. By being less controlling, less fastidious, and by stepping back a little, even small areas can be let go and allowed to quietly rewild all by themselves – with little or no help from you.

Above, left to right: *This wooden seat is rotting away, but rather than replace it, it has been let-go in a corner of the garden which is being left to run wild. Overlooked logs lying on the ground quickly start to decay and become home to a clump of wildlife-sheltering stinging nettles.*

COAXING NATURE BACK

When you create a garden from scratch, or mark out an allotment, everything starts to change. You take over the custodianship of that patch of earth for months, years, decades (perhaps even generations when a garden is tended successively by the same family). To make a garden, nature almost inevitably has to shove over, and move out of the way.

In planning a garden, we usually have to work with the existing topography (unless we can invest in major earthworks), and shape our ideas around large, established plants such as trees. But we make our mark in a multitude of ways, all of which means that nature – the wild mix of birds, animals and plants that lived there before you – is often squeezed out.

Coaxing nature back into your garden is easier than you think. Rewilding is now happening on a landscape-wide scale, as a key part of using 'natural climate solutions', to help combat our climate emergency. It goes beyond conventional conservation efforts, by allowing nature a mostly free hand to restore and take care of itself with minimal intervention.

As gardeners we cannot influence vast areas, but our modest individual efforts in adding a 'wild side' to our patches of earth, taken together, will all add up.

REWILDING YOUR GARDEN

Allowing an entire garden to run wild would undoubtedly benefit some wildlife, but it would also defeat the objective of having it in the

STUMP LIFE

This willow (*Salix* spp.) stump is all that was left after the tree was brought down during a storm. The rest of it, which stood on a semi-wild garden boundary, was logged and used to make wildlife piles (the thinner shoots were shredded and used as mulch). Rather than removing it, the stump has been left to do its own thing as a small part of the garden that is being allowed to rewild. 'Letting it be' brings multiple benefits:

1 Both birds and queen bumblebees have been exploring the hollow core, checking it out as a potential nesting site.

2 Fungi, microbes and detritivores (bugs that feed on organic matter derived from plants) are feeding on the willow's decaying heartwood, on its rotting bark, and its dying roots. In turn, they provide an invaluable food source for birds, lizards, frogs, toads, slow worms and snakes, as well as insect predators, such as ground and rove beetles, centipedes (*Lithobius* spp.), and spiders.

3 These new shoots, sprouting from the still live wood, will grow rapidly in spring and summer. In autumn they are cut off and shredded into green wood chips (page 142) and used to improve soil.

4 Evergreen ivy (*Hedera helix*) is creeping up and over the stump, providing year-round shelter for garden wildlife. Encouraged by the increased light levels, other wild species are springing up around the base.

5 Other plants,such as this wild hop (*Humulus lupulus*) are also starting to scramble over the stump, creating valuable summer cover for on-the-move small mammals, such as field voles (*Microtus agrestis*).

6 Frogs, toads, newts and snakes will take refuge in the cool, moist conditions found beneath the stump, safe from predators, and may hibernate here in winter. Hedgehogs will shelter here during the daytime in summer.

Right: Purchased 'hedgehog homes' can be buried under a layer of fallen leaves and twigs in a rewilding part of a veganic garden. Check that the entrance is at least 17 x 17cm (6.7 x 6.7in) and place it in a spot that is relatively dry, such as under shrubs or near the base of a fence.

Below: European hedgehogs (Erinaceus europaeus) thrive in scruffier, wilder gardens rich in biodiversity, because they find more food there. They will eat slugs and snails, but most of their diet comprises beetles, caterpillars and earthworms.

first place – and may well irk your neighbours (allotment and community garden sites usually have rules about keeping a plot in 'good order'). A more nuanced approach is to give nature space where it looks like it might thrive, but where it will not impinge (too much) on your gardening activities.

In a large garden, a patch of bramble (*Rubus fruticosus* agg.) in an out of the way spot, can become a thorny protective cover for small birds fleeing from cats or bird of prey. In summer, its flowers attract clouds of butterflies and other insects, followed by delicious blackberries for wildlife and you to enjoy.

The stump or trunk of a fallen or dead tree, left alone, will soon become an entire decay-driven ecosystem in its own right. Despite the tree being dead, its remains – both above and below ground – will be teeming with life.

A patch of stinging nettles (*Urtica dioica*), occupying an awkward, unused strip or corner, brings multiple positive benefits. In spring it attracts aphids, which are then eaten by

ladybirds (adults and their larvae), and by hoverfly larvae. Fresh nettle shoots can be added to cool or hot compost heaps, where they stimulate microbial activity, or can be made into a liquid tonic. In summer, the caterpillars of butterflies such as small tortoiseshell (*Aglais urticae*) feed on nettles.

WAYS TO 'LET GO' IN YOUR GARDEN

1 Ivy can be left to scramble over an old fence or wall, or climb a tree trunk. Dense, mature ivy blooms in autumn are a rich source of pollen and nectar for many insects before they hibernate for winter.

2 Allowing a patch of wild raspberries to establish benefits many insects, especially smaller bumblebees (*Bombus* spp.). In spring its sweet-smelling, pollen- and nectar-rich flowers buzz with life, and are followed by small but tasty fruits.

3 Rocks and stones, left lying in long grass and warmed by the sun, attract basking common lizards (*Zootoca vivipara*). Black and red ants will build their nests below flat stones, sending up plumes of flying ants on warm, humid days.

4 When a tree dies, our 'tidying' instinct is to remove it. Modest-sized trees (or just the trunks of taller ones) can be left to rot in situ and soon become a habitat, and a rich food source, for myriad wildlife both above and below ground.

5 Wooden fence posts, when they eventually start to rot, might attract fungi that grows on the soft, decaying wood, or woodpeckers who peck out the wood-boring insects (and their grubs) that they can hear moving inside the wooden posts.

Nature's chancers

Every veganic garden or allotment needs its chancers. These insect-attracting plants, which flower non-stop from spring to autumn and produce copious quantities of seeds – often before their last blooms fade – are the 'self-seeders'. They sow themselves where they grow, by simply shedding their seeds around them. Left alone, some will germinate and make new plants, often trying their luck in the most unlikely spots.

Opposite: *Small black Welsh poppy seeds spilling from pepperpot-like seed capsules; the pale and curved, crested seeds of pot marigold; and the flat seed pods of honesty ready to be mixed up together for a seed-scattering session in late summer.*

SEED FACTORIES

Self-seeding 'chancers' succeed because they are able to produce vast numbers of seeds in one growing season, in order to reproduce themselves. For example, a single flower of Welsh poppy (*Meconopsis cambrica*) turns into a pepperpot-like capsule containing hundreds of tiny black seeds. As they are buffeted by the wind, the dry capsules scatter the seeds far and wide; just one plant can produce tens of thousands of viable seeds.

Self-seeders can be annuals, biennials or perennials; the most valuable plants in a veganic garden are those that produce a succession of pollen- and nectar-rich flowers over a long period. They all share the advantage of being able to grow quickly, often in large numbers, and with little or no help from us – apart from removing any opportunist plants growing where they are not wanted. Most chancers tend to be hardy annuals, which germinate in spring (or the previous autumn) and are not killed by frost. Frost-tender plants do not usually self-seed easily, and are better raised under cover and planted out.

Injecting self-seeders into your garden (if there are none there already) is as simple as buying a single packet of seeds or a plant that goes on to flower and shed its seeds. Once established, the plants that grow from those seeds quickly become a vital, self-replenishing part of your garden's ecosystem. Some food plants are also prolific self-sowers.

SPOTTING CHANCERS

Self-sown seedlings can be identified by their seed leaves (cotyledons) and their first true leaves.

Borage's broad cotyledons are followed by distinctly bristly true leaves.

Pot marigold's fleshy, glistening cotyledons are followed by sticky true leaves.

The Californian poppy's grey-green cotyledons and seed leaves are delicate, thin and wispy.

FINDING THEIR PLACE

Chancers thrive in spots around your garden where other plants find it difficult or undesirable to grow. The tiny seeds of foxgloves (*Digitalis purpurea*) and Welsh poppy will find their way into the nooks and crannies in drystone walls, where they germinate and grow, often in very little soil. When they bloom, the plants often look far more natural than if we had tried to deliberately plant them. Bee-friendly alyssum grows happily in the cracks between paving, helping to soften any straight lines (and smother out weeds).

Some self-seeders are unfussy about where they grow. Pot marigolds (*Calendula officinalis*) mingling among your vegetables will lure in beneficial insects, including adult hoverflies, whose larvae devour aphids. Others, such as tall, towering teasel (*Dipsacus fullonum*), which is a magnet for all types of bees and butterflies, will

Above left: Dark-veined red mustard readily self-seeds among other crops in a food garden, producing unexpected pickings of its hot, peppery leaves.

Above right: Welsh poppies are prolific chancers. Each seed capsule can shake out hundreds of small dark seeds which help them spread throughout a garden.

chance their luck anywhere in the garden. These biennials form spiny flat rosettes in the first year (which are easy to pull up), then tall flowering stems the following summer. If they have self-sown in a border, where they are adding to the display, or in unused ground, they can be left to their own devices.

Excessive self-seeding can be curtailed by trimming off any faded flowers, or by pulling up whole plants before they reach their seed-shedding peak.

SOW, SCATTER, FLICK AND SQUIRT

Using a few simple tricks will soon populate your garden with these opportunist and beneficial chancers. Sowing them outdoors in short rows between crops or other plants is a chance to learn what the seedlings and juvenile plants look like. Once you are familiar with the different self-seeders, it is easier to nip out any unwanted plants when they are young.

A wilder, more carefree approach is to make up a mixture of self-seeders from the list below,

MUST-GROW CHANCERS

These beautiful self-seeders produce both nectar and pollen for insects, and seeds for birds.

Columbine (*Aquilegia vulgaris*)
Borage (*Borago officinalis*)
Pot marigold (*Calendula officinalis*)
Brook thistle (*Cirsium rivulare* 'Atropurpureum')
Foxglove (*Digitalis purpurea*)
Teasel (*Dipsacus fullonum*)
Californian poppy (*Eschscholzia californica*)
Buckwheat (*Fagopyrum ecsulentum*)
Sunflower (*Helianthus annuus*)
Poached egg plant (*Limnanthes douglasii*)
Honesty (*Lunaria annua*)
Sweet alyssum (*Lobelia marítima*)
Mullein (*Verbascum* spp.)
Poppies (*Papaver* spp.)
Alexanders (*Smyrnium perfoliatum*)
Verbena bonariensis

Opposite below: American land cress (Barbarea verna) is a hardy alternative to watercress that will readily self-seed if plants are allowed to flower.

mix them with some leafmould, and then scatter them randomly around your garden at any time of year. This increases the chances of some plants finding a niche where they will flourish.

To get seeds into crevices in walls, put them in the palm of your hand and then use a finger to flick them into any gaps. Another way of 'seeding' a wall is to mix the seeds with some finely-sieved soil or leafmould, put the mixture in an old cake piping bag (or a strong plastic bag), and add water to make a gloopy mud. Squeeze the bag, squirting the seed-rich mush into as many cavities (horizontal and vertical) as possible. Inoculating walls in autumn gives germinating seeds a better chance of establishing during the moister, cooler months.

Adding chancers to your cool compost heap (page 130) or wormposting bin is another way of spreading them around your garden by stealth. As the plants decay, their dormant seeds remain behind, all ready to germinate when the mature compost is used.

Above left: Blue and pink columbines have taken a chance by sowing themselves into the slate chips in this sitting area.

Above right: These Welsh poppies were 'sown' by simply flicking their tiny seeds into the gaps in this drystone slate wall.

CLIMATE-FRIENDLY

NO GARDENING REQUIRED

Because established self-seeding chancers sow themselves, they do not need sowing into pots of compost in a greenhouse, watering or feeding – or even planting out. The most that we veganic gardeners need to do is scatter their seeds into the soil ourselves, transplant young self-sown plants (such as foxgloves) to another part of our garden, or pull up and compost any surplus plants.

Being completely self-sufficient and self-renewing, established self-seeders require zero time, effort or resources. They leave no gardening footprint, putting them among the most climate-friendly plants we can grow.

Let grass grow

Leaving your previously manicured lawn to go 'wild' and grow unchecked into areas of tall, longer grass with wildflowers nestled amongst them will boost the wildlife which visits your garden, especially bugs. Less or zero mowing drastically reduces the work of feeding and watering, and the polluting high-energy inputs required for a striped and 'perfect' weed-free lawn. No- and low-mow lawns can be enriched further with young plants and bulbs.

THE PROBLEM WITH LAWNS

Traditional lawns are routinely treated with synthetic chemical weedkillers and fertilisers, and watered and mown regularly, all of which consumes vast amounts of energy and resources. Many lawn treatments, as well as the fuel needed to run petrol-driven lawnmowers, are derived primarily from fossil fuels such as oil. Burning these releases carbon dioxide, the main greenhouse gas driving our climate emergency. Lawnmowers also create local pollution as noxious fumes and noise. Keeping a lawn constantly green requires large amounts of energy-intensive mains water, while lawn fertilisers can be responsible for polluting water supplies with nitrates and phosphates.

Lawn weeds are commonly treated with hormone weedkillers. Concerns over the effect of these types of weedkiller on human health has led to some countries banning their domestic use. Clippings from a weedkiller-treated lawn can damage the growth of other garden plants. The traditional lawn might be visually pleasing, but it comes with a high environmental cost and is usually devoid of all but transient wildlife.

LETTING LAWNS BE

The more of your lawn you allow to grow taller and at different heights, including areas of tall, undisturbed grass and wildflowers, the more wildlife it will attract – especially bugs that live both on plants and on the ground. Fast-moving, slug-eating ground beetles, as well as many spiders, thrive in long grass. Wild plants once treated as weeds will now be able to grow and flower, attracting pollinators, and then produce seeds, which will in turn attract other wildlife.

Lawn weeds such as dandelions (*Taraxacum officinale* agg., page 186) provide invaluable supplies of pollen and nectar for foraging wild bees over many weeks, especially in early spring. Soil life flourishes when the chemical-intensive treatments cease.

To make your existing lawn into a more planet-friendly, flower-rich space, simply stop mowing, feeding and watering it, and using weedkiller. Decide if any paths will weave through it, or whether you want to create some islands of longer grass and wildflowers, surrounded by close-mown paths. If you are unsure about what the results might be, leave a small area unmown to begin with, then gradually expand it by stopping mowing. Log piles and ponds can be included in areas of long grass to add extra wildlife-rich habitats.

Any wild plants present will bloom during spring and summer, showing you what flowers you already have. If wildflowers are sparse, plug plants from specialist suppliers will quickly enrich your grassy areas, or you can sow and raise your own plants. Wildflower seed mixtures, or seeds collected from wild plants growing locally, can be sown in long grass during autumn; scratch the ground over first using a rake or fork, to expose bare soil. Some suitable springtime plants for let-go lawns are listed in the panel overleaf.

Clockwise from above left: *Let grass grow long around the base of trees. Close-mown lawns contrast with wilder uncut areas. Lawns can gradually be switched to no-mow. A winding path mown through long grass.*

Opposite: *Using a person-powered scythe is a wildlife-friendly and low-impact way to cut long grass and helps to minimise your gardening footprint.*

Clockwise from top: *Peat-free wildflower plug plants ready for adding diversity to a boring lawn. Orange hawkweed. Snake's head fritillary.*

FLOWERS FOR LET-GO LAWNS

PERENNIALS:

Cow parsley (*Anthriscus sylvestris*)
Harebell (*Campanula rotundifolia*)
Hogweed (*Heracleum sphondylium*)
Field scabious (*Knautia arvensis*)
Ox-eye daisy (*Leucanthemum vulgare*)
Orange hawkweed (*Pilosella aurantiaca*)
Primrose (*Primula vulgaris*)

BULBS:

Meadow saffron (*Colchicum autumnale*)
Crocus spp.
Winter aconite (*Eranthis hyemalis*)
Snake's head fritillary (*Fritillaria meleagris*)
Snowdrops (*Galanthus* spp.)
Bluebell (*Hyacinthoides non-scripta*)
Wild daffodil (*Narcissus pseudonarcissus*)

CUTTING THE GRASS

Some mown grass paths around or through wild patches allow you to observe wildlife without stepping into the long grass. Paths can be winding and sinuous, or follow more geometric lines. Using a push mower, powered by human energy, or an electric model powered from a renewable energy source, means any mowing is as low-impact as possible. Push mowers are simple and quiet to use, provide regular exercise, and rarely break down.

Cutting grass at different heights brings the widest benefits. Grass which is mown monthly to a height of around 5cm (2in) encourages low-growing 'mower-ducking' flowers such as white clover (*Trifolium repens*), bird's-foot trefoil (*Lotus corniculatus*) and common daisy (*Bellis perennis*) to flower profusely. To achieve this, set your mower's cutting height at its highest setting. Other completely uncut areas will allow grasses and taller wildflowers to mature. Field scabious (*Knautia arvensis*), knapweed (*Centaurea nigra*), ox-eye daisy and red clover (*Trifolium pratense*) all flourish in taller grass.

Areas of tall grass mixed with wildflowers will need cutting once, usually in late summer, when any flowers have faded. After cutting, leave the material to dry out so that any flower seeds drop to the soil. It can then be raked up and composted, or used as mulch. Cutting and removing the grass occasionally prevents the soil from becoming too rich and fertile, which encourages grasses rather than flowers.

Small areas can be cut using shears or a hand-held sickle. For larger areas, a scythe is quieter and therapeutic to use, and less lethal to wildlife – you can usually hear any animals moving about in the grass and let them move away first. Avoid motorised line trimmers; they cause noise and air pollution, harm grass-dwelling wildlife such as hedgehogs and slow worms, and the cutting line (often nylon) fragments in use, contributing further to insidious plastic pollution. Trimmers with fixed metal blades powered by rechargeable batteries are a better option, but always check the grass thoroughly for any wildlife before cutting.

Turning lawn into long grass

1 (Left) Decide which areas of lawn will be left entirely uncut and allowed to go 'wild', and use a sand-filled bottle to mark them out.

2 Give your rewilded lawn a head start by planting young wildflower plug plants. Make planting holes in odd-numbered groups, using a dibber or a trowel.

3 Ease the young plants into the holes, firm the soil back in around them and give the patch a thorough watering. Plant any time from spring to autumn.

CLIMATE-FRIENDLY

SOAKING UP CARBON

As they grow, all lawns absorb carbon dioxide from the air. When their roots die, and leaf fragments decay into the soil, that carbon is sequestered away as dark humus. In an intensively-managed lawn however this climate-friendly benefit is cancelled out by the carbon emissions arising from its treatments – from manufacturing the fertilisers, pesticides and weedkillers, to the energy used when mowing and supplying the mains water used for regular irrigation.

Wild lawns sequester far more carbon than their care generates, and are a quiet yet effective means of helping to slow climate breakdown.

4 (Right) The plants will soon become established, some forming clumps among the tall, unmown grass. They will gradually spread themselves further by self-seeding.

Must-grow plants

To achieve a thriving and balanced community of wildlife in your veganic garden, you will need to grow a diverse range of plants, flowering at different times of the year, to entice them. The easiest way is to grow plants with simple, single flowers in which insects can easily forage for pollen and nectar, while avoiding complex and fussy double blooms which they cannot access. Other plants, such as trees and shrubs, provide physical habitats for birds to shelter and nest in, as well as flowers and fruits. All of the plants in this section have been chosen because they are straightforward to grow, are generally available, help to boost wildlife, and are simply beautiful.

NOTE ON PLANT DIMENSIONS

Each entry gives an indication of the final height and/or spread for that plant. Where two measurements are shown, e.g. '45–60cm x 60cm (18–24in x 24in)', the first is the range of likely height, followed by the spread.

*Left: Striking pink oriental poppy (*Papaver orientale *'Kleine Tänzerin'), flower spikes of foxtail lily (*Eremurus*) and clumps of blue-flowered hardy geraniums.*

Annual and biennial flowers

Fast-growing annuals which complete their lifecycle within a year, and biennials which take two years, are among the most valuable of plants for a garden, and many will self-seed. Some flower within weeks of sowing – making them ideal for a new veganic garden – and so immediately start attracting bees and other beneficial insects. Always choose varieties with simple, single flowers, which are rich in insect-accessible nectar and pollen.

Above, left to right:
Calendula officinalis.
Dahlia *'Fascination'*.
Digitalis purpurea.

Opposite, top to bottom:
Dipsacus fullonum.
Eschscholzia californica.
Helianthus annuus.

Calendula officinalis
POT MARIGOLD
Family: Asteraceae
A fast-growing annual with slightly sticky, pale green leaves and flat, disc-like flowers, often with dark eyes that are a magnet for bees and hoverflies. Sow the large seeds outdoors in mid-spring (or in autumn for early flowers the following spring). 'Nova' and 'Daisy May' are good single varieties. Allow to self-seed among crops in a food garden. 30–45cm (12–18in).

Dahlia 'Fascination'
BEDDING DAHLIA
Family: Asteraceae
Bees and butterflies flock to the large flowers, up to 10cm (4in) wide, held above the bronze leaves of this tuberous-rooted perennial that is grown as a half-hardy summer flowering annual. Sow in mid-spring under cover or buy ready-grown plants, choosing single-flowered varieties in mixed colours; 'Bishop's Children', 'Mignon Mixed' or 'Romeo' are all good choices. Deadhead regularly to promote flowering. 45–60cm x 60cm (18–24in x 24in).

Digitalis purpurea
FOXGLOVE
Family: Plantaginaceae
The tall and unmistakeable spikes of purple-pink flowers start to open in late spring and flowering lasts for many weeks. The tubular flowers are much visited by bumblebees. Each plant can produce many thousands of self-sown seeds. The foxglove germinates during summer and produces leafy rosettes by autumn, and then

flowers the following spring. Young plants are easy to transplant to new positions. Cutting faded stems back can encourage more blooms. A biennial which sometimes becomes a short-lived perennial. *D. purpurea* f. *albiflora* has white flowers. Up to 2.5m (8ft).

Dipsacus fullonum
COMMON TEASEL
Family: Caprifoliaceae
Sow teasel seeds either in pots of peat-free compost or outdoors in spring and summer. These tall biennial plants form a flat and spiny overwintering rosette which grows quickly the following spring, sending up branched stems topped by fat, oval heads covered in successive rings of purple flowers. Butterflies and bees find the flowers irresistible. In autumn, seed-eating birds such as goldfinches (*Carduelis carduelis*) feast on the large brown seeds. Teasel stems carry vicious barbs so grow it away from any paths. A prolific self-seeder, any unwanted rosettes should be pulled up before they establish deep roots. Up to 2.5m (8ft).

Eschscholzia californica
CALIFORNIA POPPY
Family: Papaveraceae
Fast-growing, drought-tolerant hardy annuals with finely cut, pale blue-green leaves and short-lived but prolific flowers followed by narrow seed pods. Sow outdoors in spring. Prefers poor, dry soil in full sun; self-seeds prolifically in paths and on hot, sun-baked gravel areas. A favourite plant of hoverflies seeking nectar. Choose single-flowered varieties, e.g. 'Golden Values' (yellow), 'Ivory Castle' (white) or 'Single Mixed'. Up to 30cm x 15cm (12in x 6in).

Helianthus annuus
SUNFLOWER
Family: Asteraceae
Sunflowers produce either a single large flowerhead (up to 60cm/24in across), or a branching head with multiple blooms. Sow in spring, outdoors or in pots and plant out. The flowers are rich in pollen and nectar (avoid

growing 'pollen-free' varieties as these have much less insect-appeal). Birds eat the seeds in autumn/winter so leave the plants in place until spring. Try 'Hallo' (multi-headed), 'Pike's Peak' (huge single heads) or 'Pastiche' (mixed shades and ideal for using as a cut flower). Up to 5m x 60cm (16ft x 24in).

Limnanthes douglasii
POACHED EGG PLANT
Family: Limnanthaceae
The nectar-rich, yellow-centred white flowers of *Limnanthes* appear from spring onwards above glossy and divided yellow-green leaves. Sow the large black and easy-to-handle seeds outdoors in spring. It self-seeds readily and forms low-growing clumps which can be left to fill gaps along the edges of beds in a food garden. Self-sown seedlings will overwinter and flower early the following spring. The variety 'Spanish Omelette' contains two-tone, white and yellow flowers. 15cm (6in).

Lobularia maritima (syn. *Alyssum maritimum*)
SWEET ALYSSUM
Family: Brassicaceae
Low mounds of grey-green leaves with small, honey-scented flowers. Makes a good edging plant, or dotted around a food garden. Half-hardy; sow under cover in early spring, planting out after frosts. 'Carpet of Snow' has white blooms; 'Rally Formula Mixed' has pale yellow and ochre. 5–30cm x 20–30cm (2–12in x 8–12in).

Nicotiana sylvestris
TOBACCO PLANT
Family: Solanaceae
Moths are attracted to this half-hardy annual's tubular, nectar-rich flowers which flood the night garden with scent. Tall and useful for the backs of borders. Sow under cover in spring then plant after frosts. *N. langsdorffii* reaches 1.5m (5ft) tall and has scented yellow-green flowers. *N. x sanderae* 'Sensation Mixed' adds colour and scent to borders. 1.5m x 60cm (5ft x 24in).

Below, clockwise from top left: Limnanthes douglasii. Nicotiana sylvestris. Lobularia maritima.

Perennial flowers

Perennials are hardy plants which live for two years or longer and flower annually when they are mature. The most familiar are herbaceous perennials, which produce new flowering stems each year that die back in autumn; they then lie dormant over winter, sending up new shoots in spring. Perennial flowers are invaluable for a vibrant garden ecosystem because they flower unfailingly, often for many months, with only minimal care.

Anchusa azurea 'Dropmore'
BLUE BUGLOSS
Family: Boraginaceae
Forms clumps of hairy, grey-green leaves below shoots carrying lots of amethyst-blue flowers which are sought out by bees. Good border plant. Deadheading after the first flush of flowers encourages a second showing. 'Loddon Royalist' is a strong-growing variety 90cm (36in) tall, with deep blue flowers. 'Little John' reaches just 45cm (18in) tall, and has deep blue blooms. 60–90cm x 60cm (24–36in x 24in).

Astrantia 'Hadspen Blood'
HATTIE'S PINCUSHION
Family: Apiaceae
Pretty, clump-forming plants with lobed leaves for borders in sun or dappled shade. The umbrella-like flowerheads comprise small florets surrounded by papery bracts, both deep red in colour, which are popular with all kinds of bees, hoverflies and drone flies. Can be dried for use indoors. Divide large clumps in spring. *A. major* ssp. *involucrata* 'Shaggy' has long, green-tipped bracts; *A. major* 'Sunningdale Variegated' has striking cream-edged leaves and pink bracts. 30–90cm x 45cm (12–36in x 18in).

Cirsium rivulare 'Atropurpureum'
ORNAMENTAL THISTLE
Family: Asteraceae
The tall stems of this non-invasive thistle will sway under the sheer weight of visiting bees and butterflies. An attractive border plant, it needs regular deadheading to prolong its flowering period. Divide large, sprawling clumps in spring.

Above, left to right: Anchusa azurea *'Dropmore'.* Astrantia *'Hadspen Blood'.*

Its pincushion-like, sweet-scented flowerheads, measuring 3cm (1¼in) across, are deep crimson. Stop deadheading in late summer to allow the fluffy seedheads, which are eaten by birds, to form. 1.2m x 60cm (4ft x 24in).

Geranium x magnificum

HARDY GERANIUM

Family: Geraniaceae

Find a sunny spot for this clump-forming herbaceous perennial. Bees flock to the deeply veined violet-blue, saucer-like flowers, 5cm (2in) wide, which appear non-stop throughout the summer. The lobed leaves take on reddish-orange autumn tints. Shade-loving *G. macrorrhizum* 'Ingwersen's Variety' is a good ground cover plant 45cm (18in) tall, with soft pink flowers from late spring, making it an excellent source of early nectar for bumblebees. 60cm (24in).

Leucanthemum vulgare

OX-EYE DAISY

Family: Asteraceae

From a low, spreading mound of dark green leaves, tall solitary flowerheads appear, each 2.5–5cm (1–2in) across, comprising a yellow centre surrounded by white petals. Ideal for growing in long, unmown grass in a 'rewilded' lawn, these wild perennials are a magnet for butterflies and hoverflies. Plants raised from summer-saved seed and planted in late summer or autumn will start to bloom the following summer. Self-seeds profusely when established, so be ruthless with unwanted seedlings. 30–90cm x 60cm (24–36in x 24in).

Helenium 'Waltraut'

SNEEZEWEED

Family Asteraceae

Pollinators will flock to this clump-forming herbaceous perennial which flowers from late summer into autumn. Its orange-brown, daisy-like and pollen-rich flowers, with their swept-back petals, are up to 8cm (3in) across. Lift and divide dormant clumps in winter. *H.* 'Moerheim Beauty' is similar with crimson-orange blooms. *H.* 'Sahin's Early Flowerer' produces yellow flowers that turn red with age, from early summer until autumn. 90cm x 90cm (36 x 36in).

Nepeta racemosa (syn. *N.mussinii*)

CATMINT

Family: Lamiaceae

The sheer number of wild and honey bees foraging on the flowers of catmint will draw this plant to your attention. The lavender-blue flowers appear in summer on long, slightly floppy, spreading stems and go on blooming for many weeks. It makes an excellent edging plant for paths; when brushed against the hairy grey-green leaves emit a distinctive 'catmint' fragrance. Trim faded shoots back in spring, when clumps can also be divided. *Nepeta* 'Six Hills Giant' is similar but grows 90cm (36in) tall and wide. Up to 30cm x 45cm (12in x 18in).

Phlomis russeliana

STICKY JERUSALEM SAGE

Family: Lamiaceae

This sun-loving perennial, with its felted leaves, has dense, striking whorls of hooded yellow flowers up to 4cm (1½in) long, which bees forage on noisily and furiously. A good choice for a sun-baked, dry garden, it makes an attractive ground cover. It blooms non-stop from late spring to autumn. Leave the dead flower stems for winter structural interest, cutting them down in spring. Up to 90cm x 75cm (36 x 30in).

Verbena bonariensis (syn. *V. patagonica*)

TALL VERBENA

Family: Verbenaceae

Butterflies flock to the sweetly-scented heads of lilac-purple summer flowers up to 5cm (2in) across, and carried on tall, branching stems which sway in the breeze and are ideal supports for spiders' webs. Verbena also attracts day- and night-flying moths. Easily grown from seed, or from cuttings taken in spring. Often treated as an annual, plants will easily survive mild winters in well-drained soil. Readily self-seeds. Blooms from midsummer until the first frosts. Up to 2m x 90cm (7ft x 36in).

Opposite, clockwise from top left: Cirsium rivulare *'Atropurpureum'*. Geranium x magnificum. Nepeta racemosa. Verbena bonariensis. Phlomis russeliana. Leucanthemum vulgare. Helenium *'Waltraut' (centre).*

Tall perennial flowers

Big and tall perennials which reach for the skies make excellent use of vertical growing space. They also entice bees, butterflies and other flying insects, encouraging them to stop over in a garden, and then move down on to other lower-growing pollen- and nectar-rich plants nearby. These potentially giant plants live for many years. Their faded stems add structural drama to the garden in winter.

Below, left to right: Alcea rosea. Angelica archangelica.

Opposite, clockwise from top left: Cephalaria gigantea. Echium pininana. Eupatorium cannabinum.

Alcea rosea
HOLLYHOCK
Family: Malvaceae
Easy to grow from spring-sown seed, these sturdy biennials or often short-lived perennials are available in either mixed or individual colours. Their 10cm (4in) wide blooms appear non-stop throughout summer. Single-flowered varieties allow bees to forage easily. They thrive in full sun and well drained soil. Grow them at the back of borders where they can make good use of vertical space. In smaller gardens, a single plant can be used as the centrepiece of a smaller bed. Although deadheading encourages a succession of flowers, leaving some of the round, scaly seed pods to ripen lets the plant self-sow into the surrounding soil. *A. rosea* 'Giant Single Mixed' comes in pastel shades; *A. rosea* 'Nigra' has dark, single flowers. Up to 2m (7ft).

Angelica archangelica
ANGELICA
Family: Apiaceae
Big and bold angelica is usually a perennial, but sometimes plants die after flowering. Masses of small, pale yellow flowers appear in early summer, in rounded heads. They are a magnet for hoverflies and drone flies, beetles, and other less conspicuous insects. The strong faded stems add winter interest to borders, and sections of hollow stem can be used for making bug hotels (page 178). Self-seeds readily. *Angelica gigas* has purple stems/flowers and blooms in late summer. 2m x 1m (7ft x 3ft).

Cephalaria gigantea
GIANT OR YELLOW SCABIOUS
Family: Caprifoliaceae
Tall, widely-branched stems rise up from a clump of glossy green foliage, and carry a

succession of pale blooms from early summer to early autumn. Wild and honey bees, as well as butterflies flock to the sulphur-yellow flowers. Nip off faded blooms to encourage more. The lanky stems are wind-prone – you can push twiggy hazel sticks in around the clump in spring, so that the stems grow up through them. 2.5m x 1m (8ft x 3ft).

Echium pininana
GIANT VIPER'S BUGLOSS OR TREE ECHIUM
Family: Boraginaceae
This enormous plant is easy to raise from seed, grows rapidly, and self-seeds readily after flowering. It forms a dense rosette of bristly leaves, before sending up a towering spike of pale blue-purple flowers visited by bees, butterflies and moths. These half-hardy plants grow as either biennials or short-lived perennials, and need protection from frost in winter. Plant in a sunny, sheltered spot in well-drained soil. 2.5–4m x 1m (8–13ft x 3ft).

Eupatorium cannabinum
HEMP AGRIMONY
Family: Asteraceae
Clouds of butterflies will dance over the domed heads of pink-purple, pollen- and nectar-rich flowers in late summer. The blooms are carried on reddish stems carrying distinctive, cannabis-like leaves. Plants form large, spreading clumps that need reining in if they become invasive. Grows well in moist soil and is a good choice for a bog garden or the moist edges around a large pond. 1.5m x 1.5m (5ft x 5ft).

Ferula communis
GIANT FENNEL
Family: Apiaceae
This tough perennial can take up to five years before it flowers. At first it produces a mound of frothy, finely divided dark green foliage, then in summer sends up broomstick-thick green stems topped by rounded heads comprising masses of

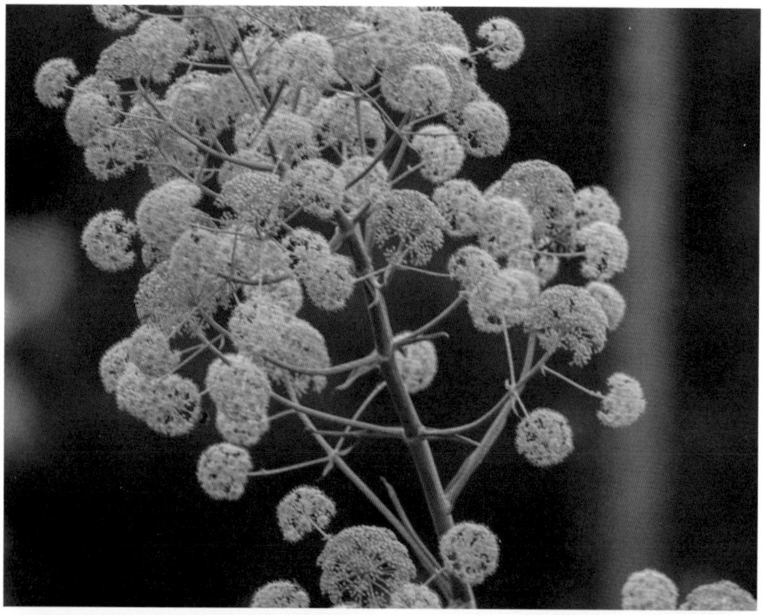

small, yellow flowers which bees, butterflies and many other insects find irresistible. Needs free-draining soil. Leave the stems for winter drama. 2.5–4m x 1m (8–13ft x 3ft).

Helianthus 'Lemon Queen'
GIANT SUNFLOWER
Family: Asteraceae
This tall perennial needs to grow in full sun where it produces a non-stop abundance of simple, daisy-like yellow flowers from midsummer to early autumn. The blooms are rich in nectar and pollen and attract bees, butterflies and other garden bugs. The showy sunflower (*Helianthus x laetiflorus*) is similar and forms 2m (7ft) tall clumps in roomy borders. 3m x 1.5m (10ft x 5ft).

Inula helenium
ELECAMPANE
Family: Asteraceae
Tall stems studded with bright yellow daisy-like flowers makes a powerful statement in a mixed border, and becomes a magnet for bees and butterflies from late summer to early autumn. Its large leaves have hairy-white undersides. Seed-eating birds such as linnet (*Linaria cannabina*) will feast on the autumn seedheads. Giant inula (*Inula magnifica*) is similar, but with large, wavy-edged leaves. It thrives in moist soil and can be grown in wild grassy areas. 2m x 1m (7ft x 3ft).

Silphium perfoliatum
CUP PLANT
Family: Asteraceae
Birds and insects will drink the rainwater that collects in the 'cup' formed by the leaf bases of this clump-forming perennial. Each daisy-like flower is up to 9cm (3½in) across and attracts large numbers of hoverflies, as well as wild and honey bees. Flowers from summer to early autumn. Compass (*Silphium laciniatum*) has similar flowers, fern-like foliage, and can reach up to 4m (13ft) tall. 1.5–2.5m x 1m (5–8ft x 3ft).

Left, clockwise from top: Ferula communis. Silphium perfoliatum. Helianthus '*Lemon Queen*'. Inula helenium.

Flowering bulbs

Bulbs flower reliably year after year and are an important source of pollen and nectar for all types of pollinator. Bought bulbs are often routinely treated with pesticides, some of which may persist as potentially harmful residues. Organically-grown and certified bulbs are guaranteed to be free of synthetic chemicals. Those taken from an established garden, where no pesticides are used, will also be safe for garden wildlife.

Allium 'Globemaster'
ORNAMENTAL ONION
Family: Alliaceae
Large round violet-purple heads of flowers up to 20cm (8in) in diameter appear on tall stems from late spring until early summer, and attract bees of all types. Plant the bulbs in well-drained soil in full sun. Cut off the faded heads to encourage strong bulbs for the following year, and allow the foliage to die back naturally. *Allium hollandicum* 'Purple Sensation' grows 90cm (36in) tall, with rose-purple heads. 80–100cm x 50cm (32–40in x 20in).

Camassia leichtlinii subsp. *suksdorfii* Caerulea Group
CAMASSIA
Family: Asparagaceae
Spikes of striking azure-blue flowers appear for many weeks from late spring onwards, and are popular with foraging bumblebees. The undersides of the long narrow leaves have an attractive blue-grey sheen. Camassia needs well-drained soil and will grow in a border, or it can be naturalised among the long grass of a wild and unmown lawn. Plant in groups of at least five bulbs 20cm (8in) apart. *Camassia cusickii* is similar, with sky-blue flowers and reaches 60cm (24in) tall. 90cm x 30cm (36in x 12in).

Colchicum autumnale
AUTUMN CROCUS, NAKED LADIES
Family: Colchicaceae
Bumblebees forage on the bright pink flowers on sunny, autumn days, as they prepare for winter hibernation. Each goblet-shaped, pollen-rich bloom is up to 8cm (3in) across. Clumps of shiny green leaves appear in spring, before dying down in summer ahead of the flowers. The corms are easy to naturalise in wild, unmown lawns and other grassy/meadow areas (do not cut the foliage until it has gone yellow and faded away). *C. autumnale* Album' has white flowers. 15cm x 15cm (6in x 6in).

Above, left to right:
Allium *'Globemaster'.*
Camassia leichtlinii *subsp.* suksdorfii *Caerulea Group.*

Crocus tommasinianus
EARLY-FLOWERING CROCUS
Family: Iridaceae
Adding generous numbers of this crocus to your veganic garden will benefit queen bumblebees searching for pollen and nectar on warm, sunny days in late winter and early spring. The corms are best naturalised by planting them in odd-numbered groups, in sunny lawns and other grassy areas. They can also be grown in wide, shallow pots. The delicate, tubular flowers come in shades of lilac to deep purple. Other early crocuses of note include *C.* 'Vanguard' (grey-mauve) and *C.* 'Romance' (yellow). 10cm x 50cm (4in x 20in).

Eranthis hyemalis
WINTER ACONITE
Family: Ranunculaceae
The bright yellow flowers bloom around the same time as snowdrops. They provide invaluable forage for winter-flying insects, especially queen bumblebees. Each 3cm (1¼in) wide buttercup-like flower is surrounded by a dark green leafy collar. Ideal for naturalising in untamed grassy areas, and underneath trees, where it forms spreading, ground-hugging clumps. Lift and divide plants straight after flowering, or source new pesticide-free plants 'in the green', which establish more easily than dry tubers. 10cm x 10cm (4in x 4in).

Fritillaria meleagris
SNAKE'S HEAD FRITILLARY
Family: Liliaceae
Ideal for naturalising in a garden with heavy, moist soil, these delicate and beautiful spring-flowering bulbs will succeed in rewilded areas, where they will flower and self-seed in long grass. Each nodding, bell-shaped pinky-purple flower has distinctively chequered petals. The narrow, grass-like foliage is hard to tell from real grasses; it is best not to cut any areas where fritillaries are growing until mid to late summer. Plant odd-numbered groups of the small fleshy bulbs in autumn. 30cm x 15cm (12in x 6in).

Galanthus nivalis
SNOWDROP
Family: Amaryllidaceae
Snowdrops are usually the first bulbs to flower in a garden. Their white, honey-scented flowers open out on warm and sunny midwinter days when overwintered bumblebees and hoverflies take to the wing. In time they make large, spreading clumps of silver-grey leaves and are ideal for naturalising in grass beneath any trees which cast dappled shade. Clumps can also be grown in mixed borders, or as part of a bug bank. Divide clumps while they are still leafy, straight after flowering. To benefit insects, always plant single- rather than double-flowered varieties. 7.5–15cm x 15cm (3–6in x 6in).

Muscari armeniacum
ARMENIAN GRAPE HYACINTH
Family: Asparagaceae
Dense clusters of small, bell-shaped flowers crowd at the tops of flowering stems in spring, providing early foraging for various wild bees. They soon form dense, spreading sheets and self-seed prolifically; remove any developing seedpods before the shiny black seeds appear. Plants thrive in sunny gravelled areas. Grape hyacinth can also be grown in shallow, well-drained containers of peat-free compost. *M. azureum* is similar, with soft-blue flowers. 20cm x 7.5cm (8in x 3in).

Nectaroscordum siculum
SICILIAN HONEY GARLIC
Family: Alliaceae
Plant this tall and distinctive bulb in odd-numbered groups of at least five bulbs in a mixed border, where it will tower over any low-growing neighbours. Bees and other beneficial pollinators are drawn to the pendulous, purple-cream flowers which open in succession over several weeks during late spring and early summer. Use the dried stems for indoor decorations. Self-seeds readily. Large clumps of bulbs can be lifted and divided from autumn until early spring. Smells of garlic. 1.2m x 10cm (4ft x 4in).

Opposite, clockwise from top left: Colchicum autumnale. Crocus tommasinianus. Galanthus nivalis. Nectaroscordum siculum. Muscari armeniacum. Eranthis hyemali. Fritillaria meleagris *(centre).*

Shrubs

Shrubs are long-lived hardy plants with woody stems, usually producing several branches from their base at or near ground level (trees have a single stem). Shrubs either keep their leaves year-round (evergreen) or drop them in autumn (deciduous). Shrubs provide food such as pollen, nectar, and autumn/winter fruits. Dense shrubs are also year-round roosting, nesting and general sheltering sites for all kinds of garden wildlife.

Above, left to right: Berberis darwinii. Buddleja davidii.

Opposite, clockwise from top left: Ceanothus *'Pershore Zanzibar'*. Hypericum olympicum. Lavandula angustifolia *'Hidcote'*. Cotoneaster horizontalis.

Berberis darwinii
BARBERRY
Family: Berberidaceae
This upright evergreen shrub flowers in mid and late spring and is an invaluable early source of nectar for bees, when few other spring flowers are available. Its orange flowers are held in hanging clusters among glossy, dark spine-toothed leaves. It also provides dense cover for roosting birds. *B. x lologensis* 'Apricot Queen' has dark orange flowers also in spring. 3m (10ft).

Buddleja davidii
BUTTERFLY BUSH
Family: Scrophulariaceae
In late summer this fast-growing deciduous shrub attracts clouds of butterflies, bees and other beneficial bugs to its elongated, nectar-rich and honey-scented flowerheads. Grow it in a mixed border with insect-attracting perennials. Prune in spring. Pink- and lilac-coloured *B. davidii* varieties are usually the most attractive to insects. *B. alternifolia* and *B. crispa* are also insect magnets. 3m x 5m (10ft x 16ft).

Ceanothus 'Pershore Zanzibar'
VARIEGATED CALIFORNIA LILAC
Family: Rhamnaceae
A striking evergreen shrub which is best grown against a sheltered sunny wall. Its golden-yellow leaves have a dark green central splash. Clusters of small, powder-blue flowers, which appear

among the colourful foliage in late spring and early summer, are popular with bees and other pollinators. The variety 'Autumnal Blue' has sky-blue flowers in late summer and autumn. Up to 3m (10ft).

Cotoneaster horizontalis
HERRINGBONE COTONEASTER
Family: Rosaceae
This deciduous shrub will clamber up against a wall, or spread in mounds over the ground. The branches, in a herringbone pattern, are covered with small dark leaves which turn deep red in autumn. In spring, bees are drawn in large and noisy numbers to the small pinkish-white sweet-scented and nectar-rich flowers. The blooms are followed by spherical red fruits 6mm (¼in) long which are eaten by birds. 1m x 1.5m (3ft x 5ft).

Hypericum olympicum
ST. JOHN'S WORT
Family: Clusiaceae
Look out for honey bees gathering pollen and nectar among the long, filament-like stamens of the yellow flowers, which are up to 6cm (2½in) across. The leaves of this deciduous shrub are grey-green. *H. olympicum* f. *uniflorum* 'Citrinum' has lemon-yellow flowers; *H.* 'Hidcote' makes a semi-evergreen bush up to 1.2m (4ft) tall and wide, with golden yellow flowers in succession over many months. 25cm x 30cm (10in x 12in).

Lavandula angustifolia 'Hidcote'
ENGLISH LAVENDER
Family: Lamiaceae
Try to include at least one lavender bush in your garden or allotment. This compact, aromatic and silver-grey evergreen shrub carries spikes of violet-blue flowers during midsummer, which wild and honey bees, butterflies and hoverflies find irresistible. Fresh flowers can be harvested and dried for use indoors. Cut faded spikes back after flowering, and then give the bush a light trim in spring. Needs full sun and well-drained soil. *L. x intermedia* 'Gros Bleu' reaches 75cm (30in) tall and has large purple spikes. 60cm x 60cm (24in x 24in).

Lonicera fragrantissima

WINTER-FLOWERING HONEYSUCKLE

Family: Caprifoliaceae

The small, strongly-scented cream flowers of this deciduous shrubby honeysuckle more than make up for its otherwise nondescript appearance. It is well worth growing in even an out-of-the-way part of the garden for its value to insects foraging for energy-giving nectar during sunny and warm winter spells, when other flowers are scarce. Red berries sometimes follow the flowers. *L.* x *purpusii* 'Winter Beauty' is similar. 2m x 2m (7ft x 7ft).

Mahonia x *media* 'Charity'

OREGON GRAPE

Family: Berberidaceae

The tall stems of this dense and slow-growing evergreen shrub carry leathery, spiny leaves, and are topped during late autumn and winter with long racemes of bright yellow flowers. The small, sweetly fragrant blooms fill the surrounding air with their scent, and are a rich source of pollen and nectar for winter-active bumblebees and other pollinators. The black-purple berries that follow are eaten by birds. Older leaves turn to shades of orange-red before they fall. *M.* x *media* 'Winter Sun' is similar. 2.5–4m x 2.5–4m (8–13ft x 8–13ft).

Rosa 'Ballerina'

HYBRID MUSK/POLYANTHA ROSE

Family: Rosaceae

This spectacular, disease-resistant rose has a spreading habit and large heads of pink, white-centred flowers, which bees find irresistible. Regularly removing faded blooms ensures that new flowers appear continuously from spring to autumn. Roses with open, single flowers are a better choice for a veganic garden; varieties where a cluster of golden stamens can clearly be seen are the most accessible to the widest range of bees, hoverflies and other garden pollinators. 1–1.5m x 1–1.2m (3–5ft x 3–4ft).

Left, top to bottom: Lonicera fragrantissima. Mahonia x media *'Charity'*. Rosa *'Ballerina'*.

Trees

Trees are hardy and long-lived woody plants, either evergreen or deciduous, usually with a single stem (trunk) from which other branches arise. They are an integral part of a garden's overall framework. In a veganic garden, trees offer roosting or nesting sites, autumn/winter food for birds, and provide spring and summer pollen and nectar for bees and other beneficial pollinators. Some trees also bear edible fruits.

Acer campestre
FIELD MAPLE
Family: Sapindaceae
A small to medium-sized deciduous tree with a compact, bushy crown, which succeeds on most soil types. In spring, clusters of small yellow-green flowers attract bees searching for pollen and nectar; entire trees will buzz with the sound of insects. Aphids feeding on the leaves will attract hoverflies. In autumn the lobed leaves turn shades of yellow, red and brown. *A. campestre* 'Nanum' is smaller, reaching 2.5–3m (8–10ft) tall. 12m x 8m (39ft x 26ft).

Amelanchier lamarckii
JUNEBERRY
Family: Rosaceae
This deciduous tree or shrub (also known as snowy mespilus) carries long heads of nectar-rich white flowers 12.5cm (5in) long in mid-spring, set against the coppery-pink young leaves, and followed by sweet and juicy black edible fruits in mid- to late summer. Its yellow-green summer leaves, 7.5cm (3in) long, turn fiery shades of red and orange during the autumn. *A.* x *grandiflora* 'Ballerina' flowers profusely and has red-purple autumn foliage. 10m x 12m (33ft x 39ft).

Below, left to right: Acer campestre. Amelanchier lamarckii.

Above, from left: Arbutus unedo. Betula pendula. Cercis siliquastrum *(top)*. Eucryphia glutinosa *(bottom)*.

Arbutus unedo

STRAWBERRY TREE

Family: Ericaeae

In autumn this glossy-leaved evergreen large shrub or tree carries clusters of white, bell-like flowers followed by round red, strawberry-like edible but largely unappetising fruits, which ripen the following spring. The reddish-brown bark is flaky, adding to this tree's appeal during winter. Needs acid or neutral soil. Much visited by bumblebees searching for nectar. *A. unedo* f. *rubra* has dark pink flowers. Compact-growing 2m (7ft) tall 'Elfin King' is ideal for a smaller garden. 8m x 8m (26ft x 26ft).

Betula pendula

SILVER BIRCH

Family: Betulaceae

An elegant deciduous tree which grows well on dry, sandy soils. It has an open canopy of branches, casting dappled shade, where birds will perch during the day and roost at night. The pretty and distinctive bark is white and peeling, becoming cracked at the base of the trunk on older trees. In spring, downy male catkins 6cm (2½in) in length appear. The leaves turn yellow in autumn. *B. pendula* 'Youngii' has a weeping habit and reaches 4m (13ft) tall. 25m x 10m (82ft x 33ft).

Cercis siliquastrum

JUDAS TREE

Family: Fabaceae

The pink flowers of this often multi-stemmed, slow-growing deciduous tree appear before the leaves in late spring and early summer, often on the thicker main branches. They are a useful food source for bees. In autumn its blue-green heart-shaped or kidney-shaped leaves turn to shades of rich yellow. *C. siliquastrum* f. *albida* has white flowers, while those of the cultivar 'Bodnant' are dark purple-pink. 10m (33ft).

Eucryphia glutinosa

EUCRYPHIA

Family: Cunoniaceae

This beautiful evergreen (or semi-evergreen), upright tree has dark green glossy foliage and flowers in mid and late summer. The cup-shaped white flowers are 6cm (2½in) wide with a central boss of gold-tipped stamens; they attract so many bees that the entire tree can appear to be buzzing and it is often heard before it is seen. *E.* x *nymansensis* 'Nymansay' is similar and grows 15m (50ft) tall. 10m x 6m (33ft x 20ft).

Halesia carolina

SNOWDROP TREE

Family: Styracaceae

This unusual slow-growing deciduous tree or large shrub produces its bell-shaped hanging flowers, which are 2cm (¾in) long, in late spring, just before its leaves appear. The winged fruits which follow are edible, with a pea-like flavour, and should be eaten when young and tender (usually midsummer). Both honey and wild bees visit the flowers, which can also be eaten in salads. The leaves turn yellow in autumn. 8m x 10m (26ft x 33ft).

Salix caprea 'Kilmarnock'

KILMARNOCK WEEPING WILLOW

Family: Salicaceae

The yellow-grey fluffy catkins of this small, deciduous weeping tree appear in mid- and late spring on bare downswept stems, and provide an early food source for foraging wild and honey bees. Its strong shape makes it useful in a border or in a grassed area. The leaves turn yellow in autumn and the bare stems add winter colour to the garden. Many willows grow very large, but 'Kilmarnock' allows a bee-friendly tree to be grown in any average-sized garden. 1.5–2m x 2m (5ft–7ft x 7ft).

Sorbus aucuparia

MOUNTAIN ASH

Family: Rosaceae

A hardy deciduous tree with divided, herringbone-like leaves that take on dazzling shades of red and yellow in autumn. Heads of fragrant, creamy-white flowers appear in late spring, and are much visited by bees. These are followed by heavy clusters of round, glossy orange-red berries which, as they swell and ripen, often weigh the tips of the branches down. Many different birds feed on the berries throughout autumn and winter, including thrushes and redwings. *S. aucuparia* var. *xanthocarpa* has orange-yellow autumn fruits. 15m x 7m (50ft x 23ft).

Above, clockwise from top left: Halesia carolina. Salix caprea *'Kilmarnock'*. Sorbus aucuparia.

Climbing plants

Climbers can be long-lived hardy plants with woody stems, usually producing several branches from their base, at or near ground level, and can be evergreen or deciduous; others are annual plants which last only a single growing season. Plants climb by using sticky roots or suckers to attach themselves to hard surfaces, by twining around other plants, or using tendrils to clamber over supports such as trellis. Climbers add vertical wildlife habitat to any garden.

Below: Clematis cirrhosa.

Clematis cirrhosa
EVERGREEN CLEMATIS
Family: Ranunculaceae
Bumblebees flit between the creamy bell-like flowers on warm, sunny days from midwinter through to late spring. Each bloom is up to 6.5cm (2½in) across and the inside of the petals is often speckled with red dots. The flowers are followed by soft and silky seedheads. Train up a trellis on a wall, tying the shoots in, or let them weave their own way through shrubs. The 5cm (2in) wide blooms of *C. cirrhosa* var. *purpurascens* 'Freckles' are covered in maroon blotches. Up to 3m (10ft).

Clematis vitalba
OLD MAN'S BEARD/TRAVELLER'S JOY
Family: Ranunculaceae
This large, fast-growing deciduous and vine-like climber is best grown where it can clamber at will over an established hedge or into shrubs or trees. Clusters of scented white flowers appear from midsummer to early autumn, and are popular with pollinators, especially hoverflies. Flowers are followed by pale wispy seedheads, which goldfinches will feed on during autumn. Plants will need support, such as wire netting or wooden trellis, to grow them against a wall. Reaches 15m (50ft).

Hedera helix
COMMON IVY
Family: Araliaceae
Ivy supports multiple wild species and is one of the most useful evergreen climbers to grow to boost the wildlife population in any garden; nesting birds, spiders and many other animals find a home there. It climbs using sticky hairs, which cling to hard surfaces such as brick and wood. Mature ivy produces bushy, non-clinging shoots which carry round heads of greenish-yellow flowers during autumn; these are nectar-rich and attract swarms of insects, including wild and honey bees, butterflies, wasps, flies and hoverflies. Queen bumblebees forage on ivy for nectar as they prepare for winter hibernation. Most of the pollen collected by honey bees in autumn is gathered from ivy flowers. Black berries follow in winter and are eaten by birds. Up to 12m (40ft).

Lonicera periclymenum
COMMON HONEYSUCKLE
Family: Caprifoliaceae
The white to yellow, red-flushed tubular flowers of this vigorous deciduous climber will fill your garden with its heady and powerful fragrance after dark. Moths, including the larger hawk

moths, feed on the flowers' nectar at night, and other insects visit by day. Let honeysuckle scramble through a hedge or up into the boughs of a tree. Birds eat the glossy red berries that follow the flowers. The variety 'Serotina' has creamy-white flowers streaked with red-purple. Height up to 7m (22ft).

Passiflora caerulea
BLUE PASSION FLOWER
Family: Passifloraceae
This exotic-looking glossy-leaved evergreen needs a sheltered wall in full sun to succeed. It climbs using twining tendrils and will clamber up fine wooden trellis. Its striking nectar- and pollen-rich 7.5cm (3in) wide flowers are blue and purple and attract wild and honey bees. Egg-shaped fruits follow the flowers and ripen to orange in autumn (they are edible but largely tasteless). *P.* 'Amethyst' can grow 4m (13ft) tall and has pale purple blooms up to 10cm (4in) wide. Can reach 12m (40ft).

Phaseolus coccineus
SCARLET RUNNER BEAN
Family: Fabaceae
Runner beans are perennial plants which we grow as half-hardy annual climbers for their

Above, clockwise from top left: Clematis vitalba. Hedera helix. Phaseolus coccineus. Passiflora caerule. Lonicera periclymenum.

Above, left to right: Solanum crispum *'Glasnevin'*. Tropaeolum majus. Wisteria sinensis.

immature edible pods. They thrive in rich soil, grow quickly in summer and soon produce clusters of red, white, pink or bicoloured flowers which attract honey and bumblebees. 'Moonlight' (white flowers), 'Firestorm' (red), and 'Red Rum' (red) are all self-fertilising varieties which do not need to be pollinated by insects, and so are useful for ensuring a crop of beans during prolonged wet spells. 'Painted Lady' has pretty red and white flowers. Up to 3m (10ft), but needs to be kept within harvesting height to pick the runner beans.

Solanum crispum 'Glasnevin' (syn. *S. crispum* 'Autumnale')

CHILEAN POTATO VINE/TREE

Family: Solanaceae

A warm sunny wall is the ideal position for this fast-growing and semi-evergreen climbing shrub, which needs training on strong trellis or wires. In summer it produces heads of purple-blue flowers 15cm (6in) wide, with brightly contrasting protruding yellow stamens and (inedible) fruits. They are attractive to all kinds of bees. The flowers bear a striking resemblance to those of the potato plant, hence the common name. *S. jasminoides* 'Album' is similar, but with fragrant pure white flowers. It grows up to 6m (20ft) in height.

Tropaeolum majus

CLIMBING NASTURTIUM

Family: Tropaeolaceae

This fast-growing hardy annual will add a splash of colour to any garden. The round, wavy-edged leaves are held, parasol-like, by a central stalk. Sow seeds in spring and allow plants to scramble over a dark evergreen hedge, or over a garden structure. They will also trail from hanging baskets. Bees will forage the red, yellow or orange flowers. 'Jewel of Africa' has cream-marbled foliage. The dark leaves of 'Empress of India' set off its bright orange flowers. 'Climbing Mixed' has green foliage and red, yellow and orange blooms. Up to 2.5m (8ft).

Wisteria sinensis

CHINESE WISTERIA

Family: Fabaceae

Allow plenty of space for these vigorous deciduous climbers with their twining stems. The scented, pea-like flowers hang in racemes up to 30cm (12in) long in spring and early summer, ahead of the foliage. Wisteria needs strong support and careful pruning to maximise flowering. 'Prolific' has strings of blueish-violet flowers, white-flowered 'Jako' and violet-red 'Amethyst' are all suitable for growing on strong supports against a wall in full sun. 12m (40ft).

Hedging plants

Hedges are living barriers or screens made up of attractive hardy evergreen or deciduous shrubs. They are used to mark out a garden's boundary, and to give privacy. The most ecologically enriching hedges contains a diverse range of flowering and fruiting plants. Birds, bees and other pollinators, small mammals, spiders and other creatures will all live and feed in, on, below and around a species-rich hedge.

Cotoneaster lacteus
COTONEASTER
Family: Rosaceae
Throughout winter, the arching branches of this evergreen shrub carry clusters of red fruits 6mm (¼in) in diameter, which birds such as blackbirds and thrushes will eat during freezing spells. The leaf undersides are felted yellow-white. In spring the scented white flowers attract wild solitary bees and bumblebees. Prune carefully, in late winter, to maintain the hedge shape. *C. simonsii* also makes a dense, semi-evergreen hedge. 4m (13ft).

Crataegus monogyna
HAWTHORN
Family: Rosaceae
In late spring this thorny deciduous shrub's white flowers fill the air with a sweet honey fragrance, and are much visited by noisy foraging bees. These are followed by fruits 6mm (¼in) in diameter which turn red in autumn, and which are a valuable winter food source for many garden birds such as blackbirds, redwings, starlings and thrushes. It is easily trimmed into a dense, formal hedge, making it popular with nesting birds. 10m x 8m (33ft x 26ft).

Below, left to right:
Cotoneaster lacteus.
Crataegus monogyna.

Elaeagnus umbellata

AUTUMN OLIVE

Family: Elaeagnaceae

Tolerant of exposure, this deciduous large shrub makes an attractive informal and scented hedge. It has leaves 10cm (4in) long which are silvery when young, later becoming bright green. In early spring, bumblebees and other wild bees flock to its highly fragrant, silvery yellow-white flowers which are 1.5cm (½in) long. These are followed by small edible fruits which ripen from silver to red by autumn. 4m x 6m (13ft x 20ft).

Hebe 'Great Orme'

HEBE

Family: Scrophulariaceae

This evergreen shrub, with its narrow, glossy leaves, makes an excellent insect-friendly informal hedge that needs little if any pruning. Its spikes of flowers 5–10cm (2–4in) long, in pink fading to white, bloom non-stop from midsummer to mid-autumn. Thrives in coastal areas. *H.* x *franciscana* 'Variegata' flowers in summer and autumn and has mauve flowers set against cream-edged leaves. 1.2m (4ft).

Ilex aquifolium

COMMON HOLLY

Family: Aquifoliaceae

Eventually making a dense, spiny, and bird-friendly evergreen hedge, this shrub has small white flowers in spring, followed by bright red berries which persist throughout winter and which are eaten in severe cold snaps by thrushes and other birds. The variety 'J.C. van Tol' is self-fertile, so will produce berries without needing to be close to other hollies. 25m x 8m (82ft x 26ft).

Prunus spinosa

BLACKTHORN

Family: Rosaceae

One of the first deciduous shrubs to flower, its white flowers stud the leafless stems in early spring, providing early nectar for bees on warm, sunny days. It makes a tough and spiny informal wildlife hedge and is less suited to formal pruning; it forms a good impenetrable boundary

for a spacious garden with wild areas. Spherical black fruits or 'sloes' 1.5cm (½in) wide ripen in autumn. 5m x 4m (12ft x 15ft).

Pyracantha 'Orange Glow'

FIRETHORN

Family: Rosaceae

The persistent and eye-catching orange berries of this thorny evergreen shrub stand out against its dark leaves, although hungry blackbirds and thrushes will often quickly strip the berries during winter cold snaps. Honey bees and bumblebees visit the sweet-scented clusters of white flowers in late spring. Mature firethorn hedges are a safe space for nesting birds. 'Soleil d' Or' has yellow berries. 3m (10ft).

Rosa rugosa

RUGOSA ROSE

Family: Rosaceae

Disease-resistant and thriving in poor soil, this tough deciduous species rose makes a low-maintenance multipurpose hedge. Its prickly stems carry wrinkled, leathery leaves which take on fiery shades of red and orange in autumn. Deep pink cup-shaped, sweet-scented flowers appear throughout the summer, attracting bees foraging for nectar and pollen. Large reddish-orange hips follow in autumn and are eaten by birds. *R.* 'Roseraie de l'Hay' has salmon-pink flowers 10cm (4in) wide. 1–2.5m (3–8ft).

Viburnum lantana

WAYFARING TREE

Family: Caprifoliaceae

Ideal for a multi-species wildlife hedge, this upright deciduous shrub has grey-green leaves that turn red in autumn. Domed heads of small white flowers open in late spring, followed by red and finally black fruits. Suits alkaline (lime-rich) soil. *V. opulus* (Guelder rose) has white flowers and red fruits. 5m x 4m (16ft x 13ft).

Above, clockwise from top left: Pyracantha *'Orange Glow'*. Viburnum lantana. Rosa rugosa.

Opposite, clockwise from top: Elaeagnus umbellata. Ilex aquifolium. Prunus spinosa. Hebe *'Great Orme'*.

Pollinator plants

This is a comprehensive list of flowering plants which have been proven – through a combination of scientific evidence and extensive garden observations – to be of value to pollinating insects foraging for pollen and nectar. Plants are included for every season of the year. Each plant's italicised botanical name is followed by its common name(s). Where 'spp.' is shown, this indicates that most if not all of the species and/or varieties of that plant are good for pollinators.

BUYING 'POLLINATOR-FRIENDLY' PLANTS

Many plants on sale are labelled as being good for pollinating insects, even though they may have been grown using synthetic pesticides and fungicides; residues of these chemicals could still linger in the tissues of the plant and cause harm to any bugs which which forage on them. To reduce the risk of inadvertently harming pollinators, always try to source organically-grown plants, seeds and bulbs (page 54).

Plants grown in peat-based compost are also inherently harmful to pollinating insects because peat mining releases carbon which is helping to drive climate breakdown (page 20).

KEY:

A = Annual
Bi = Biennial
Bu = Bulb
C = Climber
P = Perennial (herbaceous or evergreen)
S = Shrub
T = Tree

WINTER FLOWERING

Clematis cirrhosa Evergreen clematis C
Crocus spp. Winter-flowering crocus Bu
Eranthis hyemalis Winter aconite Bu
x *Fatshedera lizei* Tree ivy S
Galanthus nivalis Snowdrop Bu
Helleborus spp. and varieties Winter-flowering hellebore P
Lonicera × *purpusii* 'Winter Beauty' Winter-flowering honeysuckle S
Mahonia spp. Oregon grape S
Salix aegyptiaca Musk willow S
Sarcococca confusa Sweet box S
Sarcococca hookeriana Sweet box S
Viburnum tinus Laurustinus S

SPRING FLOWERING

Acer campestre Field maple S or T
Acer platanoides Norway maple T
Acer pseudoplatanus Sycamore T
Acer saccharum Sugar maple T
Aesculus hippocastanum Horse chestnut T
Ajuga reptans Bugle P
Arabis alpina subsp. *caucasica* Alpine rock cress P
Armeria juniperifolia Juniper-leaved thrift P
Aubrieta spp. Aubretia P
Aurinia saxatilis Gold dust P
Berberis darwinii Darwin's barberry S
Berberis thunbergii Japanese barberry S
Bergenia spp. Elephant ear P
Buxus sempervirens Common box S
Caltha palustris Marsh marigold P
Ceanothus spp. California lilac S
Cercis siliquastrum Judas tree T
Chaenomeles spp. Japanese quince S
Cornus mas Cornelian cherry S
Cotoneaster conspicuus Tibetan cotoneaster S
Crataegus monogyna Common hawthorn S or T
Crocus spp. Spring-flowering crocus Bu
Doronicum x *excelsum* Leopard's bane P
Enkianthus campanulatus Redvein enkianthus S
Erica carnea Alpine heath S
Erica x *darleyensis* Darley Dale heath S
Erysimum spp. Wallflower Bi or P
Euphorbia amygdaloides Wood spurge P
Euphorbia characias Mediterranean spurge P
Euphorbia cyparissias Cypress spurge P
Euphorbia epithymoides Cushion spurge P
Euphorbia x *martini* Martin's spurge S
Euphorbia nicaeensis Nice spurge P
Geranium spp. Hardy geranium or cranesbill P
Geum rivale Water avens P
Hebe spp. Hebe S
Helleborus spp. and varieties Spring-flowering hellebore P
Iberis saxatilis Alpine candytuft P
Iberis sempervirens Perennial candytuft P
Ilex aquifolium Common holly T
Lamium maculatum Spotted dead nettle P
Lunaria annua Honesty Bi

Mahonia spp. Oregon grape S
Malus baccata Siberian crab apple T
Malus domestica Edible apple T
Malus floribunda Japanese crab apple T
Malus hupehensis Hupeh crab apple T
Malus sargentii Sargent's crab apple T
Mespilus germanica Common medlar T
Muscari armeniacum Armenian grape hyacinth Bu
Nectaroscordum siculum Sicilian honey garlic Bu
Ornithogalum umbellatum Common star of Bethlehem Bu
Pieris formosa Lily-of-the-valley bush S
Pieris japonica Lily-of-the-valley bush S
Primula veris Cowslip P
Primula vulgaris Primrose P
Prunus avium Wild and edible cherries T
Prunus domestica Wild and edible plums T
Prunus dulcis Almond T
Prunus incisa 'Kojo-no-mai' Cherry 'Kojo-no-mai' T
Prunus insititia Damson T
Prunus laurocerasus Cherry laurel S
Prunus mume Japanese apricot T
Prunus padus Bird cherry T
Prunus pendula f. *ascendens* 'Rosea' Flowering cherry T
Prunus persica Peach T
Prunus spinosa Blackthorn S
Prunus tenella dwarf Russian almond S
Prunus x *yedoensis* Flowering cherry T
Pulmonaria spp. Lungwort P
Pyrus communis Pear T
Ribes nigrum Blackcurrant S
Ribes rubrum Common redcurrant S
Ribes sanguineum Flowering currant S
Salix caprea Goat willow (male form only) S or T

*Above: Red admiral butterfly (*Vanessa atalanta*) foraging on* Verbena bonariensis.

Salix hastata 'Wehrhahnii' Halberd willow 'Wehrhahnii' S
Salix lanata Woolly willow (male form only) S
Skimmia japonica Skimmia S
Smyrnium olusatrum Alexanders Bi
Stachyurus chinensis Stachyurus S
Stachyurus praecox Stachyurus S
Vaccinium corymbosum Blueberry S

SUMMER FLOWERING

Achillea spp. Yarrow P
Actaea japonica baneberry P
Aesculus indica Indian horse chestnut T
Aesculus parviflora Bottlebrush buckeye S
Agastache spp. and varieties Giant hyssop P

Ageratum houstonianum Flossflower A
Alcea rosea Hollyhock Bi
Allium spp. Ornamental onion (and edibles such as onions and leeks when allowed to flower) Bu
Alstroemeria spp. Peruvian lily Bu
Amberboa moschata Sweet sultan A
Amsonia tabernaemontana Eastern bluestar P
Anchusa azurea Large blue bugloss A
Anchusa capensis Cape alkanet A
Angelica archangelica Angelica Bi
Angelica gigas Purple angelica Bi
Angelica sylvestris Wild angelica Bi
Anthemis tinctoria Dyer's chamomile P
Antirrhinum majus Snapdragon A or P
Aquilegia spp. Columbine P
Arabis allionii Siberian wallflower P
Argemone platyceras Crested poppy A or P
Armeria maritima Thrift P
Aruncus dioicus Goat's beard (male form only) P
Asparagus officinalis Asparagus P
Astrantia major Greater masterwort P
Borago officinalis Borage A
Brachyglottis (Dunedin Group) 'Sunshine' Brachyglottis 'Sunshine' S
Brachyglottis monroi Monro's ragwort S
Buddleja davidii Butterfly bush S
Buddleja globosa Orange ball tree S
Buphthalmum salicifolium Yellow ox-eye P
Bupleurum fruticosum Shrubby hare's ear S
Calamintha nepeta Lesser calamint P
Calendula officinalis Pot marigold A
Callicarpa bodinieri var. *giraldii* Beautyberry S
Callistephus chinensis China aster A
Calluna vulgaris Heather S
Campanula carpatica Tussock bellflower P
Campanula glomerata Clustered bellflower P
Campanula lactiflora Milky bellflower P
Campanula latifolia Giant bellflower P
Campanula medium Canterbury bells Bi
Campanula persicifolia Peach-leaved bellflower P
Campsis radicans Trumpet honeysuckle C
Caryopteris x *clandonensis* Caryopteris S
Catalpa bignonioides Indian bean tree T
Catananche caerulea Blue cupidone P
Centaurea atropurpurea Purple knapweed P
Centaurea cyanus Cornflower A
Centaurea dealbata Mealy centaury P
Centaurea macrocephala Giant knapweed P
Centaurea montana Perennial cornflower P
Centaurea nigra Common knapweed P
Centaurea scabiosa Greater knapweed P
Centranthus ruber Red valerian P
Centratherum punctatum Manaos beauty A
Cerinthe major 'Purpurascens' Honeywort 'Purpurascens' A
Cirsium rivulare 'Atropurpureum' Ornamental thistle P
Clarkia unguiculata Butterfly flower A
Clematis vitalba Old man's beard, traveller's joy C
Cleome hassleriana Spider flower A
Consolida ajacis Giant Larkspur A
Convolvulus tricolor Dwarf morning glory C, A
Coreopsis spp. Tickseed A or P
Cornus alba Red-barked dogwood S
Cosmos bipinnatus Cosmos A
Cosmos sulphureus Yellow cosmos A
Crambe cordifolia Sea kale P
Crataegus monogyna Common hawthorn S or T
Cucurbita pepo Marrow, courgette A
Cuphea ignea Cigar flower A
Cynara cardunculus Globe artichoke and cardoon P
Cynoglossum amabile Chinese forget-me-not P
Dahlia spp. Dahlia P
Delosperma floribundum Ice plant P

Left: *Adult hoverfly on* Tagetes tenuifolia.

Delphinium elatum Candle larkspur P
Dianthus barbatus Sweet william Bi
Dictamnus albus Dittany P
Digitalis spp. Foxglove Bi
Dipsacus fullonum Common teasel Bi
Echinacea purpurea Purple coneflower P
Echinops spp. Globe thistle P
Echium vulgare Viper's bugloss A
Elaeagnus angustifolia Oleaster S
Erica cinerea Bell heather S
Erica erigena Irish heath S
Erica vagans Cornish heath S
Erigeron spp. Fleabane
Eriophyllum lanatum Golden yarrow P
Eryngium alpinum Alpine eryngo P
Eryngium giganteum Miss Willmott's ghost P
Eryngium planum Blue eryngo P
Eryngium x *tripartitum* Eryngo
Erysimum spp. Wallflower P or S
Escallonia spp. Escallonia S
Eschscholzia californica California poppy A
Eupatorium cannabinum Hemp agrimony P
Eupatorium maculatum Joe Pye weed P
Euphorbia cornigera Horned spurge P
Euphorbia donii Spurge P
Euphorbia sarawschanica Zeravshan spurge P
Ferula communis Giant fennel P
Foeniculum vulgare Common fennel P
Fragaria x *ananassa* Garden strawberry P
Fuchsia spp. Hardy types S
Gaillardia x *grandiflora* Blanket flower P
Gaura lindheimeri White gaura P
Geranium pratense Meadow cranesbill P
Geranium spp. Cranesbill (summer-flowering) P
Geum spp. Avens (summer-flowering) P
Gilia capitata Blue thimble flower A
Glandularia x *hybrida* Garden verbena A
Glebionis segetum Corn marigold A

Above: *Oriental poppy* (Papaver orientale).

Gypsophila elegans Annual baby's breath A
Hebe spp. Hebe S
Helenium spp. Helen's flower P
Helianthus annuus Common sunflower (excluding pollen-free varieties) A
Helianthus debilis Cucumberleaf sunflower A
Heliopsis helianthoides Smooth ox-eye P
Heliotropium arborescens Common heliotrope A
Heracleum sphondylium Hogweed Bi
Hesperis matronalis Dame's violet, sweet rocket P
Hydrangea anomala subsp. *petiolaris* Climbing hydrangea C
Hydrangea paniculata Paniculate hydrangea (choose varieties with fertile flowers: 'Kyushu', 'Big Ben', 'Floribunda', 'Brussels Lace') S
Hylotelephium spectabile and varieties Ice plant P
Hylotelephium telephium Orpine P
Hypericum olympicum Mount Olympus St John's Wort S
Hyssopus officinalis Hyssop S
Iberis amara Wild candytuft A
Ilex aquifolium Common holly T
Inula spp. Inula P
Jasminum officinale Common jasmine C
Kalmia latifolia Mountain laurel S
Knautia arvensis Field scabious P
Knautia macedonica Macedonian scabious P
Koelreuteria paniculata Pride of India T
Lathyrus latifolius Broad-leaved everlasting pea P
Laurus nobilis Bay tree S
Lavandula angustifolia English lavender S
Lavandula x *intermedia* Lavandin S
Lavandula stoechas French lavender S
Lavatera olbia Tree lavatera S
Lavatera trimestris Annual lavatera A
Leucanthemum x *superbum* Shasta daisy P
Leucanthemum vulgare Ox-eye daisy P

Left: Sun-loving sage, Salvia officinalis.

Liatris spicata Button snakewort P
Ligustrum ovalifolium Garden privet S
Ligustrum sinense Chinese privet S
Limnanthes douglasii Poached egg flower A
Limonium platyphyllum Broad-leaved statice P
Linaria maroccana Annual toadflax A
Linaria purpurea Purple toadflax P
Lobularia maritima Sweet alyssum A
Lonicera periclymenum Common honeysuckle C
Lychnis coronaria Rose campion Bi or P
Lychnis flos-cuculi Ragged robin P
Lysimachia vulgaris Yellow loosestrife P
Lythrum salicaria Purple loosestrife P
Lythrum virgatum Wand loosestrife P
Malope trifida Large-flowered mallow wort A
Malva alcea Greater musk mallow P
Malva moschata Musk mallow P
Matthiola incana Hoary stock Bi
Mentha aquatica Water mint P
Mentha spicata Spearmint P
Monarda didyma Bergamot P
Myosotis spp. Forget-me-not Bi
Nemophila menziesii Baby blue eyes A
Nepeta spp. Catmint P
Nicotiana alata Flowering tobacco A
Nicotiana langsdorffii Langsdorff's tobacco A
Nicotiana sylvestris Flowering tobacco A
Nigella damascena Love-in-a-mist A
Nigella hispanica Spanish fennel flower A
Oenothera spp. Evening primrose Bi
Olearia spp. Daisy bush
Onopordum acanthium Cotton thistle Bi
Origanum onites Pot marjoram S
Origanum 'Rosenkuppel' Marjoram P
Origanum vulgare Oregano, wild marjoram P
Paeonia spp. Peony
Papaver orientale Oriental poppy P
Papaver rhoeas Common poppy A
Parthenocissus tricuspidata Boston ivy C
Penstemon spp. Beard-tongue P
Perovskia atriplicifolia Russian sage S
Persicaria amplexicaulis Red bistort P
Persicaria bistorta Common bistort P
Phacelia campanularia Californian bluebell A
Phacelia tanacetifolia Fiddleneck A
Phaseolus coccineus Scarlet runner bean A
Phlomis spp. Sage S
Phlox paniculata Perennial phlox P
Photinia davidiana Stranvaesia S
Phuopsis stylosa Caucasian crosswort P
Pileostegia viburnoides Climbing hydrangea C
Polemonium caeruleum Jacob's ladder P
Potentilla spp. Cinquefoil P or S
Prostanthera cuneata Alpine mint bush S
Ptelea trifoliata Hop tree S
Pyracantha spp. Firethorn S
Reseda odorata Garden mignonette A
Ridolfia segetum False fennel A
Robinia pseudoacacia False acacia T
Rosa spp. Rose S
Rosmarinus officinalis Rosemary S
Rubus fruticosus agg. Blackberry S
Rubus idaeus Common raspberry S
Rudbeckia spp. Coneflower P
Salvia spp. Sage A or P
Sanvitalia procumbens Creeping zinnia A
Scabiosa spp. Scabious A or P
Sidalcea malviflora Checkerbloom P
Solidago spp. Goldenrod P
Sorbus aria Common whitebeam T
Sorbus aucuparia Mountain ash, rowan T
Spiraea japonica Japanese spiraea S
Stachys byzantina Lamb's ear P
Stachys macrantha Big sage P
Stokesia laevis Stokes' aster P
Symphoricarpos albus Snowberry S
Tagetes patula French marigold A

Tagetes tenuifolia Tagetes A
Tamarix ramosissima Tamarisk S
Tanacetum coccineum Pyrethrum P
Tanacetum vulgare Tansy P
Telekia speciosa Yellow ox-eye P
Tetradium daniellii Bee-bee tree T
Teucrium chamaedrys Wall germander P
Thymus spp. Thyme S
Tilia x *europaea* Common lime T
Tilia maximowicziana Lime T
Tilia oliveri Lime T
Tilia platyphyllos Broad-leaved lime T
Tithonia rotundifolia Mexican sunflower A
Trachymene coerulea Blue lace flower A
Trollius spp. Globeflower P
Tropaeolum majus Garden nasturtium A
Verbascum spp. Mullein Bi
Verbena bonariensis Tall verbena P
Verbena rigida Slender vervain A
Veronica longifolia Garden speedwell P
Veronica spicata Speedwell P
Veronicastrum virginicum Culver's root P
Viburnum lantana Wayfaring tree S
Viburnum opulus Guelder rose S
Vicia faba Broad bean A
Weigela florida Weigela S
Zauschneria californica Californian fuchsia S
Zinnia elegans Youth and old age A

AUTUMN FLOWERING

Aconitum carmichaelii Carmichael's monk's hood P
Actaea simplex Simple-stemmed bugbane P
Anemone hupehensis Chinese anemone P
Anemone x *hybrida* Japanese anemone P
Arbutus unedo Strawberry tree T
Campanula poscharskyana Trailing bellflower P
Ceratostigma plumbaginoides Blue-flowered leadwort P
Chrysanthemum spp. and varieties Chrysanthemum P
Clematis heracleifolia Tube clematis P
Colchicum spp. Autumn crocus Bu
Crocus spp. Autumn-flowering crocus Bu
Dahlia spp. and varieties Dahlia P
Elaeagnus pungens Silverthorn S
Elaeagnus x *submacrophylla* Ebbinge's silverberry S
Fatsia japonica Japanese aralia S
Hedera colchica Persian ivy C
Hedera helix Common ivy C
Helianthus x *laetiflorus* Perennial sunflower P
Leucanthemella serotina Autumn ox-eye P
Machaeranthera tanacetifolia Tansy-leaf aster A
Salvia spp. Autumn-flowering sage P
Symphyotrichum spp. and varieties Michaelmas daisy P
Tilia henryana Henry's lime T

FLOWERS ATTRACTIVE TO MOTHS (AND OTHER NOCTURNAL INSECTS)

Growing nectar-rich plants which also flower at night (some also release scent) will attract moths, which in turn become food for bats. The following will all help entice moths to your veganic garden.

Buddleja davidii Butterfly bush S
Buddleja globosa Orange ball tree S
Centaurea spp. Knapweed A or P
Centranthus ruber Red valerian P
Cynara cardunculus Globe artichoke and cardoon P
Echinacea purpurea Purple coneflower P
Erica cinerea Bell heather S
Eryngium giganteum Miss Willmott's ghost P
Hebe spp. Hebe S
Hedera helix Common ivy C
Hylotelephium spectabile and varieties Ice plant P
Hesperis matronalis Dame's violet, sweet rocket P
Jasminum officinale Common jasmine C
Lonicera periclymenum Common honeysuckle C
Lychnis coronaria Rose campion Bi or P
Lychnis flos-cuculi Ragged robin P
Matthiola longipetala subsp. *bicornis* Night-scented stock A
Nicotiana alata Flowering tobacco A
Nicotiana langsdorffii Langsdorff's tobacco A
Nicotiana sylvestris Flowering tobacco A
Oenothera spp. Evening primrose Bi
Salix caprea Goat willow (male form only) S or T
Silene latifolia White campion Bi or P
Symphyotrichum spp. and varieties Michaelmas daisy P
Verbena bonariensis Tall verbena P

Below: *Cardoon (Cynara cardunculus) flowers attract insects by day and at night.*

Disease-resistant and climate-resilient vegetables

Climate breakdown is driving increasingly chaotic growing seasons that no longer follow weather patterns which were once familiar to gardeners. To make sure we reap some reward for our gardening efforts, it makes sense to grow plant varieties which have been developed to both resist diseases – some of which could become more unpredictable as our climate changes – and to perform well during extreme weather conditions, such as unseasonal hot/cold or wet/dry spells.

Most seed and plant listings now include vegetable varieties which have been bred to resist everyday diseases, together with those which have been proven to perform in less than ideal growing conditions. It is worth checking catalogues regularly for new and improved varieties, which are being developed all the time. The following list of varieties show good resistance to common diseases, or perform well in less than optimum conditions.

CARROT ROOT FLY

F1 'Flyaway'
F1 'Maestro'
F1 'Resistafly'

BRASSICA CLUBROOT DISEASE

All of the following vegetable varieties show resistance to soil-borne clubroot disease caused by the fungus-like pathogen *Plasmodiophora brassicae*.

Cabbage:
F1 'Cordesa' (savoy, autumn/winter)
F1 'Red Lodero' (round red, summer/autumn)
F1 'Kalibro' (round, summer)
F1 'Kilaton' (round, autumn/winter)
F1 'Kilazol' (round, autumn/winter)

Cauliflower:
F1 'Clapton'
F1 'Zaragoza'

Broccoli (calabrese):
F1 'Komodo'
F1 'Moncano'

Brussels sprouts:
F1 'Crispus'
F1 'Cryptus'

Swede:
F1 'Invitation'
'Marian'

PARSNIP CANKER ROOT ROT

'Avonresister'
F1 'Albion'
F1 'Archer'
F1 'Gladiator'
F1 'Javelin'
F1 'Picador'

POTATO/TOMATO LATE BLIGHT DISEASE

Potatoes: Several potato varieties claim resistance to late blight (*Phytophthora infestans*), but the 'Sarpo' potatoes show exceptional resilience against this devastating fungal disease. They also have dense, weed-suppressing foliage (haulms), crop heavily and will store well without sprouting for long periods.
'Sarpo Axona' (red, maincrop)
'Sarpo Blue Danube' (blue, maincrop)
'Sarpo Kifli' (white, maincrop)

'Sarpo Mira' (red, maincrop)
'Sarpo Una' (red, second early)

Tomatoes: Tomatoes grown under cover in a greenhouse or polytunnel, where their leaves stay constantly dry, are far less susceptible to late blight and other airborne fungal diseases. Outdoor crops can suffer severe damage, especially as increasingly extreme weather makes our growing seasons chaotic and unpredictable. If you are only able to grow your tomatoes outdoors, the following varieties all show good, proven resistance to blight.

F1 'Cocktail Crush' (cordon, red)
F1 'Crimson Blush' (cordon, red beefsteak)
F1 'Crimson Cherry' (cordon, red cherry)
F1 'Crimson Crush' (cordon, red)
F1 'Crimson Plum' (cordon, red plum)
F1 'Fantasio' (cordon, red)
F1 'Ferline' (cordon, red)
F1 'Koralik' (bush, red cherry)
F1 'Lizzano' (bush, red cherry)
F1 'Losetto' (bush, red cherry)
F1 'Mountain Magic' (cordon, red)
F1 'Romello' (bush, red cherry)
F1 'Summerlast' (bush, red cherry)

SELF-FERTILE/POLLINATING RUNNER BEANS

Climate breakdown means we now experience increasingly turbulent and unpredictable spells of weather, often right in the middle of the peak gardening season. The following runner bean varieties have all been bred to be self-fertile and 'set' (form pods) during both cool, wet weather, when few insect pollinators, such as wild bees, are on the wing, and in dry and extremely hot spells, when fertilisation and pod-setting often fails. The bicoloured flowers of the 'Tenderstar' variety will also add a welcome splash of beauty and colour.

'Aurora' (pink flowers)
'Firelight' (red flowers)

Above, left to right: *Broccoli F1 'Monclano'. Blight-resistant tomato F1 'Crimson Cherry'. Parsnip F1 'Albion'.* ***Below:*** *Red cabbage F1 'Lodero'.* ***Opposite, left to right:*** *Carrot F1 'Resistafly'. Red maincrop potato 'Sarpo Mira'.*

'Firestorm' (orange/red flowers)
'Moonlight' (white flowers)
'Red Rum' (red flowers)
'Snowstorm' (white flowers)
'Stardust' (white flowers)
'Tenderstar' (pink/red bicoloured flowers)
'Wey' (white flowers)

Veganic garden year planner

SPRING

EARLY SPRING

- Spread dark and crumbly mature garden compost and/or mature leaf mould, over the surface of your no-dig beds, smothering any weeds.
- Move any bug hotels which have been kept dry over winter back to their original spots.
- Cut 12.5cm (5in) square holes all around the base of a solid wooden boundary fence, so that hedgehogs and other small wild mammals can move freely between gardens.
- Mix your own peat-free sowing and potting composts, then store them indoors until needed, in reusable compost bags.

*Below: Leave patches of lawn unmown so that wildflowers such as these tall hogweeds (*Heracleum sphondylium*) can bloom.*

- Empty out wormposting bins and sieve through the contents. Remove any inorganic materials that have not rotted down, and add part-rotted fragments to the next bin you set up.
- Mark out some areas of your lawn which can be left unmown and left to go wild, and boost the wildflower population by sowing seeds and/or planting young plug plants.
- Clean out water butts and tanks, remove any debris, giving them a wash out using eco-friendly detergent before reconnecting them to gutters and downpipes.
- Purchase fresh bags of quality and vegan-friendly peat-free compost. If you are buying from a retailer, reject any bags which are faded, torn or heavy and waterlogged.

MID-SPRING

- Bring pot-grown dandelions into an unheated greenhouse or porch to encourage early flowers, and to provide pollen and nectar for queen bumblebees.
- Start sowing seeds in an unheated greenhouse using a quality compost. On cold nights bring them indoors to encourage germination.
- Keep greenhouses well ventilated on warm, sunny days, opening both the top and louvre vents to main a good and constant air flow.
- Push home-grown twiggy plant supports in amongst tall-growing perennials so that the plants grow up and through them.
- Coppice hazels (cut them back to the base), and use the sticks either for

making green wood chips or for use as supports for food crops such as runner beans and peas.

- Stand potted, greenhouse-grown strawberries outdoors on fine days so that hoverflies and wild solitary bees can forage on and pollinate their flowers, which leads to fruit formation. On clear nights, move them back indoors, or stand against a sun-warmed wall, to avoid frost damage.
- Take photographs as a visual reminder of where spring-flowering bulbs are growing, so you can locate and transplant them later on when their leaves have died down.
- Wash down your greenhouse or polytunnel on a rainy day, which makes the job easier.

LATE SPRING

- Move tender, greenhouse-raised plants outdoors after the last frosts for 10 days before planting them.
- Remove or adjust a few of your greenhouse's highest glazing panels to create gaps which allow any insects or small birds to escape easily.
- To kick start a new garden's ecosystem, sow fast-growing annual plants with simple, single flowers, such as pot marigold (*Calendula*) to attract bees and other pollinators.
- Learn to identify the self-sown seedlings, removing any you don't want, but allowing those you want to keep to continue growing.
- Gently loosen the soil around any deep and tap-rooted weeds, ease them from the ground and put them in a tub of water to drown and die.
- Half-hardy annuals can be planted after the last spring frosts in your area. Stand them in pots outdoors for two weeks before they are planted in the soil, to harden them off. Move them to the base of a sunny wall on cold nights, and cover them with sheets of newspaper.
- Keep plants in containers well-watered as daytime temperatures rise.

Above, left to right: Plant wildflower plug plants. Support peas with hazel twigs. Spread mature garden compost over no-dig beds.

Below, left to right: Stand tender plants outdoors. Small copper butterflies (Lycaena phlaeas) *will pollinate potted strawberries. Open louvre vents on warm days.*

Above, left to right: *Keep mangetout pea 'Golden Sweet' well watered to encourage a succession of pods. Carefully remove weeds from around crops.*

EARLY SUMMER

- Ask your neighbours if they will let you have lawn mowings to provide 'greens' for your compost-making (check they don't use weedkillers).
- Use crop covers to keep adult butterflies away from the leaves of vulnerable crops, such as brassicas.
- Remove any young weeds from no-dig beds, then cover the soil with weed-repressing mulch.
- Mount regular slug/snail hunts on warm and damp evenings, specially following rain. Collect them in a container and then relocate them to a wild area well away from your garden.
- Sow fast-growing living mulches such as buckwheat and phacelia to improve soil. Letting both plants flower attracts large populations of pollinators.
- Look out for ready-grown insect-attracting plants such as single-flowered bedding dahlias and marigolds (*Tagetes*) and plant them at random in a food garden.
- Cut and chop up fresh comfrey leaves or stinging nettle shoots and brew them for two to three weeks in a covered bucket of water, to make a nutrient-rich soil/plant tonic.
- Visit a well-stocked local plant nursery and study the insect activity on the sales benches. Flowers which attract masses of different pollinators will make ideal pollinator plants for your veganic garden or allotment.

MIDSUMMER

- Water food crops infrequently but thoroughly in dry spells; water should soak deep into the soil.
- If a heatwave strikes, rather than use plastic netting, cut some leafy branches of shrubs and lay them over the roof of a greenhouse/polytunnel to create instant shade (shred them for mulch afterwards).
- Kill off tough weeds by laying them out on a dry surface in full, baking sunshine. When you are sure they are dead, chop/shred them and add them to your compost heap or bin, or drown them in a tub.
- Build large and hot compost heaps while you have plenty of 'green' and 'brown' materials available; ask neighbours if they will donate their own (veganic) garden waste.
- Check 'cool' compost heaps. If they have dried out, give them a thorough soaking with water to kick start the rotting process.
- Allow annual flowers such as pot marigolds (*Calendula*) and borage to produce and sow their own seeds.

Below, left to right: *Harvest lettuces when their hearts are firm and solid. Pick secondary shoots of broccoli to encourage more. Hunt for slugs on damp evenings.*

Above, left to right: Keep pests at bay with crop covers. Let annual flowers sow themselves. Buckwheat, allowed to bloom, attracts beneficial insects.

- Use sheets of cardboard, weighed down with stones, to cover any bare soil to keep it weed free until you are ready to sow/plant with fresh crops.
- Use rainwater rather than mains tap water to top-up the water level in a pond during prolonged spells without rain. Check that any wildlife can easily escape from a pond should it accidentally fall in.

LATE SUMMER

- Steep fresh seaweed in water until it turns brown, then dilute it 1 part seaweed water to 10 parts fresh water and use it as a foliar tonic.
- Plant new pot-grown and peat-free perennial plants so they have a chance to become established during the autumn. If the soil is dry, make a shallow, saucer-shaped depression around the plant and fill it with water so it soaks down around the roots.
- Use a sharp scythe to mow the long, yellowing grass and fading flowers in any wilder parts of the garden, and in an unmown lawn. Leave the cut stems for two weeks so that wildflower seeds drop back into the wild areas.
- Harvest food crops regularly to keep them productive over a long period. Do not leave crops such as beans and courgettes unpicked, or the plants will stop producing any more.
- Support any tall-growing plants, such as giant sunflowers, with home-grown sticks and poles, to prevent damage during summer thunderstorms.
- Lift strong and leafy dandelion rosettes and plant them in pots of peat-free compost.
- Overwintering salad crops, such as oriental greens, can be sown into your vegan-friendly compost and germinated in an unheated greenhouse. They grow quickly and will be ready for planting out three to four weeks later.
- Use 'grey water' from the kitchen and bathroom for outdoor watering if your stored rainwater supplies run out during a prolonged dry spell. Always use it fresh, and avoid splashing over the leafy parts of food crops, watering on the soil around the roots instead.

Below: Use leafy branches as instant greenhouse shading.

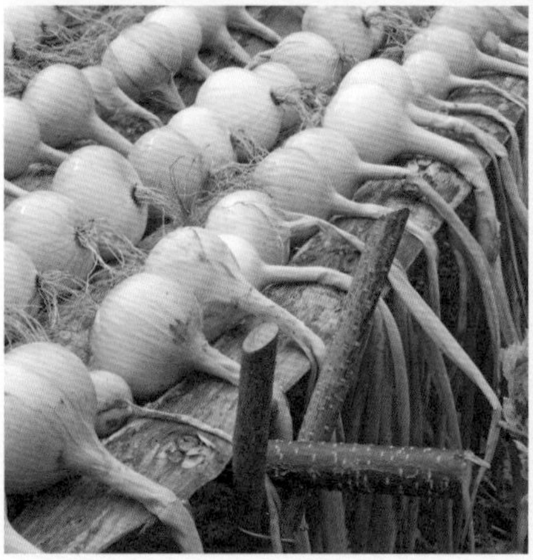

EARLY AUTUMN

- Deadhead late-flowering pollinator plants such as dahlias, to keep the blooms opening until the arrival of first autumn frosts.
- Put winter squashes and pumpkins in a sunny spot on dry days to ripen and toughen ahead of winter storage.
- Collect up any plastic plant pots and trays and store them out of sunshine, preferably in a dark shed.
- Use the warm and dry conditions in a greenhouse or polytunnel to dry off and ripen crops such as bulb onions before storing them.
- Order and plant in warm soil your plug plants of autumn- and winter-cropping salads and vegetables.
- Clear an overgrown garden or allotment of weeds by laying a thick sheet mulch, using multiple layers of overlapping cardboard weighed down with vegan-friendly organic matter.
- Collect ripe seeds of self-seeding plants, mix them with leaf mould, and flick the mixture into the crevices in drystone walls. Save some seeds and store them ready for another batch of sowing in spring.
- Boost the plant diversity in a lawn by scarifying it with a spring-tine rake to expose patches of bare soil, then sowing with a wildflower seed mixture.

MID-AUTUMN

- Plant spring-flowering bulbs in odd-numbered groups. Sourcing organically-grown bulbs means the resulting plants will be free of harmful pesticide residues.
- Carefully use a powered shredder to turn soft and sappy woody prunings into green wood chips, which can be used to improve and boost the microbial life in your no-dig soil.
- Install a new wildlife pond so it has time to settle down and achieve a natural balance ahead of spring, when wildlife such as frogs and toads might spawn there.
- Lay a sheet of wire mesh over your pond to stop it filling with falling leaves. Prop it up so that any wildlife is still free to come and go.
- Sow hardy field beans and winter tares as living mulches to avoid leaving soil bare and exposed over the winter months.
- Shred colourful woody stems such as willow and then use them as pot-top mulches after planting up containers of spring-flowering, organically-grown flower bulbs.
- Drain water tanks and butts before the first frosts to stop them being cracked and damaged.
- Collect fresh, plastic-free seaweed from along the strand line on beaches, for use as a mulch.

Opposite, clockwise from top: *Leave bruised and rotting fruit for butterflies. Teasel seeds will feed birds in winter. Tread carefully to avoid froglets and toadlets. Dry off and ripen onions under cover.*

LATE AUTUMN

- Ask neighbours to donate any woody prunings so you can turn them into mulch, or use as 'green wood chips'.
- Resist the temptation to cut down the hollow stems of fading perennial plants. These can add interest to your garden in winter and provide nest sites for wild bees in spring.

Above, left to right: *Birds will feast on sunflower heads. Hollow plant stems can be used to make bug hotels.*

- Gather up fallen leaves using a rake and store them in wire cages to slowly rot down into soil-building leaf mould. Collect extra leaves by asking neighbours if you can have theirs.
- Let fallen/bruised apples and pears stay on the ground so that adult butterflies can feed on them before entering winter hibernation.
- Make a late sowing of field beans as an overwintering and slow-growing living mulch. The leafy tops can be cut down in spring for composting, and the thick, nitrogen-rich roots can be left in the soil to rot down.
- Leave sunflowers, teasels and other plants with large seedheads after they have finished flowering so birds such as goldfinches can feed on them.
- Stack up some logs to make habitat-rich wildlife-friendly log piles around your garden or on the 'wild' edges of an allotment.
- Check if autumn-planted crops in a greenhouse need water. If the soil is dry and the plants are wilting, give them a thorough watering, but avoid getting their leaves wet.

EARLY WINTER

- Keep an eye (and an ear) out for tree surgeons working locally. Ask if they have any woody prunings, logs or chippings they need to dispose of, and offer to take them off their hands.
- Fix bird nesting boxes to walls, trees and other structures. Ideally they should face north or east, so that the entrance is pointing away from the direction of driving rain. Put bat roosting boxes under the eaves.
- Make scale plans of a new garden, or of a part of an existing garden you want to develop, starting with key features such as paths, beds, or a greenhouse or polytunnel. Mark them out using stakes and string.
- Shred any tough and thorny woody prunings and make a separate, long-term compost heap in an out of the way part of the garden. Non-thorny shreddings can be used straight away as mulch around established plants.
- Give garden structures and plant supports a check. Look out for loose fixings on walls and buildings and make repairs ahead of storms. Replace damaged greenhouse glazing.
- Move bug hotels to a drier spot, such as next to a wall with wide eaves, or into an unheated shed, to stop them becoming soaked by winter rain.
- Clean up and lubricate garden tools before storing away for winter. Rub oil into bladed tools to stop corrosion.
- Bare-root hedging plants, trees and shrubs can be planted now until early spring, providing the soil is not waterlogged, frozen or snow-covered.

MIDWINTER

- Browse seed and plant catalogues and place orders with ethical and/or co-operative suppliers. Wherever possible, choose organically-grown and certified seeds, plants and bulbs, which will be free of pesticide residues. Avoid any seeds which have been treated with chemical fungicides (usually a bright seed coating).
- Avoid any urge to 'tidy up' your garden: wildlife such as hedgehogs will still be hibernating in piles of dry, fallen leaves and compost heaps.
- When the leaves of snowdrops and winter aconites start to grow, clear them of any fallen leaves so they can thrive and bloom unhindered.
- Collect non-thorny wood chips from roadside verges – checking first that it is safe to do so – and then use them to replenish pathways in your garden or allotment, or as surface mulch.
- Build up stocks of home-made biodegradable paper plant pots and store them until spring seed sowing.
- Close all greenhouse vents and doors ahead of storms and gales, to avoid the glazing being broken by damaging gusts of wind.
- Start chitting tubers of blight-resistant potato varieties in a light and cool frost-free place.
- Stay alert for damage by slugs and snails still active in mild spells.

LATE WINTER

- Pull up or transplant any self-sown annual or biennial plants which germinated the previous summer or autumn and have been growing over winter.
- Build your own bug hotels and position them around the garden by early spring so potential guests can check them out.
- Lift and divide hardy herbaceous perennials; sourcing plants from an established garden where no pesticides have been used will ensure the plants contain no harmful residues.
- Take advantage of leafless, bare hedges to look out for an unused or abandoned greenhouse in local gardens. Ask the owner if they would be happy for you to dismantle it and give it a new home.
- Soak the soil in the beds of greenhouses and polytunnels ahead of spring sowing and planting; it can become very dry during the winter months.
- Collect any dry and hollow plant stems from garden borders and pack them inside a tin can to make a simple nest box for wild solitary bees and solitary wasps.
- Check greenhouses and polytunnels for winter storm damage and carry out repairs. Use repair tape to fix holes and tears in polytunnel coverings.
- Check the overwintering crops in an unheated greenhouse, harvesting oriental and other greens regularly, especially during mild spells. Soil under cover can dry out so if leafy crops start to wilt, water them thoroughly on a mild day.

Left: *Shred thorny brambles for slow, long-term composting.*

Opposite, clockwise from top: *Lift and divide herbaceous perennial plants while they are dormant. Add bird nesting boxes to the garden. Order bulbs 'in the green' and plant them straight away. Overwintered purple-leaved pak choi ready to harvest.*

Further information

UNITED KINGDOM

ORGANIZATIONS

Garden Organic, Ryton Gardens, Wolston Lane, Coventry CV8 3LG
tel: 024 7630 3517
www.gardenorganic.org.uk
• UK's leading gardening charity promoting organic growing. Also maintains a collection of heritage/heirloom vegetable varieties and distributes them to its members.

Growing With Grace, Clapham Nursery, Station Road, Clapham, Lancaster LA2 8ER, tel: 01524 251723
www.growingwithgrace.org.uk
• Quaker-inspired and co-operatively owned organic market garden practising closed-loop, veganic horticulture, all in large greenhouses. Occasional open days.

Hulme Community Garden Centre, 28 Old Birley Street, Manchester M15 5RF
tel: 0161 227 8198
www.hulmegardencentre.org.uk
• Community-focused urban garden centre where vegetable, fruit and herb plants are grown in vegan-friendly peat-free compost (all other plants are peat-free). Demonstration gardens, volunteering opportunities and courses.

Open Pollinated Seeds
tel: 01342 822646
www.open-pollinated-seeds.org.uk
• Information on open-pollinated vegetable varieties and their importance in maintaining genetic diversity that is available to all.

Stockfree Organic Services
www.stockfreeorganic.net
• Information and advisory service for existing and aspiring stockfree/vegan gardeners and growers (part of Vegan Organic Network).

The Vegan Society, Donald Watson House, 34-35 Ludgate Hill, Birmingham B3 1EH, tel: 0121 523 1730
www.vegansociety.com
• Charity promoting all aspects of a vegan lifestyle, with plenty of information for aspiring vegans.

Tolhurst Organic Partnership, Hardwick Estate, Whitchurch-on-Thames RG8 7RA
www.tolhurstorganic.co.uk
• Long-established experimental organic farm and the first in the world to be registered as 'stockfree', meaning no animal inputs are used. Hosts regular festivals and open days where farm-scale veganic growing can be seen in action.

Vegan Organic Network (VON), Anandavan, 58 High lane, Manchester M21 9DZ
www.veganorganic.net
• UK/international membership organisation offering advice and information on veganic gardening and growing. Publishes *Growing Green International*, hosts events and arranges open days on veganic gardens/farms. Can help you find other veganic gardeners and growers locally.

Viva! 8 York Court, Wilder Street, Bristol BS2 8QH, tel: 0117 944 1000
www.viva.org.uk
• Charity campaigning for an end to animal exploitation and in favour of a vegan lifestyle.

SEED SUPPLIERS

Most catalogues now include a limited range of organically grown and certified seeds (and sometimes bulbs and plants). The following all focus on supplying seeds which are open-pollinated/non-hybrid in origin (meaning you can save your own seeds for future use), and in some cases certified as organic.

Real Seeds, PO Box 18, Fishguard SA65 OAA, tel: 01239 821107
www.realseeds.co.uk
• Proven, non-hybrid and open-pollinated vegetable and flowers seeds for UK gardeners. Actively encourages you to save seeds for yourself.

The Seed Co-operative, Gosberton Bank Nursery, Gosberton Bank, Gosberton, Spalding PE11 4PB, tel: 01775 840592
www.seedcooperative.org.uk
• Co-operative seed company specialising in and breeding open-pollinated and locally-adapted vegetable varieties for organic gardening and growing.

Vital Seeds Ltd, Baddaford Farm, Ashburton TQ13 7NF
www.vitalseeds.co.uk
• Open-pollinated and organic vegetable, herb and flower seeds. Customers are encouraged to save their own seeds.

GENERAL SUPPLIERS

Dorset Seaweeds
www.dorsetseaweeds.co.uk
• Sustainably-harvested, organically-approved liquid seaweed products.

Implementations, Ansley Village, Nuneaton CV10 9PG, tel: 02476 392497
www.implementations.co.uk
• Copper/bronze gardening tools.

The Natural Gardener, Scotts Lane, Knowbury SY8 3JP, tel: 01584 890092
www.thenaturalgardener.co.uk
• Range of natural/sustainable products for veganic gardening, including dried seaweed and peat-free coir products.

Plastic Free Gardening, 83a Mill Hill Road, London W3 8JF
www.plasticfreegardening.com
• Fairtrade natural rubber seed/plant cell growing modules.

Sarpo Potatoes Ltd, Siambra Gwynion, Llandygai, Bangor LL57 4BG
tel: 01248 364260, www.sarpo.co.uk
• Blight-resistant 'Sarpo' potatoes.

The Shropshire Seaweed Company, Sea-Chem Ltd, Unit 18, Horton Court, Hortonwood 50, Telford TF1 7GY
tel: 01952 677002, www.sea-chem.co.uk
• Liquid seaweed products.

Tamar Organics, Cartha Martha Farm, Rezare, Launceston PL15 9NX
tel: 01579 371087
www.tamarorganics.co.uk
• Extensive mail order catalogue offering products for organic/veganic gardening.

The Organic Gardening Catalogue, Long Road, Paignton TQ4 7SX
tel: 0344 967 0330
www.organiccatalog.com
• Extensive mail order catalogue offering products for organic/veganic gardening.

VEGAN-FRIENDLY, PEAT-FREE COMPOSTS

The majority of peat-free compost (soil mix) and soil improver on sale does not specify whether or not it is vegan-friendly. You will need to ask retailers and/or check a brand's website for further information. The following suppliers are transparent about the suitability of their products for veganic growing.

Melcourt Industries Ltd, Boldridge Brake, Long Newnton, Tetbury GL8 8RT
tel: 01666 502711
www.melcourt.co.uk
• SylvaGrow is a professional-grade peat-free compost range, the majority of which is vegan-friendly.

Earth Cycle, Woodhorn Business Centre, Woodhorn Lane, Oving, Chichester PO20 2BX, tel: 01243 781730
www.earthcycle.co.uk
• Peat-free, plant-based soil conditioner, topsoil and mulch (NB other products contain animal manures).

Fertile Fibre, Withington Court, Withington, Hereford HR1 3RJ
tel: 01432 853111
www.fertilefibre.com
Vegan/vegetarian-friendly, organically-certified compost (soil mix) based on coir.

Dalefoot Composts, Dalefoot Farm, Heltondale, Penrith CA10 2QL
tel: 01931 713281
www.dalefootcompost.co.uk
• Lakeland Gold is a vegan-friendly, organically-certified soil improver/compost enhancer made from composted bracken (NB other products contain sheep's wool).

Bloomin Amazing, Rainbarrow AD Plant, Martinstown, Dorchester DT2 9JF
tel: 01305 267886
www.bloominamazing.com
• Nutrient-rich, plant-derived and vegan-friendly digestate from anaerobic digestion (AD) plants which produce 'green' energy (methane gas). Can be used in home-made peat-free compost (soil mix).

PEAT-FREE PLANT NURSERIES

More peat-free nurseries exist than can be listed here. The following are all growers who offer a mail order service. A comprehensive up-to-date list of peat-free UK growers is available at www.dogwooddays.net. Check with suppliers that they are also using vegan-friendly compost.

Beth Chatto's Plants and Gardens, Clacton Road, Elmstead, Colchester CO7 7DB, tel: 01206 822007
www.bethchatto.co.uk
• Wide range of perennial plants recommended for 'ecological' planting. Nursery and public display garden.

Bluebell Cottage Gardens and Nursery, Lodge Lane, Dutton, Warrington WA4 4HP, tel: 01928 713718
www.bluebellcottage.co.uk
• Flowering perennial plants grown using chemical-free pest controls, using minimal plastic. Nursery and public display garden.

British Wildflower Plants, Main Road, North Burlingham NR13 4TA
tel: 01603 716615
www.wildflowers.co.uk
• Over 300 wildflower species supplied as plug plants.

Caves Folly Nurseries, Evendine Lane, Colwall WR13 6DX, tel: 01684 540631
www.peatfreeplants.org.uk
• Wide range of perennials, herbs, alpine plants and bulbs.

Hardy's Cottage Garden Plants, Priory Lane Nursery, Freefolk Priors, Whitchurch RG28 7FA, tel: 01256 896533
www.hardysplants.co.uk
• Comprehensive range of herbaceous perennial plants.

Organic Plants, Delfland Nurseries Ltd, Benwick Road, Doddington, March PE15 0TU, tel: 01354 740553
www.organicplants.co.uk
• Organically grown and certified vegetable, herb and flower plug plants.

Rosybee Plants for Bees, Steventon Road, East Hanney OX12 0HS
tel: 07710 096734
www.rosybee.com
• Chemical-pesticide-free range of plants which are proven to attract bees and other pollinators.

The Edible Garden Nursery, Moorland Barn, Whiddon Down, Okehampton EX20 2QL, tel: 01647 400301
www.theediblegardennursery.co.uk
• Extensive range of common and unusual food plants, including herbs.

ORGANICALLY-GROWN BULBS

Some catalogues list a limited range of organically grown and certified flower bulbs. The following all supply good selections of mail order bulbs grown to organic standards.

Natural Bulbs for Organic Gardeners, Noorderlaan 26, 2182 GZ Hillegom, The Netherlands, tel: 2354 77900
www.naturalbulbs.co.uk

Organic Bulbs,
email: hello@organicbulbs.com
www.organicbulbs.com

Flowerbulbsinc.co.uk, Hemmerbuurt 36, 1607 CJ Hem, The Netherlands
tel: 0203 318 4418
www.flowerbulbsinc.co.uk

Sarah Raven's Kitchen & Garden Ltd, 1 Woodstock Court, Blenheim Road, Marlborough SN8 4AN
tel: 0345 092 0283
www.sarahraven.com

The Organic Gardening Catalogue, Long Road, Paignton TQ4 7SX
tel: 0344 967 0330
www.organiccatalog.com

IRELAND

Irish Seed Savers Association, Capparoe, Scarriff, County Clare, tel: 61 921866
www.irishseedsavers.ie
• Charity conserving the genetic diversity of Ireland's food crop varieties. Organic demonstration gardens and workshops.

The Organic Centre, Rossinver, County Leitrim, tel: 71 985 4343
www.theorganiccentre.ie
• Charity demonstrating organic gardening, including orchards; workshops.

Brown Envelope Seeds, Ardagh, Church Cross, Skibbereen, County Cork
tel: 083 1874 637
www.brownenvelopeseeds.com
• Organically-certified, open-pollinated vegetable seeds.
Fruit Hill Farm, Veyranno Ltd, Colomane, Bantry, County Cork P75 HV08
tel: 027 50710
www.fruithillfarm.com
• Supplier of products for organic gardening, including peat-free compost.

UNITED STATES

Vegan Agriculture Network
www.goveganic.net
• Network of gardeners, growers and farmers using veganic techniques.
Annie's Heirloom Seeds
tel: 1 800 313 9140
www.anniesheirloomseeds.com
Burpee Seeds and Plants, W. Atlee Burpee & Co, 300 Park Avenue, Warminster PA 18974, tel: 1 800 888 1447
www.burpee.com
Seed Savers Exchange, 3094 North Winn Road, Deborah, Iowa 52101
tel: 563 382 5990
www.seedsavers.org
• Conserving, growing and sharing heirloom seeds and plants.
Wicked Tulips Flower Farm, 90 Brown Avenue, Johnston, RI 02919
email: teamtulip@wickedtulips.com
• Bulb growers working toward organic, pesticide-free bulb production.
Fedco Seeds
www.fedcoseeds.com
PO Box 520, Clinton, ME 04927
• Organic seeds, potatoes, bulbs, trees, and plant-based soil improvers.
NOFA Organic Land Care Programme, The Northeast Organic Farming Association of Connecticut
tel: 203 408 6819
www.organiclandcare.net
ctnofa@ctnofa.org
• Information, training and certification to support urban organic methods.

CANADA

Vegan Agriculture Network
www.goveganic.net
• Network of gardeners, growers and farmers using veganic techniques.
Canadian Organic Growers, 56 Sparks Street, Suite 600, Ottowa, ON K1P 5B1
tel: 613 216 0741, www.cog.ca
• National organic growing charity.
Vegeculture
www.vegeculture.net
• Technical information on veganic farming, growing and gardening.
Greta's Organic Gardens, 399 River Road, Gloucester, Ontario K1V 1C9, tel: 613 521 8648
www.seeds-organic.com
• Certified organic vegetable seeds.
Salt Spring Seeds, Box 444, Ganges PO, Salt Spring Island, BC V8K 2W1,
tel: 250 537 5269
www.saltspringseeds.com
• Untreated, open-pollinated and non-GMO heritage (heirloom) organically grown vegetable seeds.

AUSTRALIA

Commonwealth Scientific and Industrial Research Organization, CSIRO Publishing, Unipark, Building 1 Level 1, 195 Wellington Road, Clayton, Victoria 3168, tel. 03 9545 8400
www.publish.csiro.au
• Publications on eco-friendly sustainable gardens, food and low-water gardening.
Sustainable Gardening Australia, 6 Manningham Road West, Bulleen, Victoria 3105, tel. 03 8850 3050
www.sgaonline.org.au
• Non-governmental, non-profit-making organization raising awareness of the environmental consequences of conventional gardening practices, and providing realistic and sustainable alternatives. Email newsletter.
Digger's Club, Heronswood, 105 Latrobe Parade, Dromana, Victoria 3936
tel: (03) 5984 7900, www.diggers.com.au
• Eco gardening club specialising in heritage (heirloom) seeds and plants, with two demonstration gardens.

NEW ZEALAND

Koanga Institute
tel: (06) 838-6269
www.koanga.org.nz/gardens
• Supports access to heritage (heirloom) food plants; offers seeds grown using sustainable methods, and workshops.
Soil and Health Association, PO Box 9693, Marion Square, Wellington 6141 tel: 09 419 4536
www.organicnz.org.nz
• New Zealand's largest membership organization supporting organic food and farming.
Oakdale Organics, tel: 0210 411 370
www.oakdale-organics.co.nz
• Organically certified heritage (heirloom) vegetable and herb plants.
Weathersfield Organics
tel: 021 892 505
www.weathersfieldorganics.co.nz
• Certified organic herb and vegetable starter plants.

SOUTH AFRICA

Biogrow, Private Bag X15, Suite 116 Hermanus, 7200
tel: 028 313 2054
www.biogrow.co.za
• Eco plant foods, bio-stimulants and natural pest, disease and weed controls.
Kitchen Garden, 12 Ursula Road, PO Box 136, Pringle Bay 7169, tel: 082 820 9646
www.kitchengarden.co.za
• Seed-sprouting kits and seeds.
Sustainable, Unit 4, 13 Bell Crescent, Westlake Business Park, Cape Town 7495, tel: 021 701 2028
www.sustainable.co.za
• Affordable eco-friendly products, including those for water conservation and composting.
Talborne Organics (Pty) Ltd, 9 Tungsten Street, Ekandustria, Bronkhorstspruit, PO Box 1256, Cullinan, Gauten, 1000, tel: 061 454 9632
www.talborne.co.za
• Manufacturer and distributor of organically accredited fertilisers.

Index

JOHN WALKER is an award-winning gardening and environment writer with over 40 years' experience in horticulture, teaching and the garden media. He trained at the botanic gardens in Birmingham and Cambridge, and at the Royal Botanic Gardens, Kew, where he gained the Kew Diploma in Horticulture. He was features/deputy editor of Garden Answers magazine, and contributing editor of Kitchen Garden magazine. John writes about greener, ecologically renewable gardening for national newspapers and magazines, and is the author of *How to Create an Eco Garden: A Practical Guide to Sustainable and Greener Gardening*, and *Weeds: An Earth-Friendly Guide to their Identification, Use and Control*. He is slowly coaxing a climate-friendly veganic garden from a previously bracken-riddled hillside at his home in Eryri, North Wales. John has won the British Garden Media Guild Environmental Award three times. He can be found at www.earthfriendlygardener.net.

Acknowledgements

For Richard Ellis
and in memory of Colin Leftley 1958–2017

Published by Lorenz Books
an imprint of Anness Publishing Ltd
www.lorenzbooks.com; info@anness.com
© Anness Publishing Ltd 2022

Publisher: Joanna Lorenz
Design: Adelle Mahoney
Special photography: Colin Leftley
Illustrations: Liz Pepperell
Artwork concepts: John Walker
Index: Marie Lorimer
Production: Ben Worley

The author and publisher would like to thank the following for allowing photography to take place in their gardens: Sue Beesley, Bluebell Cottage Gardens and Nursery; Garden Organic, Ryton Gardens; Nick Hamilton, Barnsdale Gardens; Judith Hughes, Pen Y Buarth; Delia Lanceley, Pant Ifan; Tatton Park Gardens; Peter Woollam, Hough Garden.

John Walker would also like to thank Caroline Boyce (Miscanthus) and Sally Nex (chalk soil).

Other picture acknowledgements:
(t=top, b=bottom, l=left, r=right, m=middle):
With thanks to Suttons Seeds (240–1) and Hotbin Composting (135b). John Walker: 6bl, 10, 12bl, 15tr, 17ml, bl, 34br, 35br, 36, 37, 38tr, b, 39, 40tr, 41br, 43tr, 45tr, b, 46 (all), 49tl, tr, 50tr, 53t, bm, br, 54br, 56t, ml, ml (bulbs), 74, 75, panel (sow a green manure), 76, creeping thistle, bramble, compost heap, chickweed, dandelion, 78tr, 80, 85br, 89tl, b, 93, 94tl, 95tl, tr, 97, 99bl, tr, 101br, 109tl, 112tl, 114, 116br, 118, 119, 120, 121 (all), 126tl, 131, 133t, 134r, 136t, 137tr, bl, bm (watering heap), 138, 139, 140tl, ml, 142br, 143, 144b, 148tr, 149t (both), 150 (all), 151, panel: reclaimed slate, shredded chips, 154tl, tr (both), 155, 158m, bm, br, 159, 161t (both), 164tl, 167t, 171tr, 175br, 177br, 183br, 184, 186, 189 (all), 191tr, 192, 193, 194 (all), 195bl, bm, br, 196tr, 197, 199tl, tm, br, 201, 201tl, bl, 205br, 214m (sneezeweed), 220mr (snowdrop), 229tr, 232mr, 240br, 243bm, 245tm, tr, b, 246t, 247tr, 248, 249bm, br, 256. Thanks to Shutterstock for additional images.

All rights reserved. No part of this publication may be reproduced, stored in a retrieval system, or transmitted in any way or by any means, electronic, mechanical, photocopying, recording or otherwise, without the prior written permission of the copyright holder. A CIP catalogue record for this book is available from the British Library.

The advice and information in this book are believed to be accurate and true at the time of going to press, but neither the author nor the publisher can accept legal responsibility or liability for any errors or omissions nor for any loss, harm or injury that comes about from following this book. Utmost care must be taken when handling bladed equipment and machinery.